Conquering Innovation Fatigue

OVERCOMING THE BARRIERS TO PERSONAL AND CORPORATE SUCCESS

Jeffrey Dean Lindsay, Cheryl A. Perkins, and Mukund R. Karanjikar

WILEY

John Wiley & Sons, Inc.

Library of Congress Cataloging-in-Publication Data:

Lindsay, Jeffrey D.
    Conquering innovation fatigue: overcoming the barriers to personal and corporate success / Jeffrey D. Lindsay, Cheryl A. Perkins, and Mukund Karanjikar.
        p.   cm.
    Includes index.
    ISBN 978-0-470-46007-8
        1. Technological innovations—Economic aspects.   2. Diffusion of innovations.
        3. Success. I. Perkins, Cheryl A. II. Karanjikar, Mukund. III. Title.
    HC79.T4L555 2009
    658.4'063—dc22

                                                                    2009001906

Printed in the United States of America
10 9 8 7 6 5 4 3 2 1

To those who yearn to create,
To those who see what can be.

Contents

Foreword   xiii

Preface   xv

About the Authors   xvii

Acknowledgments   xix

Part I: Introduction   1

Chapter 1   **An Introduction to Innovation Fatigue**   3

Common Innovation Fatigue Factors:
An Overview   4

1. People Fatigue (Fatigue from the Way
   People Act)   5
2. Fatigue Factors in the Organization
   (Strategy, Culture, Actions)   6
3. External Fatigue (Factors in the
   Environment)   6

Nine Leading Fatigue Factors   7

Incentives and Innovation: It's Not Just About
Profit   8

EmpowerPlaygrounds and the
Light of Innovation   9

Tesla's Sacrifice   11

Chapter 2   **The Funnel vs. the "Horn of Innovation™"**   **15**
             The Rise of the "Invention Horn"   21

         **Part II: People Fatigue—Problems
             at the Individual Level**   **27**

Chapter 3   **Enduring Innovation Fatigue:
             Another Look at Television**   **29**
             One Perspective: Farnsworth, the Wronged
                Inventor   30
             Lessons (First Perspective)   33
             The Other Immigrants: Another Perspective   34

Chapter 4   **Fatigue Factor #1: Theft and Exploitation**   **39**
             Unrequited Innovation: The Pain of Others
                Getting Credit   41
             Avoiding "Theft" within the Corporation (Loss
                of Recognition)   43
             Avoiding Theft: Tips for Corporate Inventors
                and Corporations   46
             Exploitation of Inventors and Entrepreneurs   46
             Exploitation and Patent Shortcuts   47
             Avoiding Deception 101: Do Your Due
                Diligence and Seek Advice   48

Chapter 5   **Fatigue Factor #2: Innovator Deficiencies**   **51**
             The Dangers of Unhealthy Pride   51
             The Gatorade® Syndrome   52
             Inability to Let Go: The One-Man Relay Race   53
             Impatience and Other Infections   54
             Reluctant Marketers   54
             Tips for Innovators   55

Chapter 6   **Fatigue Factor #3: The "Not Invented Here"
             Syndrome—An Irrational Lack of
             Exuberance**   **57**
             Devil's Advocates and Other Champions of Defeat   58
             Personal vs. Corporate Gains: Playing it Safe
                with "Not Now" or "No"   59

The Unseen Hand—or Fist?   60
Workarounds: Persistence, Networking, and
    Multiple Connections   62
Imagined NIH Syndrome: Inventor Myopia
    and the Lens of Risk   63
Tips for Innovators Taking Concepts to
    Prospective Partners   65

**Part III: Fatigue Factors in the Organization
(Strategy, Culture, Actions)   67**

Chapter 7   **Fatigue Factor #4: The Silent Innovation
Killer—Breaking the Will to Share   69**
A Lesson from Pride Rock   69
Breaking the Will to Share   70
Devaluation of the Internal Inventor   73
Fatigue by Objectives   74
Fatigue and the Weakness of Corporate
    Strengths   75
Fatigue among Senior Innovators   77
The Young Are at Risk as Well   77
Thinking with an Accent: A Diversity Problem   78
Culture Codes for Innovation and Corporate
    Innovators   80
Promotion Systems, Performance Management
    Systems   81
Listen to the Voice of the Innovator   83
Learnings   84

Chapter 8   **Unintended Consequences:
Reinventing HP   85**
Learnings   90

Chapter 9   **Fatigue Factor #5: Fundamental Flaws in
Decision Making and Vision   91**
The Armada Effect: Fatigue Through
    Reshuffling   91
Leaders Listening to the Wrong Voices—Like
    Shareholders?   93
The Foolishness of Crowds Revisited: iPod®
    Skepticism   93

Errant Metrics in Evaluating Innovation 95
The Danger of Focusing on Cost Alone:
    Dismembering the Ecosystem 99
Learnings 100

Chapter 10   **Fatigue Factor #6: Open Innovation
Fatigue** **103**
"The Statement We Read to People Like You" 105
Competitive OI and Connecting with a
    Personal Touch 107
Lessons from the British Navy: Why the Cure
    for Scurvy Took 200 Years to Be Implemented 108
Learnings 110

Chapter 11   **Case Study on Overcoming Fatigue:
Hi-Tech Gems from the "Low-Tech" Paper
Industry** **113**
"Go Find Out" 115
18 Months of Solving the Wrong Problem—And
    Paul's Conversion on the Road
    to . . . Cambridge 116
Skepticism, Uncertainty, and Encouragement 117
Standing His Ground 119
Certifiably Nuts: Finding the Right Problem
    to Solve 120
Connections for Success—and Disappointment 121
Labor Pains: Birth is Just the Beginning 124
Learnings 125

Part IV: External Fatigue Factors **127**

Chapter 12   **Fatigue Factor #7: Patent Pain: Barriers to
Intellectual Property Protection** **129**
Judicial and PTO Hurdles to Protecting Good
    Inventions 130
Enforcement Fatigue 132
KSR: A Potential Fatigue Factor from the
    Supreme Court 133
Fatigue and Weak Property Rights 134

Business Method Fatigue   136
Global Fatigue: The Demise and Rise of
   International Intellectual Property Rights   140
Learnings   143

Chapter 13   **When Questionable Patents Are Allowed
to Sprout: Another Form of Patent Fatigue   147**
"We Didn't Know Where to Turn": A Patent
   Battle over Sprouts   148
Innovating for Quality   149
The Lawsuit   150
Aftermath   155
Learnings   156

Chapter 14   **Fatigue Factor #8: Regulatory Pain:
Challenges in Policy, Regulation, and Law   159**
Safety Regulations and the Dangers of Risk
   Aversion   160
Sarbanes-Oxley: the Dangers of Averting
   Financial Risk   163
Sometimes It's Not Enough to Be Innocent   164
Crimes of Omission: When Regulations
   Aren't Enforced   166
Recommendations to Innovators   167

Chapter 15   **Orion Energy Systems: Creative Solutions to
External Fatigue   169**
Innovation in Business Methods   173
Orion Asset Management   176
More Lessons from Orion   177
Leading Others to Innovate   178

Chapter 16   **Fatigue Factor #9: University-Industry
Barriers   181**
Skipping School Again: Driving Companies
   Away from U.S. Universities   182
The Bayh-Dole Act   182
Tax-Free Bonds and the University: Additional
   Barriers to Collaboration   184
Misaligned Incentives   185

Other Barriers   186
Fatigue in Universities   187
Global Perspective   188

Chapter 17 **Innovation Fatigue in the Pulp and Paper**
            Industries (Forest Bioproducts): Why
            "Innovestment" Matters   **191**
            A Proud History of Innovation   193
            The Need for Innovation—and
              "Innovestment"   196
            The Microcosm at the 'Tute   197
            Other Fatigue Factors for the Industry 200
            A Few Recommendations   201
            Learnings   204

            Part V: Further Guidance   **205**

Chapter 18 **Guidance for the Lone and Corporate**
            Inventor   **207**
            Completing the Circuit of Innovation 208
            Expanding the Scope of Intellectual Assets:
              Trademarks and More   211
            The Need for Multidisciplinary Skills: Da Vinci
              in the Laboratory   212
            Endurance and Patience: Still Vital for
              Innovators   215
            Recommendations to Innovators   217

Chapter 19 **Energizing Theory: Disruptive Innovation**
            and Disruptive IA   **219**
            Introduction to Disruptive Innovation 220
            The Theory of Disruption or the "Christensen
              Effect"   221
            Facing the Barriers   224
            A Proposed Solution: Disruptive Intellectual
              Asset Strategy   224
            Insights from Kimberly-Clark's Efforts 226
            A Few Recommendations   228

Chapter 20   **Further Guidance for Management**   **231**
Creating a Culture that Inspires Inventors and
   Innovators   231
Case Study: Multidisciplinary Innovators in the
Oil and Gas Industry and the Rise of Inficomm   234
The Future Oil Field and Need for Data   236
Solutions from an Unexpected Place   236
Open Innovation as an Energizing Factor:
   Completing the OI Circuit   237
Open Innovation Fatigue Revisited:
   The Persistence of Closed Innovation   239
Corporate Energizer: Communities of Practice
   to Support Innovation   241
University Considerations   242

Chapter 21   **Da Vinci in the Boardroom?**   **245**
Adding Value to Open Innovation, or, New
Lessons from the Renaissance   245
Da Vinci and Open Innovation   247

Chapter 22   **The Impact of Financials on Innovation**   **249**
How to Measure Financials and Their Impact   250
   Traditional Financial Metrics   250
   Profit Per Employee   251
Innovation Metrics   252
How Financials May Hinder Innovation   254
   Tough Times Make Slashing R&D Budgets
     More Tempting   254
   Focus on Innovation Can be Lost During
     Reorganizations or Mergers   255
How Financials Can Help Drive Innovation   255
Possibilities for Positive Organizational Change   256
Enhancing Corporate Culture   257

Chapter 23   **Guidance to Government and Policy**
Influencers   **261**
Listen to the Voice of the Innovator   261
Existing Framework   262

Diversity: The Need to Value and Encourage
Innovation from Many Sources   263
Support Innovation with a Global Vision of
Success   265
Thoughts on Removing External Fatigue
Factors   266
Keep It Simple   267

Chapter 24   **Summary**   **269**

Index   275

Foreword

Innovation is hard work. No matter where you are in the innovation process, there are traps that can slow you down or worse yet, cause you to surrender. As an inventor in a research organization, I experienced this first hand. As a corporate leader, the biggest challenge I currently face is where the next big idea will come from and how it can be guided and nurtured into a commercial success.

In *Conquering Innovation Fatigue*, Lindsay, Perkins & Karanjikar take a unique approach to highlight what we can learn from the from the metaphor of innovators as immigrants who must overcome many new barriers and challenges in their journey to business success. By drawing upon case studies, they tell stories of success and advances in innovation—and how to turn the drain of fatigue into creative energy to be captured by individuals and organizations.

If innovation were easy, we wouldn't be talking about it. This book challenges the reader to look at the role they play in the innovation process. Whether you are an inventor, a corporate leader or a policy maker, there are practical examples on how the role you play will either amplify or dampen innovation. There are recommendations that you can implement immediately. For corporate leaders and policy makers, it reminds us to listen to the neglected voice of the innovator. By beginning with targeted innovation inspired by the right strategy and enabled with the right minds—we can breathe life into innovation for our company—or our nation.

In this book, you will find useful tools to guide you through the steps you need to take to inspire, nurture and energize your innovation efforts—be they personal, corporate or national. Some are new and others are useful reminders of steps we should be taking on a daily basis. It will teach you how to:

- Recognize and overcome the nine major innovation fatigue factors.
- Prepare for successful licensing or marketing of inventions with holistic intellectual assets ("360° IA™") and other tools for success.
- Use the "Circuit of Innovation™" model that guides innovators in connecting their products to the marketplace.
- Avoid the unintended innovation-killers that can result from well-meaning corporate policies and actions.
- Exploit low-cost intellectual assets (not just patents!) to increase the odds of success with disruptive innovation, or reduce the risk of competitive disruption.
- Turn the problematic "innovation funnel" upside down to create more efficient, targeted innovation using the new "Horn of Innovation™" paradigm—a rich music-inspired model that makes much better use of innovator skills and business strategy.
- Tap the innovation power of Da Vinci (but probably not the Da Vinci you know!), as described in sections on "Da Vinci in the Boardroom" and "Da Vinci in the Laboratory."
- Strengthen open innovation for success, including university-industry collaboration.

Good Luck as you navigate the innovation journey!

Jean E. Spence
Executive Vice President
Research, Development & Quality
Kraft Foods

Preface

There is a personal side to innovation that is often overlooked. In our personal experiences and in our interactions and interviews with numerous innovators, we have found that there are many lessons from the "voice of the innovator" that are often missed when innovation is discussed. Innovation always begins at the individual level, in the minds of human beings. Standing between prospective innovators and success are a host of "innovation fatigue factors" that can discourage and hinder innovation. These fatigue factors affect both individuals—whether employees or independent inventors and entrepreneurs—and entire organizations.

After an overview in Part One, we explore the fatigue factors and their solutions in Parts Two through Four, corresponding to fatigue factors at three levels: individuals, organizations, and the external environment. Finally, in Part Five we explore broader "energizing factors" with further recommendation to individuals, corporations, and policy makers. Sprinkled throughout are case studies of the good and the bad, of the pains of innovation fatigue and the joys of successful innovation.

In addition to what we feel is an original perspective, we offer several original case studies and concepts that may be useful for others. These concepts include the innovation paradigm called "the Horn of Innovation™"—an innovator-centric model that turns the familiar "innovation funnel" around. We also present the "Circuit of Innovation™"—an electrical metaphor for bringing the energy of innovation to the market, "Da Vinci in the Boardroom™"—an approach to innovation that couples open innovation with multidisciplinary talent, and "Disruptive Intellectual Asset Strategy"—an effort to fill a gap in the literature on disruptive innovation by showing how low-cost, proactive intellectual asset strategy can overcome some of the barriers to pursuing disruptive opportunities or averting disruptive threats. (We generally prefer to speak of intellectual assets (IA) rather than intellectual property (IP), a subset of IA that lacks defensive publications and other valuable elements that are not strictly owned.)

Our work is intended for three groups: (1) entrepreneurs and innovators, including the often-overlooked corporate employee involved in R&D or other creative operations, as well as lone inventors, university researchers, and start-ups; (2) corporate leaders and strategists, including those developing strategies for innovation and intellectual assets; and (3) policy makers and influencers.

Through it all, we emphasize innovation at the personal level, seeking to help aspiring innovators find solutions in their spheres of influence. At the same time, we encourage business and political leaders to listen to the "voice of the innovator" and to consider unintended consequences that many tactics and policies may have on innovation.

We often invoke the metaphor of the innovator as an immigrant in a foreign land to describe the gaps that can exist between aspiring innovators and those who don't speak their language or understand their ways. Leaders of companies, institutions, and even government agencies who learn to deal with the "foreign" nature of innovation can give needed help to "immigrant" innovators and realize added economic success. Open innovation, for example, is a concept based on learning to embrace the foreign. While many speak of it, few succeed because they fail to bridge cultural divides or make their processes "immigrant friendly."

The story of innovation often involves a journey into unfamiliar territory where at least one person—sometimes an entire company or more—becomes the stranger in a strange land, facing barriers that can bring fatigue and despair. Others have made this tiring journey and can help us understand the path to success. The path of innovation does not need to be so difficult. As we discuss in our chapter on the "Horn of Innovation™," innovation, like the cornucopia of Greek mythology (based on a goat's horn that could turn wishes into reality), can truly turn the visions of the human mind into rich bounties that enhance life on this planet. There's no reason to let fatigue get in the way.

Our quest to help others overcome innovation fatigue will be an ongoing effort. The blog at *InnovationFatigue.com* will provide additional thoughts, resources for readers, and a place to share your feedback and experiences. Please join us there as we seek to help more innovators, entrepreneurs, and leaders find the path to innovation success.

About the Authors

Jeffrey D. Lindsay, Ph.D., Director of Solution Development at **Innovationedge** (Neenah, Wisconsin) and former Corporate Patent Strategist at Kimberly-Clark, is an innovation enthusiast with over 100 patents in numerous areas. Prior to 13 years of experience in the innovation community at Kimberly-Clark, Jeff was an Associate Professor at the Institute of Paper Science and Technology on the Georgia Tech Campus. Jeff is a registered U.S. patent agent with a Ph.D. in Chemical Engineering from Brigham Young University, where he was a National Science Foundation Graduate Fellow. Jeff is chair of the Forest Bioproducts Division of the American Institute of Chemical Engineers and is a member of the Licensing Executives Society. Jeff blogs at InnovationFatigue.com and SharpIP.com.

Cheryl A. Perkins is a sought-after keynote speaker and innovation thought leader who has traveled the world for more than 25 years to present her expertise in innovation to executives and innovation leaders. Cheryl is the founder and President of Innovationedge, a strategic global innovation consultancy that helps executives define their strategy and deliver breakthrough innovations, and helps inventors create strategic corporate partnerships for commercial success. Before founding Innovationedge, Cheryl served as Kimberly-Clark's Senior Vice President and Chief Innovation Officer, where she led the global health and hygiene company's innovation and enterprise growth organizations. Cheryl was named by *BusinessWeek* as one of the "Top 25 Champions of Innovation in the World." She is also Chair of the International Congress on Co-Development, a leading forum advancing open innovation. Cheryl blogs at InnovationEdge.com/blog.

Mukund R. Karanjikar, Ph.D., is a senior associate at Technology Holding LLC (Salt Lake City, Utah), a firm specializing in commercialization of breakthrough innovations focused on the area of energy and environment. Prior to Technology Holding, he was a consultant assisting energy companies in creating innovation alliances. He also worked with Chevron Technology Ventures LLC (Chevron Corporation) and Rallis India Limited (a TATA enterprise). He has published articles on topics including idea management, new product development, and open innovation. Mukund has a Ph.D. in Chemical Engineering from Auburn University and a Bachelor of Chemical Engineering degree from the University Institute of Chemical Technology, Mumbai, India. He serves on proposal review boards of the National Science Foundation and the Department of Energy, and is Chair of the Management Division of the American Institute of Chemical Engineers.

Acknowledgments

Numerous people and organizations have assisted our work. We thank the clients of **Innovation**edge for sharing their experiences and their passion for innovation, and giving us an opportunity to make a difference. We thank our families for their support and encouragement. Thanks to John Cronin, Ted Farrington, Casey Hill, Ivan Schrodt, Rob Williamson, and Terry Adams for early encouragement and ongoing discussions with Jeff in intellectual asset and business strategy. Thanks to Verna Allee for important inspiration on ecosystems for innovation. We appreciate the information and guidance we received from Neal Verfuerth, Paul Rasband, Henry Chesbrough, Merrilea Mayo, Steve Goers, Frank Crikelair, Ashley Crikelair, Nancy Edwards Cronin, Doug Dugal, Mahendra Doshi, Nicole Marshall, Walter Reade, Kendra Lindsay, Meliah Lindsay, Fung-jou Chen, Mark Perkins, Alexander B. Magoun, Woody Rice, Chakshu Kalra, A.S. Rao, Anil K. Gupta, Amy Achter, Tom Mildenhall, Rosann Kaylor, Rex Lewis, Oliver Schwabe, Scott Rickert, Robert Gruetzmacher, Nancy Hermanson, and many others, including some who prefer anonymity. Thanks to the Management Roundtable for opportunities to help lead others in open innovation. Thanks also to Mark Benyo of Benyo Designs for creating the fatigue factor icons and providing other assistance.

PART

I

INTRODUCTION

An Introduction to Innovation Fatigue

"Ingenuity should receive a liberal encouragement."

Thomas Jefferson

Exhibit 1.1   Are there better paths to avoid fatigue in the maze of innovation?

Conquering innovation fatigue begins with understanding the journey of innovators at a personal level. It begins with recognizing the "fatigue factors" they face and then seeking for solutions to help them reach success. A useful metaphor for the innovator's journey is that of the immigrant. In nearly every nation, there is a history of tension between established citizens and newcomers. The newcomers generally lack resources, don't understand how "the system" works, and struggle to understand the language of the natives. They may be ridiculed for their different ways and mistrusted by those in power, but the newcomers who persevere and conquer often reshape history and create prosperity for generations to come.

In the world of business, the brightest minds seeking innovation are sometimes like immigrants standing on a strange new shore, filled with visions of success but often facing harsh barriers. Who can they trust? Where should they go? How do they find shelter and protection? In fact, many great innovators like Nikolai Tesla, the father of the electric age, were literal immigrants who faced severe challenges in realizing their visions. Though each story is unique, there are several common classes of "innovation fatigue factors" that hinder individual and corporate success in innovation today as in the past. Understanding and overcoming these barriers is vital not only to individuals—whether corporate employees, university researchers, lone inventors or entrepreneurs—but also to corporations and nations themselves.

Innovation is the successful translation of new concepts into economic value and the process of creating and realizing value from that which is new. Whether it's a technology, product, process, or method of doing business, innovation goes beyond invention and discovery to involve the social aspect of changing behaviors such as how we eat, shop, dress, or drive.[1] The pathway from an idea or invention to broad change in society is often complex and multifaceted, like the journeys of immigrants as they become established in a new land.

For inventors and entrepreneurs, there are always risks, delays, and pains on the route to innovation, but greater success and speed is possible with the right approach and the right help. Our goal is to help prospective innovators, entrepreneurs, and corporations succeed sooner, more visibly, and more profitably (for those who care about profits). Innovation fatigue can be conquered.

Common Innovation Fatigue Factors: An Overview

Few things make creative people wearier than empty talk about innovation. Leaders may boast of innovation, but a different impression arises when one talks to frustrated and alienated inventors, or surveys the missed continents of opportunity that were somehow circumnavigated. Some of them may sincerely seek innovation but lack the know-how to make it happen. How do we find real success in innovation?

Are companies facing innovation fatigue? Based on our experience, yes, many are. Supporting evidence comes from several sources, including a 2007 study by Boston Consulting Group/ *BusinessWeek* polling 2648 senior executives. BCG reports that "top executives worldwide are more upset than ever about the slow pace of innovation at their companies."[2] Also reported is that only 46 percent of the executives are happy with the return on their innovation investment, and only 66 percent rank innovation as a top-three priority, down from previous years. Many who would like to increase the pace of corporate innovation find their innovation engines sputtering. What's going wrong?

One concerned CEO is Jean-Pierre Garnier of GlaxoSmithKline. He speaks of the "innovation malaise" in the pharmaceutical industry and blames declining R&D productivity for the massive erosion in shareholder value in pharmaceutical stocks, where share price on the average plummeted from 32 times earnings to just 13 over a few years.[3] Other industries such as IT, industrials, and discretionary consumer products have shown steady erosion in shareholder returns over the past decade.

Many publications praise various organizations for their commitment to innovation based on actions and statements from those at the top. While leaders are talking innovation, our interviews and experiences sometimes show that their prospective innovators are beset with "innovation fatigue." Leaders often fail to understand the frustrations of innovators in the organization. As a result, the actual innovation performance of many organizations may be far below their potential, contributing to the statistics indicative of innovation fatigue.

In our discussions with inventors and entrepreneurs over the years, we have found persistent themes about the disincentives innovators face. In general, we find that fatigue factors can be grouped into three broad categories pertaining to individuals, organizations, and external factors.

1. People Fatigue (Fatigue from the Way People Act)

"People fatigue" includes the personal flaws of individuals, including inventors and those they work with. Greed, for example, can result in theft from the inventor, while excessive demands from the inventor can also block progress. Arrogance or excessive pride from others can result in the "Not Invented Here" (NIH) syndrome that can shut down opportunity, while the same flaws in the inventor can hinder the cooperation needed to work with allies.

We recognize that all fatigue factors ultimately reflect some aspect of human nature, though it may be implemented at the corporate or governmental level. Nevertheless, we assign fatigue factors to the people category when they arise from one-on-one interactions with individuals in which an undesirable trait of one party tends to destroy potential success of an innovation or discourage future innovation.

2. Fatigue Factors in the Organization (Strategy, Culture, Actions)

Many fatigue factors arise from strategies, policies, and cultures in an organization. We focus on corporations, though some of the principles apply to other entities as well. We consider, for example, the impact of errant metrics or poor decision making in evaluating opportunities. There are also process-related fatigue factors due to structures and systems in corporations. For example, weak performance management systems and incentives can contribute to innovation fatigue. At the strategic level, "open innovation fatigue" results in many missed opportunities. One of the most critical issues for corporations, though, is the tenuous thread that links the "will to share" of the creative employee to the intellectual asset engines of the corporation. When trust is breached or other discouragements befall prospective innovators, innovation engines can quickly shift into neutral, unbeknownst to management. Factors that make innovators feel devalued are one part of this problem. We address these issues and suggest solutions.

3. External Fatigue (Factors in the Environment)

Beyond the fatigue factors that arise from individuals and organizations, a host of external factors can contribute to innovation fatigue. These environmental factors can include barriers to protecting and exploiting one's intellectual assets (IA) arising from patent systems, legislation, regulation, and other aspects of government policy. Also included are roadblocks to open innovation such as barriers to university-industry cooperation from legislation and tax policy.

Within the scope of these three classes of fatigue factors, we explore nine specific fatigue factors:

Nine Leading Fatigue Factors

People Fatigue:

1. Theft of the invention and exploitation of inventors.
2. Innovator deficiencies (e.g., unreasonable expectations, impatience, unhealthy pride).
3. The NIH syndrome ("Not Invented Here").

Organization-Level Fatigue (Strategy, Culture, Actions):

4. Breaking the will to share (loss of cooperation from the innovation community).
5. Fundamental flaws in decision making and vision.
6. Open innovation fatigue (corporate barriers to external innovation and collaboration).

External Fatigue:

7. Patent pain: barriers to intellectual property protection.
8. Regulatory pain: challenges in policy, regulation, and law.
9. University-industry barriers.

The factors can be grouped as shown in Exhibit 1.2, illustrating that similar themes occur in each of the three main categories of fatigue factors. Whether at the individual, organizational, or external level, factors can be grouped in terms of threats to intellectual property and trust, barriers to collaboration, and flaws in judgment and behavior (including corporate and governmental behaviors or policies). The classifications are not crisp, for some fatigue factors can cross groupings and categories, but these groupings may be helpful in analyzing innovation barriers and finding solutions.

To conquer invention fatigue, we must understand the impact of fatigue factors at the people, organizational, and external levels, recognizing that whatever the level, the harmful impact is on individuals, whether inventors or entrepreneurs, whether self-employed or within a corporation or institution. This requires not only understanding the fatigue factors that beset innovators, but first understanding the personal incentives that drive innovators.

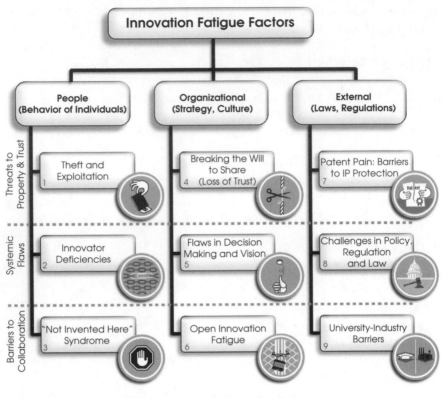

Exhibit 1.2   Grouping of leading fatigue factors

Incentives and Innovation: It's Not Just About Profit

We are passionate about innovation, for it is much more than a source of profit: it is also a source of fulfillment and even joy to the innovator and others. Joseph Schumpeter, in his economic surveys of innovation and entrepreneurship, spoke of motivations such as the "will to conquer" and the "joy of creating, of getting things done, of simply exercising one's energy and ingenuity."[4] But where there is joy and victory, there can be anguish and fatigue. All three of us have experienced the joys of innovation success and the bitterness of innovation setbacks as various "fatigue factors" are encountered. A missing element in much of the literature on innovation, in our opinion, is the personal voyage that individuals experience, including individuals on teams within corporations, as they seek to bring an idea into reality. The fatigue factors that cause weariness and frustration, the energizing factors that give encouragement and hope, the personal drive to move forward in spite of resistance, and the joys and sorrows of innovation throughout that journey must be understood if we are to keep innovation alive and build healthy cultures of innovation.

The profit motive is only a part of that picture. Even seemingly modest inventions can end up contributing to the quality of life, or may contribute to larger ends such as saving lives and preventing crime. The desire of the innovator to make a difference, even if it is just seeing a new product on the shelf, is a surprisingly common sentiment. While many of us desire financial returns, for some inventors, a higher inspiration fuels their passion. Ben Markham is one such individual.

EmpowerPlaygrounds and the Light of Innovation

Ben Markham is the innovator behind an exciting new venture that is transforming lives in Africa. The inspiration occurred while Ben and his wife were living in Ghana on a humanitarian and religious mission after he retired from a long career as a chemical engineer at ExxonMobil. Ben observed that the children of West Africa rarely had toys to play with and school classrooms were frequently quite dark. Many school buildings were simple concrete shells with few windows and no electrical power, often far too dark for effective education. One day he saw an article about a rotating ring device for pumping water from shallow wells. He wondered if playground equipment such as a merry-go-round could be designed to produce electricity from children at play. As he discussed his desire to make schools more fun for children, local citizens helped him recognize an even higher priority: education. The students in rural schools were handicapped in their studies by the lack of lighting at home and hands-on experience with mechanical and electrical devices. When they weren't in school, they were expected to be doing manual labor required on the family farm while it was light. When chores ended, it would be too dark to study or do homework. With these handicaps, almost unthinkable in many Western nations where lighting and labor saving devices are taken for granted, the vast majority of rural Ghanaian students are unable to pass the tests required to advance to high school. Future opportunities for children could be vastly improved by access to lighting and exposure to hands-on science education.

As Ben contemplated this challenge, a "revolutionary" concept emerged: merry-go-rounds at schools could be connected to small wind power generators creating electrical power for recharging portable LED lanterns. Students would control lighting in the school and at home for studying after dark. "It was far more difficult than I thought it would be," Ben told us.[5] The technical challenges of generating a steady voltage for charging a low-cost automotive battery involved many factors and several unfruitful avenues. With the help of creative students and professors volunteering their assistance at Brigham Young University-Idaho and BYU in Provo, Utah (Ben's alma mater), Ben was able to make his invention more practical while meeting high standards of safety and reliability. Ben also insisted that as much as possible be made locally in Ghana.

The basic concept was simple, but as with most innovations, more than just technology is involved. Innovation in the business model is often needed to bring the product or service to life. Ben requires that the headmaster of any targeted school have a reputation of honesty. Further, he found that the leaders of the school need to be committed to the project. He tests for commitment by asking them to write a proposal explaining how they will administer oversight of the lamps, since there may be only 30 lamps for 100 students, for example. Ben has no preconceived right answer in mind, but wants to see the leaders develop a reasonable plan to meet student needs. The very act of preparing the proposal is also a useful measure of commitment.

With the merry-go-round generator as a first invention, Ben founded a charitable organization, EmpowerPlaygrounds,[6] to deliver the invention to schools. There were other challenges to overcome, including local regulations regarding schools and import regulations that initially threatened to impose high duties on equipment. These external factors have been dealt with, and now EmpowerPlaygrounds is moving ahead to serve additional schools. *"I'm doing this for no other reason than to help the children in Africa,"* Ben told us. What a wonderful motivation for innovation. Their primary need now is for additional funds to continue empowering students across Africa.

The result of Ben's work has been successful where implemented. Kids love the special merry-go-round and love the freedom to study even when it's dark. Ben's vision has now grown beyond merry-go-rounds. Ben continues collaborating with others in pursuit of further inventions, with the goal of an entire playground of devices that can help provide power for large schools. The merry-go-round alone is helpful for schools of about 100 to 150 children. With his recently developed power-generating swings and zip-lines (pulley-suspended rope cables that allow users to travel from high places to low, creating electricity from a generator attached to a pulley on one end), Ben is well on his way to achieving his vision and experiencing more of the joy that meaningful innovation can bring.

Tesla's Sacrifice

Motives higher than profit fueled the work of another inventor who helped bring light to others. In this case, billions of others. Nikola Tesla, one of the greatest inventors and innovators of all time, ushered in the electric age with his revolutionary vision of efficient alternating current (AC) power. His systems for generating, transmitting, and operating motors and other devices from AC power are the foundation for much of the technology in the modern world. He also was the father of the radio and other wireless broadcast technologies, in addition to generating hundreds of patents in dozens of areas.

After arriving penniless in the United States, this Serbian immigrant from present-day Croatia would face several of the fatigue factors discussed in this book: he may have been denied recognition for important innovations he created for Thomas Edison; he faced intense opposition in his pursuit of AC power from Edison himself; he was sometimes ridiculed by others not only for his foreign appearance and ways but for his "impossible" ideas;[7] and he even had his personal belongings confiscated by a powerful agency of the United States government—the now defunct Office of the Alien Property Custodian, created by an executive order to deal with purported enemy threats from aliens in World War II. (The confiscation of his property—inspired by rumors that Tesla had invented a death ray—may not have been too troubling to him since it occurred shortly after his death in 1943, but it was a final insult to this great immigrant and an illegal act since he was not an alien but a U.S. citizen since 1891.)

What inspired this immigrant to persist in innovation? Wealth and recognition were not his goal, as he wrote in his autobiography— indeed, his disdain for corporate profits may have contributed to

Exhibit 1.3   A high honor for Tesla from his homeland of Serbia—printed during a time (1993-1994) when hyperinflation was a devastating external fatigue factor for local entrepreneurs

trouble later in life when he faded from the limelight and died in relative poverty. Rather than wealth, Tesla sought the heroic path of the inventor who makes the world better.[8] He even voluntarily tore up his contract to spare George Westinghouse the burden of royalty payments to him after the "Current Wars" with Edison left Westinghouse financially strained. He wrote that the betterment of mankind was "the difficult task of the inventor who is often misunderstood and unrewarded. But he finds ample compensation in the pleasing exercises of his powers and in the knowledge of being one of that exceptionally privileged class without whom the race would have long ago perished in the bitter struggle against pitiless elements."[9]

Corporations, governments, and others sometimes fail to appreciate the intrinsic incentives for innovation that go beyond financial reward. That failure can result in unintended discouragement of innovation as leaders assume all is well as long as financial incentives and written expectations are in place. Sadly, pay can be great but incentives to truly innovate may be absent when the intrinsic incentives are ignored or when trust is breeched (see Chapter 7). On the other hand, we are aware of corporate leaders who point to the importance of intrinsic incentives as justification for not offering financial incentives for innovation. This can sometimes be indicative of a culture profoundly lacking in the intrinsic incentives as well, or one suffering from fatigue factors such as devaluation of the innovator.

For corporate employees, we have found that money *per se* is rarely the driving force for leading inventors, though none have complained about receiving it and it is certainly an enabling factor. Indeed, financial incentives for inventors can stimulate additional innovation or can motivate extra-mile efforts to generate intellectual assets. However, recognition, respect, appreciation from peers, the chance to make a difference in the marketplace, the thrill of seeing a concept take life, the satisfaction of being included in major projects, and many other intrinsic factors play important roles.

Are there other Teslas in our midst whose brilliant potential is dimmed by our unwillingness to listen, cooperate, and help an innovator who thinks with an accent?

Whatever the personal incentives driving innovation, many of the fatigue factors we have outlined above stand as threats to success. Before we explore them in detail, we take one more step in understanding the often overlooked personal interaction of innovators with innovation systems, especially those used in corporations. This exploration will use another metaphor where we offer a twist—and perhaps a few curves—on some traditional models of innovation. Our goal is to build a framework for understanding how innovators, at the personal level, must be considered in the full spectrum of innovation efforts to enhance efficiency and reduce innovation fatigue.

Notes

1. Everett M. Rogers, *Diffusion of Innovation* (New York: Free Press, 1962). Rogers defines diffusion as "the process by which an innovation is communicated through certain channels over time among the members of a social system" (Rogers, 4th ed., 1995, 5), as cited by G. David Garson, "Diffusion Theory," North Carolina State Univ., http://faculty.chass.ncsu.edu/garson/PA765/diffusion.htm (accessed Oct. 13, 2008).
2. "Executive Briefing: Is Innovation Bogging Down?", *Investors Business Daily*, May 29, 2007, A6.
3. Jean-Pierre Garnier, "Rebuilding the R&D Engine in Big Pharma," *Harvard Business Review*, 86, no. 5 (May 2008): 68-76.
4. Joseph A. Schumpeter, *The Theory of Economic Development: An Inquiry Into Profits, Capital, Credit, Interest, and the Business Cycle*, transl. by Redvers Opie (Brunswick, NJ: Transaction Publishers,1983, orig. in German, 1934), 93.

5. Ben Markham, interview by Jeff Lindsay, Sept. 12, 2008.
6. See www.EmpowerPlaygrounds.org.
7. Margaret Cheney and Robert Uth, *Tesla, Master of Lightning* (New York: Barnes and Noble, 1999), 13.
8. Ibid., vi.
9. Nikola Tesla, *My Inventions: The Autobiography of Nikola Tesla* (Williston, Vermont: Hart Brothers, 1982), as cited by Wikipedia contributors, "My Inventions: The Autobiography of Nikola Tesla," *Wikipedia*, http://en.wikipedia.org/wiki/My_Inventions (accessed Nov. 16, 2008).

CHAPTER

The Funnel vs. the "Horn of Innovation™"

One of the most useful and common metaphors for visualizing the front end of the innovation process is the funnel. The broad end of the funnel (see Exhibit 2.1) represents the many concepts that are considered as a company does early stage exploration. Possibilities are progressively winnowed as the funnel converges into a narrow pipeline of projects to be launched. Henry Chesbrough in his groundbreaking book *Open Innovation*[1] invoked that model to compare conventional in-house innovation to open innovation, in which inventions and concepts from outside can enter the pipeline at various stages of development. In any case, the standard model of new product development is funicular—and very slow, with only a few carefully selected concepts dripping from the end of the pipeline into the market. Open innovation increases the input to the funnel and can accelerate output, but from the perspective of innovators at the broad end, only a tiny fraction of their efforts will be among the few "survivors" that have any hope of impact on the market.

In other words, the innovation funnel can be hostile territory for prospective innovators as much of their creative effort is lost in the massive waste streams disappearing from the funnel or trapped in endless vortices of indecision. For some industries, the funnel model may be the most reasonable approach. In pharmaceuticals, for example, it makes sense that only one winning drug of many

15

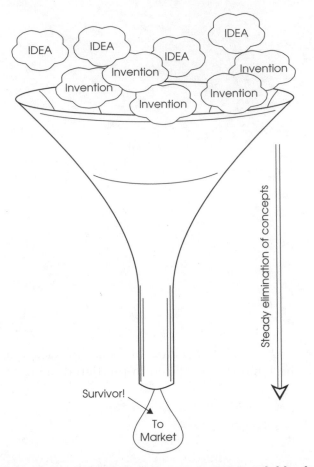

Exhibit 2.1   The funnel of innovation, a common model to describe the winnowing of early stage concepts to select innovations to commercialize

thousands of candidates should make it to market due to the high uncertainties and risk involved. However, in industries with different constraints, a different paradigm may help.

Instead of the flow of innovation growing weaker and weaker to a trickle from the narrow end of the pipeline, what would happen if we turned things around and considered innovation as a horn (see Exhibit 2.2)? In a "French horn model of innovation," directed energy from the innovator enters the pipeline at one end—the mouthpiece. This "inspiration" goes through internal bends, transforming itself

Exhibit 2.2   The French horn: an alternative to the funnel?

as it interacts with the constraints of the instrument, and then expands out of the bell (the open funnel) into the environment—the marketplace.

Unlike the fixed notes on a piano, playing a given note on a horn requires delicate adjustments by the hornist in the vibration or "buzz" of the lips, the position of facial muscles, and even the shaping of the hand that is placed in the flared opening (the bell) of the horn, a unique aspect of modern horn playing. Hitting a desired note involves an iterative feedback loop as the hornist senses the sound coming from the horn and its interaction with the environment (e.g., how it blends with other musical instruments), and constantly makes adjustments to achieve the desired effect. If the feedback loop is cut off, the music can quickly become out of tune.

In our paradigm of the "Horn of Innovation™," the hornist is the prospective innovator. In the corporate version of this model, the hornist may represent R&D staff, and other inventors and innovation engines within the corporation. In other contexts, the hornist may be a university professor, a graduate student, an entrepreneur, the CEO of a start-up, a lone inventor or team of innovators. The efforts of innovators to breathe life into their inspired ideas (recalling the Latin root *spirare*, to breathe) should not be mostly wasted breath, as in traditional funnels of innovation, but should consistently contribute to delivered output that affects the environment, where the audience and the music hall represent the market. The acoustic input from the hornist, the buzz of vibrating lips, initially sounds rough and non-musical, but it is systematically transformed into melodious notes as that input is refined, shaped, and mellowed by the nonlinear pipeline—the midsection of the horn—with its many curves, bends, valves, and changing diameter. This is shown in Exhibit 2.3.

The transformation of the raw buzz in this midsection represents the contributions of other teams, interactions with partners, and adjustments in response to important constraints. The innovation system encompassed in the horn includes sound innovation channels that provide alternate pathways when needed, as do the valves in the physical horn. Finally, what exits into the marketplace is further refined with hands-on guidance. "Handstopping," an important practice in playing the French horn, involves placing a hand in the open end (the "bell") of the horn where it can be used to shape the final sound (timbre and volume) and make fine adjustments to the pitch. The hand can represent management and others, including the innovator, working together to ensure that the output is on key, fits the score (the business plans), and follows further on-the-fly guidance from the director.

The feedback loop involving the hornist is absolutely critical to the success of the output. Think of the difficulties if the hornist were isolated from the output and could not sense what emerged from the bell. This is what happens with many corporate innovation groups, where technical people are kept isolated from much of the business and market activity that could have better guided their creative work. Many innovation personnel have complained about the lost vision and knowledge that has occurred when they are required to simply hand off their inventions to other groups without being involved in the shaping of the output to meet market needs. Being "out of the loop" is one of the most common frustrations we hear from innovators in corporations.

To further complicate things, imagine a hornist with a poorly copied, hard-to-read score, or perhaps with an outdated score that might even have the wrong music, or without any score at all. Without clear and accurate guidance, constant feedback and iterative adjustments, and involvement in the modification and reshaping of the notes, it might take hundreds of hornists to get a few successful notes—somewhat like the traditional innovation funnel.

The transformation of the "innovator's buzz"—however inspired it may be—to a melodious tune aligned with the rest of the orchestra to please the marketplace requires tremendous transformation

The Horn of Innovation

From Inspiration & Buzz to Efficient On-Target Output:
An Iterative, Inclusive Process with Cross-System Feedback

Feedback Loop: Sense & Adjust

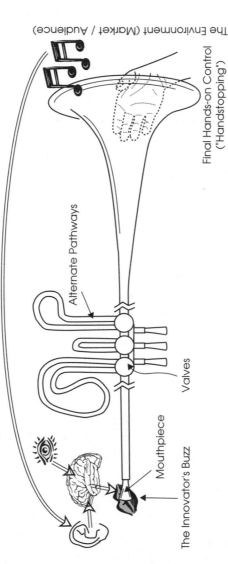

The Environment (Market / Audience)

Alternate Pathways

Final Hands-on Control ("Handstopping")

Mouthpiece

Valves

The Innovator's Buzz

Steady Refinement and Mellowing from Sound Pathways and Interaction with Constraints

Exhibit 2.3 A simplified, stretched-out horn illustrating the "Horn of Innovation™," a metaphor for enhancing innovation success

within the instrument. It requires direction and feedback at many levels. When done properly, the innovator's efforts are less likely to result in wasted breath and more likely to be part of targeted, directed, aligned innovation in which the innovator is included and has a hand in the final success of the efforts. In other words, success can come when the innovator's "buzz"—inspiration, the initial idea—is coupled with perspiration (the work) and aspiration (the vision) in an environment where the innovator is connected to the right sources of feedback and guidance.

Interestingly, in the physics of the horn, positive feedback from the acoustic waves inside the horn also affect the vibration of the lips, helping the lips to open and close at the proper frequency of the horn.[2] By analogy, the corporate inventor can benefit from feedback from the corporate system as concepts progress and move toward commercialization (see Exhibit 2.4). Internal feedback during the early stages as well as external feedback during market testing and commercialization can guide the efforts of inventors and improve their performance. Without that, there can be lots of noise but little music. Again, the model of the "Horn of Innovation™" calls for increased involvement of the innovation community in

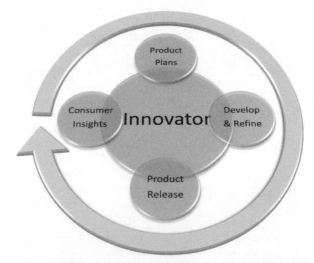

Exhibit 2.4   The iterative feedback loop of successful innovation involves innovators throughout the process

corporate new product development efforts, and for targeted efforts which are less likely to waste the energy of star performers. Less wasted energy means less fatigue among innovators.

In this model, there is still dissipated and trapped energy. In fact, much of the acoustic energy in a physical horn during play is held within its tubing in the form of standing acoustic waves.[3] This energy, in a sense, is delayed and kept in reserve, like many new product concepts, but much of it will eventually leave the bell and enter the environment in some form. Some of the internal energy is dissipated through the walls of the horn. Further, some of the energy expended by the hornist is lost at the lips and never makes it into the horn. Perfect efficiency is not achieved—there will still be some winnowing and loss, but far more of the expended effort results in output to the environment than in the traditional funnel model. This requires more training and skill on the part of the innovators, higher quality corporate systems for directing and transforming inventive input, and aggressive feedback systems that can quickly learn from the market and make iterative adjustments, with innovators closely coupled to the system, ensuring that innovative energy is on key to meet the needs of the market.

Some may see the concept of a hornist following a score from someone else as a poor model for an innovator, so we could extend the analogy to the case of the hornist as composer, perhaps in a solo work, or as an improviser in a jazz group, where the music played is innovation in action. However, delivering pleasing melodies from the horn, regardless of who wrote the score and who is directing, requires artistry and creative interpretation from the hornist that goes far beyond rote labor. The hornist is an artist who actively participates in the creation of a musical experience for the audience, regardless of who composed the sequence of notes being played.

The French horn offers still further insights into innovation, as we see in a brief review of history.

The Rise of the "Invention Horn"

Horns in various forms date back thousands of years, but only in recent history became able to play enough notes to be of use in formal music. Before about 1750, the sound produced could only be controlled with the lips and was governed by the fixed internal acoustics and natural harmonics of the horn. Only a few notes could be played, and complete scales were out of the question. Then German hornist A.J. Hampel is said to have discovered an improved way to control the pitch of the horn by placing his hand in the flared opening and adjusting hand shape and position.[4,5] With the discovery of "hand stopping," notes could be played that were not in the harmonic series. Full scales were possible and new possibilities arose for melodic playing. His innovation is considered to be one of the most important in the development of the horn. (As with many innovations, there are legitimate questions about misappropriated credit. Other hornists in the 1720s may have already practiced the technique.[6])

The invention might have faded if Hampel had not made efforts to teach it to others who had the energy and skills to carry it to others. Hampel taught a gifted student, Giovanni Punto, who further improved the technique and carried it across Europe, developing a large network of influential people to draw attention to the possibilities of the horn. The new potential of the "French horn" (the name of this largely Germanic or Alpine instrument is another possible case of unfairly allocated credit) would inspire Beethoven and others.[7,8] Whether in music or nanotech, enlisting the help of people with the right connections can make all the difference in the success of an innovation.

What we can learn from A.J. Hampel and the horn doesn't stop there. Hampel went on to collaborate with a talented instrument maker in Dresden, Johann Werner. Together they designed a new horn with a set of detachable tubing sections, "crooks," that could alter both the mouthpiece and the middle of the horn, allowing a broad range of transpositions to be achieved. Coupled with hand-stopping, the new horn could play a full chromatic scale in any key.

What did Hampel and Werner call the fruit of their collaborative invention? It was called the *Inventionshorn*—the Invention Horn[9] (also known as the Orchestra Horn). How appropriate! After steady refinements from 1750 to 1755, the horn was no longer a raucous and occasional "special effect" in music, but was "firmly established as a refined musical instrument and became a regular member of the symphony orchestra"[10]—thanks to the enduring innovations of Hampel, who built on the work of others, collaborated with skilled professionals to convert his ideas to reality, and gained the support of highly connected influencers to spread his innovations throughout the musical world.

The "Horn of Innovation™" is the fruit of successful innovation practices and also a symbol or model for several aspects of innovation.

Hampel's system of crooks reminds us of open innovation, where adjustments to the pipeline can be made by plugging in the desired capabilities from without. Need a different technology in your pipeline? Plug in a section from a collection of available "crooks" (a term we hope does not describe your outside partners!) to alter the output.

The horn originated as a tool for extending the human voice, making it easier for the shepherd to call to his flock or for one person to call others. It is thus a symbol of communication and of spreading information and influence to many, a reminder of the social efforts required in converting ideas to innovations that others adopt. We also see the horn as a symbol of "the voice of the innovator," a theme we use to describe the insights that come from understanding innovation and its challenges at the personal level. Later in this book, we call upon corporate leaders, policy makers, and others to listen to the often neglected voice of the innovator in their decision making.

In Latin, the word for horn is *cornu*, as in *cornucopia*, the symbol of abundance and plenty from a rich harvest. This stems from a Greek myth about the goat Amalthea who raised Zeus on her milk. When a horn broke off during play with Zeus, Zeus gave it back to her—now a unicorn—with the added power that the horn could grant wishes to whoever had it. Thus, the horn is also a symbol of converting ideas into reality, of fulfilling unmet needs with the abundance that innovation creates, originating with human thought.

The horn also reminds us of the need for endurance and stamina in innovation, for the hornist must be able to constantly buzz the lips with proper embouchure (the use of facial muscles and the shaping of the lips while playing) throughout performances and rehearsals, which can easily lead to soreness and fatigue. Constant delivery of air, especially during long series of connected notes, also requires stamina. Doing this well in front of an audience also requires courage and the confidence to take risks.

Continuing the analogy with the hornist as innovator, let us consider handstopping. Even with the benefits of valves in modern horns, a hand in the bell is still needed to improve and shape the sound.

By altering hand position, a shift of as much as a half tone can be achieved, in addition to shaping other aspects of the sound. Feedback from the environment to the ear can identify the need for regular adjustments provided by the hand in the bell—analogous to the guidance of management. Achieving the targeted output based on the written score requires the creative work of innovators, iterating in response to feedback from the marketplace and guidance from management and others who shape and adapt innovation for success. This iterative approach is similar to that advocated by Clayton Christensen for disruptive innovation, where learning quickly from the marketplace is essential to developing new products in unpredictable areas.[11]

The concepts from the "Horn of Innovation™" may help produce more directed and cost-effective innovation. By beginning with targeted innovation inspired by the right strategy and enabled with the right minds, companies can breathe life into their "Horn of Innovation™," iteratively guiding the tone produced as results flow into the marketplace. With targeted efforts and cross-system feedback, more people will see some tangible result of their work and can be energized by that experience, even if the note produced was initially off-key and needed a little handstopping.

Naturally, the score itself needs to be carefully composed and suited for the audience. Country music at a jazz fest may cause frustration for all the players involved. But even the best score will fail without the artistic contributions of the players and their inclusion in the feedback loop inherent to live music.

More effective learning from the marketplace is essential for the success of many innovations. For example, Kleenex® facial tissue was actually launched as a cold cream removal aid—a niche product. However, numerous letters from the public revealed that the soft tissue was valued for its role as a disposable handkerchief. Learning from the marketplace, not from research prior to launching, allowed Kimberly-Clark to completely reposition their tissue product to become one of the world's most famous and useful brands, offering a classic example of a disruptive innovation. With a better feedback loop according to the "Horn of Innovation™," the process might have been much faster and more efficient.

Again, the "Horn of Innovation™" is not meant to replace funnel-based paradigms in all cases, but when it is applicable, its concepts can increase innovator efficiency and reduce some common sources of innovation fatigue. However, some of the lessons learned from considering the horn model can be helpful even when a funnel approach best describes the constraints of an industry's new product development system. For example, improved feedback loops involving inventors and other prospective innovators can be helpful in most cases. Other widely applicable concepts include (1) learning rapidly and iteratively from the market-place, (2) creating internal systems that take the buzz of innovators and transform it progressively with innovators included in the process, and (3) generally listening to the "voice of the innovator"—a voice that, when coupled with the right systems, guidance, and encouragement, can create inspiring benefits for the rest of the world.

Notes

1. Henry Chesbrough, *Open Innovation: The New Imperative for Creating and Profiting from Technology* (Boston: Harvard Business School Press, 2003).
2. Matthew Panayiotou, "The French Horn," *MatthewPanayiotou.com*, 2005, www.matthewpanayiotou.com/articles/fhorn/?page=all (accessed Nov. 9, 2008).
3. Ibid.
4. Thomas Bacon, "A Brief History of Horn Evolution," *HornPlanet.com*, 2008, www.hornplanet.com/hornpage/museum/history/horn_history1.html (accessed Nov. 7, 2008).
5. "Horn (Instrument)," *Wikipedia*, http://en.wikipedia.org/wiki/Horn_(instrument) (accessed Nov. 7, 2008).
6. Thomas Bacon, "A Brief History of Horn Evolution: 2. Crooks and Hand Horns," HornPlanet.com, 2008, www.hornplanet.com/hornpage/museum/history/horn_history2.html (accessed Nov. 7, 2008).
7. Ibid.
8. Gary Smith, "Giovanni Punto [Johann Wenzel (Jan Václav) Stich] (1746–1803), "*TheMozartForum*, www.mozartforum.com/Contemporary%20Pages/Giovanni_Punto_Contemp.htm (or http://tinyurl.com/gpunto) (accessed Nov. 9, 2008).
9. John Humphries, *The Early Horn: A Practical Guide* (Cambridge, UK: Cambridge University Press, 2000), 28–29.
10. Bacon, "A Brief History of Horn Evolution."
11. Clayton M. Christensen and Michael E. Raynor, *The Innovator's Solution* (Boston: Harvard Business School Press, 2003).

PEOPLE FATIGUE—PROBLEMS AT THE INDIVIDUAL LEVEL

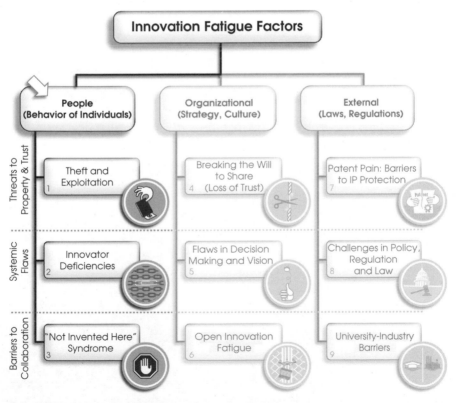

Exhibit 3.1 Fatigue factors at the individual level

Enduring Innovation Fatigue

ANOTHER LOOK AT TELEVISION

Quiz time. Can you name the inventors of any of the following?

- The first incubator for infants
- The PPI Projector, forerunner of modern air traffic control systems
- An atomic fusion system using "fusors," the first device that could clearly demonstrate production of controlled fusion reactions (still in commercial use as a neutron source)
- The "image dissector," a camera tube for converting an image into an electronic signal that can be transmitted
- The "image oscillite," a cathode ray tube receiver that could display images captured by the image dissector
- The first completely electronic television system

If your list mentioned Philo T. Farnsworth at least once, congratulations! You're among the tiny minority that has heard of this inventor. If you listed him for every invention, you get full credit. Now, who invented television? This could be a trick question, for no single answer is accurate. Many inventors played a role, but significant contributions of Philo Farnsworth to television were largely ignored in the press until recently. With a resurgence of interest, the Farnsworth story is now being told, often framed as a David vs. Goliath tale in which Goliath won and stole the invention and fame from the rightful owner, illustrating the fatigue factor of theft, among others. That tragic story stirs our sympathies and teaches valuable lessons for prospective innovators. However, there is another side to the story, and it may be even more instructive.

One Perspective: Farnsworth, the Wronged Inventor

One more question: What does a potato field have to do with television? The connection provides an instructive example of how great inventors draw upon experiences all around them to solve problems in other fields.

At age 13, growing up in Rigby, Idaho, Philo T. Farnsworth thought about electricity and electronics as he worked on the family farm. The boy contemplated the challenge of television, which then could only be achieved at the crudest level using rotating mechanical means of breaking up an image into an electrical signal, an approach that could never reach the speeds needed for meaningful image transmission. A year later, as he plowed a field, making regular scans back and forth, one row at a time, he realized that an image could be electrically dissected into rows and assembled row by row, stitched together by the eye. Thus was born the concept of the electronic television system he would later demonstrate and patent. Though many inventors contributed to the development of the modern television, part of the credit must go to Philo. In 1927, at just twenty years of age, he conducted the first demonstration of a television system that did not rely upon mechanical means like spinning disks for dissecting an optical image to create an electrical signal.[1] The same year he filed a patent for an entire television system. *Wired Magazine* recently named the potato field that Philo plowed in Idaho as one of the unlikely places where great inventors had their "Eureka!" moments.[2]

Farnsworth's journey was far from easy. In a sense, he would be shunned by the elite citizens of academia and business as a foreigner, a mere farm boy without the right credentials. This attitude from others may have contributed strongly to the barriers he faced. Or was the problem the inability of this immigrant innovator to learn the language and ways of the established citizens and gain the mentoring and advanced education he needed to succeed?

FIRST TELEVISION CAMERA · USA

Philo T. Farnsworth   20c

Exhibit 3.2   Farnsworth honored on a U.S. stamp in 1983

When the Farnsworth family moved to Provo, Utah, young Farnsworth began to take some courses, but his father died and he had to work to support the family. Farnsworth persisted, and soon received funding from two businessmen from California. Filled with new hope, he married his childhood sweetheart and went to California, where the living room of his Hollywood home would become his laboratory. Finances became tight again, and he turned to his backers for more. Fortunately, he soon had something valuable to show them, a patent on the electronic television. Things were looking up when he received favorable publicity and an offer from a Philadelphia radio company to bring his research (equipment and staff) to them for a collaborative effort.

Some of the greatest opposition he faced would come from one of the most powerful forces in the early world of electronics: RCA. The fatigue factors were many and overwhelming, as told in several sympathetic accounts such as Vince Horiuchi's "Mormon Farm Boy: Inventor of Television."[3]

In 1930, RCA's president, David Sarnoff, hired Vladimir Zworykin, a Russian immigrant who had also been pursuing television. Zworykin visited Farnsworth and reported back. Some say Sarnoff was impressed with the work. Others say his main interest was in Farnsworth's patent. Either way, Sarnoff soon offered Farnsworth $100,000 for the rights to his work. Farnsworth and his backers declined, upsetting Sarnoff. RCA soon developed the iconoscope, a camera tube similar to the image dissector of Farnsworth, which some suspect may have been a reverse engineering of Farnsworth's invention.

Sarnoff launched a patent battle (an "interference") in which RCA claimed that Zworykin was the real inventor of Farnsworth's Image Dissector concept, that Farnsworth was infringing Zworykin's patent, and that the patent rights should belong to RCA. Farnsworth felt this was an outrageous move aimed at defrauding him from his patent. A lengthy, costly legal battle ensued and continued over the next four years to determine who should receive the patent for the television. This interference proceeding would tie up Farnsworth for lengthy interrogations by RCA lawyers, hindering his own work to further advance television and imposing heavy burdens and costs in defending his patent. The battle centered on Claim 15 of Farnsworth's 1930 patent #1,773,980, "Television System," filed in 1927:

> 15. An apparatus for television which comprises means for forming an electrical image, and means for scanning each elementary area of the electrical image, and means for producing a train of electrical energy in accordance with the intensity of the elementary area of the electrical image being scanned.

This simple claim essentially describes what Farnsworth conceived as a teenager in Rigby, Idaho: a means for forming an electrical image using scanning. RCA claimed that this claim should belong to Zworykin for his 1923 patent application for the iconoscope, which eventually issued as U.S. Pat. No. 2,141,059 in 1935. While Zworykin's patent shows some significant concepts in the direction of electric television, the Patent and Trademark Office (PTO) ruled that Zworykin's use of photoelectric globules did not fit Farnsworth's definition of electrical image for Claim 15. There was also no physical evidence presented (notebook entries or specimens) to show that Zworykin's 1923 invention was successfully constructed.[4]

In 1934, the PTO ruled that Farnsworth was the rightful inventor and that RCA had no right to make the invention of Claim 15. RCA had 16 months to appeal, and waited until the last day to file. The process wore on, but after losing all appeals in multiple cases against Farnsworth's patents, in 1939 RCA finally capitulated and agreed to license Farnsworth's patents for $1,000,000. This was the first patent that RCA ever licensed. While Farnsworth had prevailed, he still felt drained.

During World War II, television production was suspended by the U.S. government. After the war, Farnsworth's patents had little life left, and his position was looking desperate. With RCA's publicity efforts, Sarnoff and Zworykin were being called the true inventors of television. Farnsworth had a nervous breakdown. His wife said, "He had put his whole life into this, and he felt he had spent all this time and energy for nothing because he didn't think his patents would still be valid." This was the nadir of innovation fatigue. While television would become one of the most important inventions in his lifetime, his role was largely unknown, and only recently was the story retold when Farnsworth's wife, in her 90s, wrote a biography called *Distant Vision*.[5]

Farnsworth endured innovation fatigue factors of many kinds, but kept innovating, generating many valuable technologies but also spending most of what he had in the futile quest for nuclear fusion in the home. At the time of his death, he held 300 domestic and foreign patents, little wealth and very little recognition for what he had achieved.

Now recognition for his work is growing. He has been given an honorary Emmy. There is a statue of him in the Capitol. A peak was named after him in the Oquirrh Mountains of Utah where television station antennas sit. The U.S. Postal Service commemorated him with a stamp in 1983. (See Exhibit 3.2.) *Time* declared him one of the 20 most important scientists and thinkers of the 20th century, while *U.S. News & World Report* called him one of the world's greatest inventors. Brigham Young University turned his life into a stage play called *A Love Affair with Electrons*.[6] In 2007, another play, *The Farnsworth Invention* by Aaron Sorkin debuted at the LaJolla Playhouse and later opened on Broadway; it was generally sympathetic to Farnsworth.[7]

Lessons (First Perspective)

Lessons? First, Farnsworth would not have had a chance without patents. Frankly, a more thorough intellectual asset strategy might have helped, including a series of related patents around key television inventions. Proper protection for major inventions remains critical today, though some of the rules and strategies have changed. Second, we can see the pain that the pride of others can cause, as some people refused to believe that a man without an elite education and vast resources could have accomplished what Farnsworth did. Finally, we see the importance of connecting with the right people and getting help from the right sources. A generous source of funds was essential for Farnsworth's early success. Beyond that, his lack of connections to major sources of financial and media power may have put him at a severe disadvantage.

Farnsworth's biggest challenge may have been his "immigrant" status. A foreigner to the elite halls of the established citizens of electronics and business, this rough and unschooled farm boy from Idaho was truly an alien. He produced a brilliant advance, but failed to gain the acceptance of the elite. He needed the assistance and recognition of others. A strong company as a partner early on could have made the difference, perhaps.

The case of Philo T. Farnsworth begins with the inspiring triumph of a lone inventor but ends as one of the sadder stories of innovation fatigue. While it may discourage some, let us remember that Farnsworth did succeed. He helped bring television to the world, he prevailed in court, and history is beginning to remember him as "the father of television." With the right team of partners, a marketing strategy and a more holistic intellectual asset strategy, we believe things could have turned out much better.

That's where we might be tempted to leave the story— Farnsworth as victim of corporate greed and theft, dying unrecognized for one of the greatest inventions ever, succumbing to innovation fatigue but triumphing nonetheless, even if posthumously. However, there is another reasonable perspective that demands consideration.

The Other Immigrants: Another Perspective

Dr. Alexander B. Magoun, Executive Director of the David Sarnoff Library in Princeton, New Jersey, has kindly offered us several insights into another side of the Farnsworth story, particularly the legacy of David Sarnoff and Vladimir Zworykin, both immigrants from Russia. Magoun is also the author of *Television: The Life Story of a Technology*.[8] Magoun's review of the play, *The Farnsworth Invention* made several salient points:

The flaws with the play are not in Sorkin's mash-up of history and fiction. . . . They appear in the effort to make a tragedy out of a conflict between an inventor and an innovator. There are lots of brilliant inventors, but many of their inventions or patents never make it to the factory or the consumer, because of technical drawbacks, someone else's better idea, the lack of entrepreneurial support, the wrong market, or the wrong cultural moment for the right market. There are arguably fewer brilliant entrepreneurs who have a vision, a place for particular inventions and products within that vision, and a sense of what the right market will bear. . . . Sarnoff invariably "wins" because as innovator he commands the financial and intellectual resources to take the best inventions and organize the groups necessary to turn them from paper ideas into a popular commercial product.[9]

Magoun makes the point that the real lesson of Farnsworth's story is the need to nurture brilliant young people like Farnsworth and to help them gain the education and build the relationships needed to succeed.

He also argues against claims that Zworykin stole anything from Farnsworth. Rather he and Sarnoff "did what Thomas Edison did with electric light: take an invented, impractical technology and—with a great deal of support from engineers, scientists, technicians, marketers, investors, and customers—turn it into a commercial system that we and the rest of the world have used ever since."[10]

Magoun has pointed out that Farnsworth's television system, as exciting as it was, suffered from serious flaws related to its inability to store image information and the resulting need for painfully intense light on a subject to produce a visible image. If Farnsworth's patent indeed had limited commercial potential on its own, it may have been a serious error to refuse Sarnoff's offer for $100,000 and the opportunity to join forces with Sarnoff to more rapidly move toward commercialization.

In spite of the $1,000,000 Farnsworth eventually received, Farnsworth wasted much of that pursuing an impractical invention, nuclear fusion for the home. With the right mentoring and connections, he might have found better inventive battles to fight.

Zworykin, on the other hand, pursued innovation with the benefits of advanced education, business mentoring, and extensive financial support. Zworykin, like Sarnoff, was an immigrant from Russia. With Sarnoff's help as a visionary entrepreneur with financial and political means, Zworykin would ultimately receive about 120 U.S. patents and receive the United States' highest scientific honor, The National Medal of Science, awarded in 1966 by President Lyndon B. Johnson. Ultimately, Magoun calls us to respect the inventors Farnsworth and Zworykin, and "remain in awe of Sarnoff, the innovator" for his work that enabled the video age.[11]

Whatever one makes of the Farnsworth-Sarnoff controversy, this added perspective brings additional lessons. First, an inventor's sense of being robbed may not always represent reality. Second, few major innovations are the work of a single inventor. Others are almost always needed to fill in the gaps, guide development, and form connections with sources of capital. Third, Farnsworth needed help in understanding and appreciating the limitations of his own work. His confidence in what he had to offer may have been excessive and a barrier (see Fatigue Factor #4).

We find compelling elements in both perspectives of the story, and recognize that reality is rarely a simple story of good versus evil. We recommend considering both perspectives, while drawing one's own conclusions about who, if anyone, should be called the "father of television."

Notes

1. Howard B. Rockman, *Intellectual Property Law for Engineers and Scientists* (Hoboken, NJ: John Wiley & Sons, 2004), 337–349.
2. Mathew Honan, "Photo Essay: Unlikely Places Where Wired Pioneers Had Their Eureka! Moments," *Wired Magazine*, March 24, 2008, www.wired.com/culture/lifestyle/multimedia/2008/03/ff_eureka (accessed April 4, 2008).
3. Vince Horiuchi, "Mormon Farm Boy: Inventor of Television," *Salt Lake Tribune*, March 20, 2000, www.adherents.com/people/pf/Philo_Farnsworth.html (accessed April 5, 2008). See also Rockman, *Intellectual Property Law*, and Paul Schatzkin, *The Farnsworth Chronicles*, (Pts. 1–11), www.farnovision.com/chronicles/index.html (accessed Oct. 12, 2008).
4. Rockman, *Intellectual Property Law*, 344.
5. Elma G. "Pem" Farnsworth, *Distant Vision: Romance and Discovery on an Invisible Frontier* (Salt Lake City, UT: Pemberly Kent Publishers, 1990).
6. Ibid.
7. See, for example, Paul Schatzkin, "The Farnsworth Invention: Fact-v-Fiction," www.thefarnsworthinvention.com (accessed Oct. 12, 2008).

8. Alexander B. Magoun, *Television: The Life Story of a Technology* (Westport, CT: Greenwood Publishing Group, 2007).
9. Alexander B. Magoun, "Farewell to The Farnsworth Invention?", *The David Sarnoff Library Blog*, March 6, 2008, http://davidsarnoff.blogspot .com/2008/03/farewell-to-farnsworth-invention.html (accessed Sept. 12, 2008).
10. Alexander B. Magoun, "David Sarnoff, Vladimir Zworykin, and The Farnsworth Invention," *The David Sarnoff Library Blog*, Dec. 3, 2007, http://davidsarnoff .blogspot.com/2007/12/david-sarnoff-vladimir-zworykin-and.html (accessed Sept. 13, 2008).
11. Ibid.

CHAPTER

4

Fatigue Factor #1

THEFT AND EXPLOITATION

Theft and exploitation of inventors is more common than many might think, but the perpetrators often don't fit common stereotypes. Theft as a fatigue factor occurs when some other person or organization apparently steals an invention from an inventor. Theft as a fatigue factor also occurs when the recognition for an innovation goes to a less deserving party than the primary inventors, something that can even happen with a corporation. Exploitation is analogous, often due to attempts to take advantage of vulnerable or naïve inventors with the intent of taking money or intellectual property (IP) with little value returned.

The stories of lone inventors wronged by big corporations sometimes receive significant attention in the media. A famous example is Robert W. Kearns, the inventor of the intermittent windshield wiper who took his invention to big U.S. automakers, had it rejected, and then watched them commercialize his invention. The patent battles were lengthy and painful, going all the way to the Supreme Court, but he prevailed and won US$30 million. This drama is the subject of a 2008 film, *Flash of Genius*. When focusing on drama, historical and legal detail often becomes fuzzy. The "flash of genius" once said to be required for patentability was long repudiated when Kearns received his 1967 patent. Further, the courts found that the infringement from Ford and Chrysler was not "willful," as Ford has reminded viewers.[1] On the other hand, the fatigue Kearns experienced may be understated by cinema. The patent battles cost him at least two decades of his life, his job, his marriage, and more.[2] His obsession in achieving his legal goals and his unwillingness to accept an earlier settlement with Ford may have been mistakes. Sometimes the price for complete victory versus a painful compromise is far too high.

With cases like Kearns' well known to industry and with improved litigation opportunities for patent holders since the early 1980s, most major corporations now have strong internal policies against anything that could be construed as theft of a patented invention. We find many inventors afraid to take their inventions to large companies because they have been warned about corporate theft, but this is contrary to our experience. There are still dangers to avoid, but we encounter a disproportionate amount of fear based on reports of alleged outright theft.

On the other hand, many in the business world have encountered incidents where individuals in one company appear to have stolen ideas or technology from a partner. Many companies have faced negative experiences in which a vendor or supplier appears to have shared proprietary technology with competitors, or even filed patent applications on technology they picked up from the company. In some cases, the actions of both parties perhaps were in good faith and misunderstanding occurred or the relationship failed to properly delineate IP rights in the first place (contracts with inadequate attention to future IP are a common cause of frustration). However, real theft does occur, often as a result of an individual acting contrary to corporate standards, or sometimes as a result of a more serious corporate problem.

In some other cases, inventors victimized by alleged theft are actually wrong. History is filled with examples of independent minds creating similar inventions or making similar discoveries at roughly the same time, almost as if the inventions were inevitable in the technological climate of the time.[3] Stephen Stigler, a statistics professor at the University of Chicago, captures one aspect of this in "Stigler's Law of Eponymy," which holds that "No scientific discovery is named after its original discoverer."[4] (Naturally, Stigler attributes the discovery of this "law" to someone else.) When two different parties come up with similar inventions or discoveries, it is common to assume wrongdoing was involved, especially when they had some form of contact. However, dramatic stories of good vs. evil in the world of invention may sometimes overlook the complex nuances of reality in business and law, as we saw in Chapter 3.

Strong and consistent documentation, attention to legal detail, and cautious screening of partners can help reduce the threats for corporations and inventors, as we discuss hereafter.

Unrequited Innovation: The Pain of Others Getting Credit

A common theme among disgruntled inventors throughout history is the tendency for others to get credit for what they felt was their original concept. In some cases, embittered inventors are simply wrong, failing to recognize the immaturity of their concept and the significance of later work. However, in many cases, credit—either in the form of publicity, patents, royalties, or historical recognition—does not go where credit is due.

Consider the significance of the first recording of the human voice, an event that has been celebrated for decades as one of humanity's great steps forward, thanks to the vision and brilliance of the inventor of the phonograph, Thomas Edison—or was that Edouard-Leon Scott de Martinville?

Edouard-Leon Scott, a Frenchman born in 1817, went to his grave bitter about the world's failure to give him and the nation of France the recognition that went to Edison. Scott apparently was the first to record sound and the human voice, doing so two decades before Edison. Scott's name finally made headlines in the spring of 2008 when audio historians used digital tools to replay the sound of a woman singing "Au Claire de la Lune" from a recording Scott made on April 9, 1860, 17 years before Edison received his patent for the phonograph and 28 years before Edison successfully demonstrated the playback of recorded sound.[5] Scott's recording was done on a "phonoautogram" that recorded sound as a series of squiggles on soot-blackened paper. It was meant for analysis, not as a tool for replaying sounds, but with the help of scientists Carl Haber and Earl Cornell at Lawrence Berkeley National Laboratory, the squiggles, only recently uncovered at the Académie des Sciences in Paris, were digitally replayed using a virtual stylus.

As Edison gained fame for the phonograph, Scott railed against the alleged injustice. In a memoir he published in 1878, he accused

Edison of "appropriating" his methods and of missing the real point of his work. The goal was not replaying sounds, but "writing speech, which is what the word phonograph means." (Perhaps modern speech-to-text technologies owe a hat tip to Scott.) Echoing a lament of many inventors, Scott wrote, "Where are the rights of the discoverer versus the improver?" Not only did he feel a personal affront, but he suggested that France herself had been slighted, saying, "Come, Parisians, don't let them take our prize."

With all due respect to Scott, there is no evidence that Edison was aware of his work. As visionary as Scott was in recording sound, his work did not provide a way for replaying it. Edison remains the father of sound *reproduction*, and appears to have been an independent inventor of recorded sound.

We have encountered many inventors with similar frustration, wondering how their discoveries could have been unrecognized while a later improvement by a competitor resulted in fame and lucrative opportunities. Sadly, inventors often fail to recognize the limitation of their own inventions, seeing all the potential that the public might miss because of fatal flaws and limitations. The "improvement" of sound reproduction from a recording offers a world of benefits that an unplayable recording does not. The innovation that brings the improvement to the world of the consumer or allows it to solve real world problems can be the difference between a curiosity and a revolution. MP3 players existed before the iPod®, automobiles existed before the Model T, and computer networks existed before the Internet, but each provided benefits that brought the product to the public and gave the concept a life of its own. Improvements that fuel the social aspects of innovation— widespread adoption—are often where the real money and recognition may be found.

Perhaps if Scott had not let this discouragement cause innovation fatigue, he might have gone on to do more to advance his vision and change the world. Instead, he went to his grave bitter, focused on the past. In a sense, he dropped his horn of innovation and walked away after playing a few notes to an inattentive audience.

Innovators must not let apparent injustices hold them back. We'll offer guidance on how to reduce the risk and better protect your invention, but there is always the possibility that the invention will fail or won't be recognized, or that the profit and glory will go to someone who pursues a "minor" improvement. The journey is uncertain, but those who endure the frustration and keep innovating are more likely to find the success they deserve.

Avoiding "Theft" within the Corporation (Loss of Recognition)

Corporate inventors don't own their patents or inventions and have little that can be stolen from them, other than recognition. But when this is stolen or not properly given, it can be a fatigue factor that can hinder the effective future contributions of the unrecognized employee.

In one case, a friend of ours graduated with a Ph.D. from a major university and joined a Fortune 100 company. In his first week on the job, he had two bright ideas that he shared with an adjacent group and they recognized that he had something valuable. He was so excited to be contributing so quickly. The next week the manager of the other group called for a formal meeting to discuss solutions to current challenges. The solutions discussed were the ideas that this new employee had shared, but the source of the ideas was conveniently left out. When the new employee learned about it, he was outraged and resolved to no longer freely share his ideas with others in the company. We hope he gets over it and continues innovating. On the other hand, how unfortunate it was that credit for innovative thinking was withheld. Either way, it was not a great way to begin a career.

Another prolific and collaborative inventor shared this account with us:

> Some of my best ideas were inspired by other creative minds seeking a solution to a technical problem or my own curiosity about a technology and how to use it in simple process. But I ran into a real road block with a jealous manager.
>
> I was told by this manager to submit all ideas through him and that he would determine the merit, not the process [for handling] inventions. The same manager would claim these ideas as his and want his name as the inventor on occasion. I was also given a limit on the number of ideas I was allowed to submit. I was also asked to write an application for another employee so he could claim the work as his own and advance the individual's career.

I did make a decision to brighten my world of invention. I began giving ideas to others. I would seed a discussion with a topic and create an invention with a co-worker. I knew I was doing it to get around the manager. This allowed the ideas to be submitted within the co-worker's team and me as a secondary inventor. The idea was to seed the system with ideas. The best would rise to application. The manager was furious with my practice and tried at every opportunity to discredit my work.

The funny part to the whole story: one of my best ideas I gave to a large group knowing that it would be a winner. Mass customizing was it. I even had the mock ups made before anyone else knew about it. I worked with the attorneys to bypass the existing art. It was also the application the manager wanted me to write [thinking it was] for another employee. . . .

I made the choice to circumvent a bad manager with little integrity. I taught others the spirit of invention. I have reaffirmed my belief in the most valuable resource: PEOPLE. It is where innovation lives.

In corporations, recognition for the invention can be controlled by management and given to favorites or others instead of the internal inventors. From the perspective of the inventor, this may seem like a form of theft. In some cases, it's also an offense in the eyes of the law that can result in invalidation of a patent when incorrect inventors are intentionally listed, particularly in the U.S. Examples that we have encountered via reliable sources include managers who insisted on adding their names to patents from subordinates with little basis for the addition, or inventors in one group who were allegedly excluded for personal or political reasons by another group in charge of the patent filing for a particular project. Such complaints may often lack credibility, but many corporations would do well to examine their processes for determining inventorship, at least for any patents to be filed in the United States. Does a patent attorney interview the apparent inventors to ensure that they have contributed to at least one claim in the application? Do they check to ensure that actual inventors have not been left off? Sometimes attorneys work with one lead inventor and take the word of that person in listing the inventors—an approach that could one day have serious repercussions for that company. Inventorship matters not just to motivate inventors, but also for the validity of the patent itself. A patent issued with improper inventorship can be in jeopardy under U.S. patent law if a court rules that there was intent to deceive regarding inventorship.

Several years ago in one major corporation, in a meeting of numerous U.S. employees in R&D, a manager reportedly spoke about inventorship and erroneously told the group that employees should not complain if they did not get listed as an inventor on a patent based on their work. We understand that he explained that inventorship would be determined *by management as a business decision*, and that sometimes it would be helpful for business reasons to list just one person instead of the group that contributed to a patent. This is outrageously wrong. Inventorship in the United States is a matter of law, not a business decision, and business leaders need to ensure that no actions are taken that would jeopardize proper inventorship.

Many internal and sometimes external conflicts over inventorship can be avoided by training employees to keep proper records. Notebooks as well as invention disclosures or other suitable documents should be used. Facilitators who conduct brainstorming sessions should be trained to record who contributes ideas that might lead to patentable material. Those who contribute may wish to record their ideas in a laboratory notebook. Notes summarizing contributions should be circulated to allow those present to make corrections.

Inventor recognition events and incentives for contributors to intellectual assets can help inventors feel recognized, but when recognition is withheld or given to the wrong people, fatigue rather than encouragement can result. When cash awards are offered for filed and issued patents, a practice we generally recommend, pains must be taken to keep the process transparent without favoritism or game playing. If negative behaviors are identified such as contention, gaming the system, or exclusion of legitimate inventors, management may consider training, coaching, or changing details of the incentive system. One large company abandoned their cash incentives after encountering some negative behaviors and began giving a simple medallion instead. But many companies have successfully added cash incentives to recognize the extra efforts required by those who create intellectual assets, often with bonuses for assets that generate significant value.

Avoiding Theft: Tips for Corporate Inventors and Corporations

To reduce the risk of theft, inventors, entrepreneurs, start-ups, and corporations must take many steps to fully protect their intellectual assets. Diligent use of non-disclosure agreements (NDAs) is needed when sharing inventive concepts with others, even trusted vendors and partners. NDAs help create a paper trail that can deter theft. Further, after the agreement has been signed and the disclosure of confidential matter has occurred, it is often important to follow up with a letter to the other party specifying the nature of the confidential matter disclosed. Be sure to keep a copy. The follow-up letter is frequently neglected, even by major companies, making it difficult to know just what was disclosed when and to whom. Keeping a paper trail can reduce risk and provide resources for legal redress if theft occurs. Naturally, inventive work should also be documented in a laboratory notebook or other means to provide clear information about inventorship.

For those seeking to work with outside groups, careful screening can reduce risk. If a prospective partner has a track record of questionable ethics, it's best to avoid working with them. If questionable ethics are encountered after a partnership begins, it's usually best to walk away and cut one's losses quickly rather than hoping that the ethics will improve.

If collaborative work is being pursued, other legal documents such as a cooperative agreement or memorandum of understanding should be in place in addition to NDAs.

Exploitation of Inventors and Entrepreneurs

In the early days of **Innovation**edge, Cheryl Perkins worked with an attorney to file a trademark application for the term Innovation Edge®. Shortly after it was granted, we began receiving official-looking documents from what appeared to be international trademark agencies with "invoices" to complete our European registration with a Web site. Each document showed our recently published trademark and requested over $2000 for registration, payable to an office in Switzerland. It looked official, but a careful examination revealed several problems. First, there was no telephone number to call to verify details. There was also no evidence that this was in response to a request we had made. Most telling, there was fine print at the bottom in bad English indicating that this was for registration in their private database and not on behalf of any government organization. One fraudulent invoice was mailed from the Slovak Republic.

We received similar fraudulent requests shortly after merely submitting another registration for a trademark. After blogging about this experience, we received a comment from another firm saying that they had just received a similar bill and would have paid it if they hadn't seen our post. Sadly, enough entrepreneurs or their assistants fall for these frauds that multiple operators are plying this trade with apparent success.

Once an inventor gets a patent, a variety of mailings or even phone calls may follow expressing interest in the patent. The solicitation may speak of the vast potential of the patent and offer help in commercialization. These tend to be form letters prepared without any real homework. There are businesses that provide legitimate and valuable services to inventors and patentees, and some of them may use unsolicited mailings, but we urge inventors to exercise great caution when strangers approach you eager to help—for a fee. Do your homework, understand their track record, talk to satisfied customers, check out the stories, and ask tough questions.

We've also heard stories of firms (marketing, legal, regulatory consulting, etc.) helping inventors and entrepreneurs with services that seemed essential, but with nothing to show for the services except a stack of bills. One startup company we worked with needed some guidance on regulatory issues and hired a consulting firm with impressive experience and connections to regulatory agencies. When they called to discuss their case, the firm decided that one person on the call was not enough and brought in an entire team. Each person allegedly on the call would be the basis for an additional billable hour at a surprisingly high rate. The startup was also billed for several cans of soda consumed during the call ($5 a can!). After a couple of calls and a few newsletters from the firm, the startup had a bill of over $10,000, but they were no further along in their knowledge of how to cope with the regulatory burdens they faced.

Exploitation and Patent Shortcuts

Among some inventors, we have seen an unfortunate pattern involving provisional patent applications. We have encountered inventors who felt that they already had protection because they had obtained inexpensive coverage with an unusually inexpensive provisional application that also proved to be unusually incomplete, and essentially worthless in terms of protection. Relying on a provisional application can do great harm if the provisional is not thorough enough to support the regular utility filing in the future.

A provisional application is a relatively new option in the United States that can be filed at low cost ($105 as of this writing for electronic filing). It allows one to get an early priority date, but the application will not be examined and expires in one year. It can be converted into a regular utility application or used as the basis for a priority date in a subsequent utility application, if the utility application is filed within one year of the provisional's date. Many inventors have been misled by the seemingly low quality requirements of the provisional application. It only provides a priority date for material that is properly described in sufficient detail that one of ordinary skill in the art could practice the invention. To ensure that it is an "enabling" disclosure, the provisional should be drafted with nearly the same care given to a regular utility application. It can be a powerful tool when the invention is not finalized, for a series of provisionals can be filed throughout the development process, and multiple provisionals can be used for priority claims in a subsequent utility application, if filed within a year of the earliest provisional being relied on.[6]

Inadequate provisional applications aren't always offered at budget prices, either. We've seen inventors pay thousands for a brief, incomplete filing. Beware promises of quick and easy coverage without much effort. Ask detailed questions about the scope and breadth of the application and other quality factors. Ask to see examples of related work with provisionals. If there are just a couple paragraphs of text, look out.

Avoiding Deception 101: Do Your Due Diligence and Seek Advice

As obvious as it is, many inventors fail to do basic homework when they try to move their inventions ahead. For example, many fail to explore the background of a prospective partner or firm they might work with.

Lone inventors and small start-ups aren't the only ones who need to do basic diligence to avoid deception. We have seen far too many examples of major corporations entering into agreements with partners that in retrospect had warning signs pointing to possible deception. Falling in love with a partner or deal too early can lead to squinting when eyes need to be very wide to spot warning signs. Whenever you begin the diligence for a business relationship, have the attitude that the wisest action may be to walk away if warning signs are found.

Where should one turn to get advice for the complex challenges involved in protecting an invention and advancing a business opportunity? How can you know who to trust and what pitfalls to avoid? Small companies, lone inventors, and start-ups especially need to seek reliable guidance to know who to trust and who delivers. One place to start is with trustworthy, experienced people and groups in your own network such as:

- Experienced innovators with successful market launches
- Retired corporate innovators and product developers
- State-funded innovation networks and technology councils as well as venture centers or entrepreneur assistance groups at universities or technical colleges
- University tech transfer personnel

Get referrals, do your homework, keep your eyes open, ask plenty of questions, and move forward cautiously—making sure to carefully document and protect your intellectual assets.

Notes

1. Ford Motor Company, "Flash of Genius: Key facts About the Intermittent Windshield Wiper Issue," Press Release, 2008, www.ford.com/about-ford/news-announcements/featured-stories/featured-stories-detail/resolved-more-than-20-years-ago (or http://tinyurl.com/fordfacts) (accessed Oct. 3, 2008).
2. Matt Schudel, "Accomplished, Frustrated Inventor Dies," *Washington Post*, February 26, 2005, p. B01, www.washingtonpost.com/wp-dyn/articles/A54564-2005Feb25.html (accessed Oct. 3, 2008).
3. Malcolm Gladwell, "In the Air: Who Says Big Ideas Are Rare?", *The New Yorker*, May 12, 2008, pp. 50–60.
4. Wikipedia contributors, "Stigler's Law of Eponymy," *Wikipedia*, http://en.wikipedia.org/wiki/Law_of_eponymy (accessed Oct. 28, 2008).
5. Jody Rosen, "Researchers Discover Pre-Edison Recording: American Historians Play a Song from Frenchman's Sound Machine," *International Herald Tribune*,

March 28, 2008, p. 3. This is the source for much of the following information about Scott's invention and complaints.

6. For a detailed discussion of some complexities in this area, see Maria Eliseeva, "Danger and Use of Provisional Applications," AIPLA Advanced Patent Prosecution Seminar, San Francisco, CA, June 9, 2005, www.patentbar.com/AIPLARS2005-c-2.ppt (accessed July 17, 2008).

CHAPTER 5

Fatigue Factor #2

INNOVATOR DEFICIENCIES

"An inventor is simply a fellow who doesn't take his education too seriously."

Charles F. Kettering (1876–1958)

In the chain that links ideas to successful innovation, sometimes the innovators, however brilliant, provide the weak link that leads to innovation fatigue. Some of the most painful challenges innovators face arise from their own weaknesses, most of which can be overcome. For example, inventors sometimes take themselves and their inventions far too seriously. Unreasonable expectations arising from unhealthy pride or impatience have killed or stalled commercialization of many brilliant inventions. Other deficiencies, such as a reluctance to market one's work, can also sweep great concepts into the trash bins of innovation fatigue. Innovator deficiencies, if unchecked, can sometimes crush all hope for market success.

The Dangers of Unhealthy Pride

Unhealthy pride refers to the all-too-human tendency to place excessively high value on one's own work and opinions. This results in the dangerous inability to take good advice or learn from others or to change when change is needed. For inventors, it can lead to delusional ideas about the value of one's invention. The gap between reality and delusions from unhealthy pride can thwart progress and, in the end, cause severe innovation fatigue for inventors.

The Gatorade® Syndrome

When selling, it is human nature to place higher value on your product than you would if you were a buyer. When it comes to inventions, however, inventors can sometimes be their own worst enemies by putting unreasonably high value to their product. The reality is that most patents and most inventions are worthless. For those that do have value, the average is far less than the few famous patents or brands that inventors and entrepreneurs usually think about. It seems as though every inventor thinks their patent will launch the next Gatorade®, that famous brand whose University of Florida patent has brought tens of millions of dollars in licensing revenue. Such patents are extremely rare, but commonplace in the dreams of inventors.

When an inventor imagines that a patent obtained with relatively little investment (or sometimes its just a patent application, or even just an idea) is going to instantly bring in millions of dollars, reasonable offers may be instantly rejected and or even be viewed as insults. There may be value to be extracted from the patent, but the licensee must first have evidence of future success, and this generally requires substantial investment and time.

So what's a patent worth? The value of a patent is related to the strength of the patent (breadth of claims, thoroughness of the prior art search, extent of description, soundness of drafting, etc.) and the commercial potential of the technology. The more work the inventors have done, the better. That's partly because the additional work reduces risk for the licensee. Risk and value are always related. An estimated dollar value can range from zero to billions, but most patents may simply have no measurable value in the market. For companies who acquire portfolios of patents, a typical price paid for a utility patent family that fits their portfolio and meets other quality criteria might be around $50,000. That's for patents good enough to kindle serious interest in others. Similar numbers, often far below the expectations of inventors or the corporations who own the patents, have come from experience in patent auctions at

Ocean Tomo, a company working to increase the marketability of patents via an auction system. Both patent owners and many outside observers have been surprised at the relatively low winning bids. Again, a patent by itself is rarely of much value. Often it is access to other things such as market channels, trade secrets, trademarks, manufacturing capital, and human capital that make the difference between a patent protecting a valuable business and being little more than an expensive publication.

We have heard many passionate inventors insist that their invention is worth billions, not just millions, of dollars. This figure is often obtained without any proven sales or manufacturing capability and without consideration of competitive capabilities. A few rare products may reach that level, but unrealistic expectations can ensure that a concept never gets off the ground.

Inability to Let Go: The One-Man Relay Race

Imagine a relay race in which the first runner refused to pass the baton and kept running the entire race himself. Team members reached out for the transfer but were ignored as the sole runner rushed past them, clinging to the baton. The runner would soon grow weary and be outflanked by fresh competitors. In some cases, fatigue would overwhelm the runner long before the finish line was in sight.

We have seen several cases where an inventor or initial leadership team essentially doomed their business by their unwillingness to share control or ownership with those who had the resources to help it grow. Unfortunately, the skills needed for the invention or early development are often not the skills needed for commercialization or business growth. Founders need to recognize early that the long-term success of their business usually involves some surrender of control, and then work to make sure that others involved will have the skills and vision required for success.

In addition to transferring some of the leadership to others, inventors at the earliest stages need to build a team to help them with critical aspects of their project. It cannot be a one-woman or one-man effort. Inventors need help in identifying the marketing strategy, preparing an intellectual asset strategy that compliments the marketing strategy, and crafting and delivering the pitch to prospective partners when licensing is desired. Inventors who cut corners and rely on their own talents may succeed, but they often will spend years doing what could have been done quickly with the right help.

Impatience and Other Infections

In a world where numerous barriers need to be overcome even under the most ideal situations, impatience on the part of an inventor (or innovating company) can be fatal. We understand how anxious inventors can be to see their project become a success, but patience is the watchword for success. Licensing a technology to a major company can take many months for a tentative decision to be made, and then many more months of testing, market research, and further development, and may still ultimately result in "no." Some become angry when there is delay or failure of others to appreciate their work, but patience and gentle persuasion will often do more good than heated reactions. The "fiery spirits" of innovators that Joseph Schumpeter praised must sometimes be tamed for innovation to survive.

Impatience is deadly when combined with financial desperation. Inventors whose financial situation makes them overly anxious for gains from their invention quickly will rarely realize much benefit from the invention. They may sell their rights far too cheaply or take frantic steps that trample on opportunities.

We encourage innovators to brace themselves for a long journey and not to have unrealistic expectations of fast returns. It might be wise to remember some lessons from the history of healthcare innovation, like the two centuries it took for the cure to scurvy to become adopted by the British Navy (see Chapter 10), or the decades it took for basic sanitary practice to be practiced in hospitals after Ignaz Semmelweis demonstrated that it saved lives (see Chapter 18). Patience will almost always be needed when the goal is to change the way people and organizations behave.

Reluctant Marketers

"Nothing happens until someone sells something." This famous quote has been attributed to several people, including Peter Drucker and Thomas Watson of IBM. One executive we know from a major manufacturing company used it at the end of almost every presentation he gave within his company. Most entrepreneurs and businessmen understand the saying, but many prospective innovators do not. Many technically oriented inventors look down on the profession of marketing and view selling as somehow beneath them, but *selling in one form or another is the only way to turn an invention into real innovation.* The reluctance to sell one's work must be viewed as one of the more serious deficiencies an inventor or prospective innovator can have.

A retired leader in academia told us how years ago the technical work of one of his top professors had attracted the interest of several companies anxious to invest. Going against the advice of his leaders, the professor resisted outside assistance in technology transfer and insisted that he handle it all himself. However, he was unwilling to engage in marketing. The technology remained unused and undeveloped. On the other hand, some of the most successful examples we have seen of professors impacting society are those who ardently market their work—constantly speaking, presenting, networking, promoting, and reaching out to industry and others to sell their ideas and capabilities.

The world does not generally beat a path to the door of great inventors. They must beat a path to the world. They must let the world know what their innovation is, why it can make life better, why it's different, and why they should believe—and then ask them to take action (spend money, provide support, commercialize, etc.). Those who recognize their weakness here can seek out training and enlist help from others. Technology transfer offices in universities tasked with marketing of university inventions may also need outside assistance to do this vital task well. Ultimately, innovation is all about marketing. Without it, nothing changes, no matter how great the results were in somebody's lab or garage.

Tips for Innovators

- Keep expectations rooted in reality.
- Recognize that your innovation may be terrific, but there are many challenges to overcome before it becomes a hit. Patience, humility, and diligence are needed.
- Don't try to do it all alone. Get the expertise you need.
- Remember, "nothing happens until someone sells something."

6

Fatigue Factor #3

THE "NOT INVENTED HERE" SYNDROME—AN IRRATIONAL LACK OF EXUBERANCE

Alan Greenspan once worried about the "irrational exuberance" of investors. Industry, on the other hand, sometimes suffers from an irrational lack of exuberance in confronting innovation, especially when the source is from a "foreign" entity such as someone in a different department of the corporation or someone outside the corporation. While "innovation" remains the mantra, only familiar kinds of innovation from insiders or trusted allies are welcome. "Not Invented Here" (NIH) syndrome is one of the most common barriers facing innovators and it occurs at many levels. (See Exhibit 6.1.) It often appears to be an organizational and process issue, but we include it under "People Fatigue" because it commonly is a manifestation of unhealthy human pride or various forms of human foolishness (or even basic misunderstanding on the part of inventors) rather than poor corporate strategy. For its cousin at the level of corporate strategy and vision, see Chapter 10, "Open Innovation Fatigue."

The theme of inventors as immigrants is especially applicable when "NIH" reigns.

From a market perspective, the tendency of corporations to quickly reject foreign innovations, almost as if antibodies were present, is an irrational act. It is not in the self-interest of the corporation.

Exhibit 6.1   Individuals and teams afflicted with NIH syndrome can impose hostile barriers to innovation

However, it may be in the self-interest of some, as we'll discuss below. "NIH" syndrome need not result in a quick "no." In many cases, it is manifest as endless delays from people who find it safer to say "not now."

One might assume that "NIH" rarely comes from someone wearing the corporate hat, but this may be a dangerous and unfair assumption. Many practitioners of NIH would be sincerely offended if told that something other than the corporate good guides their behavior. Understanding true intent is difficult. Those displaying "NIH" behavior may be sincerely trying to help the corporation, but in too many cases, there are clear indications of selfish motivations for NIH behavior that arguably hurts the corporation.

Devil's Advocates and Other Champions of Defeat

One CEO we interviewed discussed some of the fatigue factors he had encountered in his career. He cited an individual in one major consumer products company whom he feels is slowly destroying the future of that company. Outside ideas ultimately pass through him, a man who initially treats external inventors and prospective partners with warmth and interest. However, he soon finds logical reasons why the external invention should be rejected. "There are always a hundred reasons to reject an innovation," the leader explained, "and he'll find them all." His work looks logical and objective, but the result is always the same: external innovation is killed, and it's killing the company.

We've encountered similar people in a variety of companies, often some of the most technically proficient and respected employees. They often make it a point to play "devil's advocate" to the point of destroying all hope for the invention, or they go the extra mile to create a negative scenario that senior management may accept.

These innovation killers pose as gatekeepers protecting the corporation, but they may keep out potential friends and foes alike. Sometimes their motivation is personal pride, not wanting others to look like "better inventors." Sometimes there is a personal agenda of avoiding potential competition for their own pet projects. They often justify the negativism by saying they are only playing "devil's advocate"—surely an innocent activity, right? But who's playing advocate for business success and innovation? Often no one when the devil's advocates are in charge. Management must develop an eye for "champions of defeat" who may keep outside innovation forever outside. If devout devil's advocates aren't cast out from at least a few circles, companies will have a devil of a time innovating. We're not saying they need to be exorcized from the corporation, but they need to be in a role where they won't kill emerging or incoming innovation.

Personal vs. Corporate Gains: Playing it Safe with "Not Now" or "No"

Scott Adams in *Dilbert and the Way of the Weasel* offers a valid insight:

> For every person who thinks up a magnificent breakthrough idea, there are a hundred people who are nothing more than mindless and unimportant implementers of the idea. The reason for the imbalance in numbers is that the implementers tend to kill the people with the great ideas in order to cut down on the workload.[1]

Workload reduction can be a genuine fatigue factor in many corporations. In some cases, it may be hard to escape from the "play it safe" approach of just saying no to innovation. However, another safe route for many is to not say no or yes, but simply "not now." Anxious innovators can be led along for years in some cases waiting for decisions to be made by groups who lack the leadership or courage to make firm decisions.

Many midlevel managers accept the illusion of safe, profitable careers that come by doing what they are told to do and shunning risk. Unfortunately, innovation always involves risk. Unless innovation failure is accepted as the cost of finding innovation success, managers will avoid risk and squelch or delay innovations, preferring instead to make safe, minor advances instead of real progress. The culture of the corporation plays a huge role in this.

When managers don't feel personal motivation to drive innovation, it will be driven out or driven elsewhere, if it's not too late. In some cases, the innovation may be implemented while the innovator is left behind. Here's an example from Scott Adams again, a story sent to him from a reader:[2]

> Dr. Mr. Adams,
>   For several years, I submitted plans and suggestions to my boss to enable electronic access to procurement contracts. Not seeing any opportunity for self-aggrandizement, my Pointy-Haired Boss never promoted the plan. One day a weasel co-worker took my plan to another department whose boss approved it. They both received $2,500 suggestion awards, and the plan was sent to me for implementation.

Ouch! Rewarding the wrong person is another good way to promote innovation fatigue, as we will discuss in more detail later. Rewarding someone else *and* creating extra work for the real but unrecognized originator is innovation fatigue with a vengeance.

The Unseen Hand—or Fist?

In considering the pervasiveness of "Not Invented Here" symptoms, one can only wonder why corporations seem to make so many decisions that appear to be counterproductive and even irrationally harmful. An appeal to economics may be helpful here, building on Adam Smith's unseen hand.

The power and even the magic of free markets is so basic and simple, but widely misunderstood. We wish to affirm the creative power of personal liberty. That power comes when individuals are free to make choices about what to buy, sell, make, and consume. These choices will naturally be based on self-interest. When many individuals have this freedom and a free market exists, it is remarkable how effective the market can be in collectively motivating people to make choices that can also benefit others. The power of the free market was described by the Scottish economist Adam Smith in his 1776 masterpiece, *The Wealth of Nations*. The free market works through combination of personal freedom and the mechanism of *price* as a tool for conveying vast amounts of information across the marketplace.

In a market of, say, 300 million people, how many motorcycles should be made? What styles should be offered? What price should be charged? It would take a tremendous amount of research for a committee of bureaucrats to come up with a defensible answer and it would still probably be wrong. If too few are made, there will be shortages, or waste if too many are made. If the price is too high, they won't sell. Too low, and the companies that make them receive no profit and go broke (or require bailouts).

No one person knows how many are needed. In a free market, if there aren't enough, high demand relative to small supply will result in price increases which motivate increased production. Models that don't sell will result in fewer orders and lower prices. The mechanism of price, when merchants are free to vary it and competition can exist, conveys information to let the market know when more production is needed or when more outlets are needed. Freedom and the mechanism of price lead to resources being allocated to meet consumer demand without extensive research. *Self-interest* is the fuel behind all of this activity. With the free flow of information conveyed via price, self-interest can result in efficient allocation of resources to produce the goods that people want, almost as if an "unseen hand" were guiding the collective decisions of all the players in a choreographed dance.

The freedom to pursue self-interest, while often healthy in a law-abiding and decent society (those are important provisos!), can become a serious problem *inside a corporation*, when the unseen hand becomes more like an "unseen fist" that stops progress and squashes innovation, or simply plugs the "Horn of Innovation™."

The rational, self-focused behavior that Adam Smith described as salutary for individuals in a free market can become a force of destruction in a corporation. It can kill needed projects, destroy intellectual capital, and shut down innovation engines. How is this possible? Within a corporation, the free flow of information is stopped and personal actions are shielded from the exchanges of the marketplace. Further, there is little free competition for available resources. Thus, a person of power in a corporation can make choices that are good for him or her, but bad for the corporation.

The corporation in the marketplace is more like an individual. The corporation should seek rational decisions in its self-interest (remaining within the norms of the law and basic morality). If that were happening, the collective behavior of corporations would mirror that of individuals and free markets would be efficient with the "unseen hand" lifting all boats. In reality, corporations often make puzzling decisions that are not in their long-term interest and are difficult to rationalize.

In a sense, sometimes the corporate mind acts as if it has been taken over by dangerous parasites whose decisions reflect personal interests rather than the good of the host. They use their power to block some of the free flow of information that is needed to efficiently respond to the needs and opportunities of the marketplace. This could be considered corporate mental illness. Corporations must take steps to secure the free flow of needed information and to ensure that managers are acting in the best interests of the company, lest the parasitic effect siphon off significant value and destroy the host.

Workarounds: Persistence, Networking, and Multiple Connections

External innovators when selling a product or a service may not always be able to contact the correct person within a targeted corporation. The variety of personal risks within the corporation offers a compelling argument for seeking out and connecting with the right people. It also calls for building relationships with multiple individuals as a way of increasing the odds that one of your contacts will be wearing a corporate hat and possibly even feel motivated to give external innovations a chance.

We have found many inventors who have knocked on the doors of a targeted company but were turned away coldly because they didn't reach the right people. In some cases, we have had inventor clients tell us there was no hope with a particular company that had already seen and rejected their idea, only to have decision makers in that company express sincere interest in the innovation after we contacted them. Typically, these decision makers had never heard of the invention that supposedly had been carefully considered and rejected. The problem was that the inventors had contacted the wrong people who might not have the broader corporate perspective needed to recognize the benefits of the invention, who might see it as a threat to their own projects, or who might not enjoy the responsibility of bringing external innovation into the company.

For internal prospective innovators, the various risks other individuals face means that good networking is needed, especially with experienced mentors who understand the political barriers and can provide the right help, or maybe even serve as a champion for the concept. The persistent prospective innovator with political sensitivity, patience, and the wisdom to listen to good mentors will be more likely to succeed.

Imagined NIH Syndrome: Inventor Myopia and the Lens of Risk

While "Not Invented Here" syndrome is a real plight for many companies, many NIH tales told by inventors aren't quite what they seem. Some who claim to be victims of corporate NIH syndrome may in fact be suffering from a form of myopia. This optical defect has a cure: new glasses, or more specifically, looking through the lens of risk.

In acquiring a technology, a company faces numerous risks that the inventor may not see or appreciate. Like looking through the wrong end of a telescope, the risks that an inventor sees facing a corporation—if any are seen at all—seem small and remote. But the lens of risk that corporations must look through for every decision shows a more discouraging perspective. (See Exhibit 6.2.) Through the lens of risk, the company sees an outside inventor as an unknown entity. Does the inventor have credibility? Trustworthiness? Is there risk of deception, fraud, greedy behavior, lawsuits, and so on. What isn't being told about the invention, its intellectual assets, and alternatives? Are there safety risks? Many questions must be considered.

Exhibit 6.2   The "lens of risk" can greatly change the way opportunities are viewed

One of the most obvious but important early questions is whether the invention will actually work. The stage of development of the idea is critical. Is it just an idea that hasn't been demonstrated in any meaningful way? Companies are rarely interested in inventions at that stage, even if seemingly solid intellectual assets exist. It helps if there is at least a working prototype, but there are still many risks. Have supply chain and manufacturing issues been resolved? If so, that removes some risk and can make the concept more valuable. Is it a successful product with actual sales and proven profit potential in the marketplace? If so, the risks are much lower since years have already been spent overcoming them. Companies want to find inventions that are nearly ready for the marketplace, not ideas that will require years of development.

In addition to technical risk, market risk is another major consideration. Does the invention meet a real need in the marketplace? Will consumers or end users care? Can it be profitable? A company must also question whether pursuit of the invention may divert their

The Product	• Will it work and can we produce it? • Will it succeed in the marketplace? • Does it have meaningful intellectual asset protection? • What is the current stage of development?
The People	• Are the prospective partners trustworthy? • What legal risks does partnership pose? • How will collaboration affect our reputation? • Will there be a pipeline of opportunities?
The Process	• Is there a good cultural fit with the partner? • Do we share common objectives? • Does the partner bring knowledge and systems that can help us grow?

Exhibit 6.3   Areas of concern that a company has regarding collaboration with outside innovators

attention from where it needs to be focused. Will it really lead to a profitable competitive advantage? (See Exhibit 6.3.)

The lens of risk may differ from person to person within the corporation. Some individuals—perhaps the ones the inventor has approached—may fear competition with a pet project or worry that the project would simply add to their workload or strain their budget. Personal interest can be at odds with the good of the corporation, and failure to understand the personal lens of risk that some individuals use to view outside innovation can leave inventors utterly puzzled at the decisions that are made.

Remember, risks don't just apply to the corporation as a whole. Understanding corporate as well as personal risks may help you in bringing your product to a corporation.

Tips for Innovators Taking Concepts to Prospective Partners

- While being patient, also recognize that delay from prospective partners is the safe way for them but potentially fatal for the innovation. Push for a real answer, yes or no, and move forward or move on.

- Learn to use the lens of risk and understand what others may see as they consider your innovation. Are you working with people who are motivated to innovate?
- Develop multiple connections to assist you in driving your innovation forward.

Notes

1. Scott Adams, *Dilbert and the Way of the Weasel* (New York: Collins Business, 2002), 45.
2. Ibid.

PART

III

FATIGUE FACTORS IN THE ORGANIZATION (STRATEGY, CULTURE, ACTIONS)

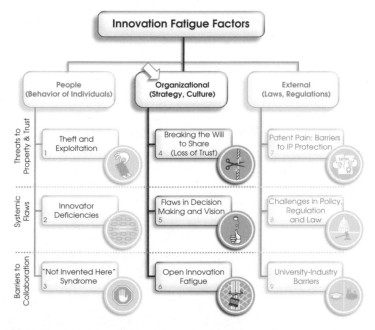

Exhibit 7.1   Fatigue factors at the organizational level

CHAPTER 7

Fatigue Factor #4

THE SILENT INNOVATION KILLER—BREAKING THE WILL TO SHARE

Innovation is surprisingly easy to stifle in an organization. Top management may think the company values innovation, while actions down on the shop floor or in the R&D ranks tell a different story. A variety of attitudes and behaviors can quickly stifle the innovation that the company needs, bringing innovative employees into a state of innovation fatigue.

A Lesson from Pride Rock

"It's the best theater I've ever seen!" These were welcome words to a small group of people from the Fox Cities of Wisconsin who had the privilege of receiving a backstage tour of Disney's *The Lion King* in Appleton's majestic Performing Arts Center in late 2007. That praise was offered by Frank Lott, the director of *The Lion King* traveling company and a man who has seen hundreds of theatres during his career. As he led the group through the intricate backstage world, he shared a story about the need to be prepared unexpected glitches, even when everything imaginable done to avoid problems. One such glitch invol mountainous prop that comes onto the s during the show, driven by re

As Pride Rock moved onto the stage for the stirring finale each evening in one city, the motion would suddenly and prematurely shut down. The cast and crew coped with it and kept the show going, but something was wrong. The crew spent days tracing the miles of wiring under the stage to find where the glitch was, without success. One night, someone noticed that the motion stopped right as a group of stagehands took a batch of wet towels and microwaved them to be hot and ready for the actors to begin cleaning off makeup after the performance. This routine of microwaving the towels happened at the same time each evening. A brief investigation revealed that electrical interference from the microwave oven was in fact hindering the transmission of the wireless signals that controlled robotic motors. The fix was simple: delay the microwaving and let the show go on.

In the world of innovation, seemingly small factors can be showstoppers that discourage creativity. To instill a vibrant culture of innovation in a company or a society, many apparently minor sources of interference should be examined for unintended consequences that might delay or stop progress. Here we will explore some of the subtle and not-so-subtle influences in corporate behaviors that may contribute to innovation fatigue.

Breaking the Will to Share

Here is   he most important lessons we offer in this book:
Emp'   aid to offer their time and energy to the cor-
p   of what may be in a contract, they will only
                  en they feel personally motivated to do so.
                  n and the "will to share" is one of the
                  te leaders. Exhibit 7.2 offers one view
                   share.
                   minds of employees to the future
                   t in many ways. This intangi-
                   ust, and respect. Extremely
                   he to develop but can be
                   eative employees, and
                   shift into neutral.
                   nerate a tremen-
                   ental gears of
                   orporation,

Exhibit 7.2   Factors affecting the "will to share" of employees

you'll just creep forward at best, no matter how much your annual report boasts of innovation.

A director in one of the world's largest and most respected corporations who came through the ranks of engineers and scientists discussed our selection of fatigue factors with us and opined that the most dangerous fatigue factor he had seen was the sudden loss of the will to share. When employees feel that trust has been breached, they may simply choose to do nothing with their great ideas, save them for themselves at a later time, or just stop ideating. On Monday, a creative employee may be enthusiastically striving to come up with breakthrough concepts for the good of the company. On Tuesday, after digesting some bitter news or unpleasant change, the employee may abandon the will to share. Additional invention disclosures may be shared, incremental advances may be pursued, but the real engines of innovation in the mind may have shut down.

Exhibit 7.3   The delicate will to share can be difficult to restore once cut

The silent killer has struck, but leaders may have no idea. It may take years for the poor productivity of a department to be recognized.

Another corporate employee tells us of a massive internal effort in which the technical community was asked to submit written proposals for "independent R&D" (IRAD) projects to support new business opportunities. The company had set aside millions of dollars for 2008 IRAD spending, and told employees that the proposals would be used to select IRAD projects. Over 50 proposals were received. However, the R&D leaders may have had their own agenda. The proposals were "summarily rejected without review," according to our source, and other pet projects were chosen for the IRAD spending. This caused a loss of trust among employees, especially those who had invested considerable time outside of work hours to prepare strong proposals. Some even quit. For those who remained, "it was a severe blow to future employee-driven innovation." The willingness to go the extra mile to share and contribute innovative thinking had been lost.

Management must actively create a culture of trust and mutual respect that can allow innovation to flourish in the corporation. They must realize that innovation requires more than employees just carrying out orders or delivering on written objectives. It requires the heart and mind of the employee sincerely seeking the good of the company, knowing that the willingness to share his or her best will also bring personal benefits and recognition. The difference between sharing a valuable idea and doing nothing can sometimes be due to something as small as a leader spending time talking to the employee, strengthening the sense of connection and softening the impact of the many disappointments that occur in corporate life. Prospective innovators want to make a difference and thrive when they feel they are respected and heard. *Are you listening to the voice of your innovators?* Do you know how engaged they are at a personal level with the objective of innovation? Are you finding ways to provide a liberal encouragement for ingenuity on your behalf?

As in the Pride Rock story, small, unappreciated factors can bring the innovation show to a rapid halt. Many of these factors deal with how the company respects its employees. When innovators feel devalued relative to others in the corporation, innovation fatigue sets in.

Devaluation of the Internal Inventor

In 2006, IBM released a study based on 760 in-depth interviews with CEOs around the world. The study, "Expanding the Innovation Horizon: The Global 2006 CEO Study,"[1] covers the many forms of innovation that CEOs are pushing for their companies. While innovation is recognized as essential for future success, the innovation being sought is increasingly from external partnerships and collaboration with others, a healthy trend. However, when asked about what sources their company relied on as sources of innovation, only 17 percent of CEOs mentioned internal R&D among the three choices allowed per respondent (see Exhibit 7.4). This suggests a low appreciation for internal R&D efforts. Indeed, internal inventors in some large corporations are increasingly viewed as having marginal value. This may reflect failure to properly tap the potential of these employees due to neglecting the value that they offer. This can be especially problematic when internal R&D is not fully

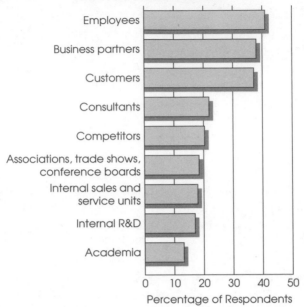

Exhibit 7.4 CEO views on major sources of innovative ideas, from IBM, "Expanding the Innovation Horizon: The Global 2006 CEO Study," 2006. Respondents could select up to three choices for the most significant source of innovative ideas for their business. Courtesy of International Business Machines Corporation, copyright 2006 © International Business Machines Corporation

aligned with open innovation efforts, thus hindering the "Horn of Innovation™" synergy that can exist when internal R&D is in tune with external efforts (see Chapters 2 and 10).

Fatigue by Objectives

Sometimes management pursues programs aimed at delivering on corporate objectives and financial goals without considering the impact on the innovation community. An example comes from Corning, one of the world's leaders in innovation for many decades, a name long synonymous with advanced "research in glass." For years, Corning's growth was assisted by scientists in a culture that provided abundant freedom and was part of the draw for working at Corning. This changed in the mid-1970s when Corning adopted the popular "management by objectives" system aimed at increasing productivity through detailed goals and timetables. As Margaret Graham and Alec Shuldiner report in their detailed and instructive tome, *Corning and the Craft of Innovation*, scientists who had long enjoyed a great deal of freedom quickly became frustrated.[2] A biologist from Corning, Ralph Messing, gave an interview to *Biotechnology Patent Digest* and described the negative impact of these productivity measures on R&D productivity.

> This [management by objectives] was the harbinger of tighter research control and a more restrictive atmosphere for industrial research efforts with less opportunity to investigate basic problems. Ultimately this type of atmosphere tends to stifle creativity, since it does not allow for failures and discretionary investigations. As productivity falls in terms of research the control becomes tighter and innovation is reduced even further. The ultimate is the transfer of authority to initiate research from the R&D Division to the Operating Division. Once this occurs, the research scientist tends to become a firefighter.[3]

There are some things in this quote which seem jarringly out of place today. The longing for the days of free-ranging scientific exploration of "basic problems" and "the pursuit of knowledge" is not a reasonable expectation for most modern corporations, but is more suitable for the university or national laboratory. However, the impact of a change in management style—changing the rules midstream—is a common source of frustration for researchers. Excessive control can also destroy a culture of innovation. Further, some reorganization efforts can lead to systematic fatigue, particularly those that relegate R&D to operations or other areas not likely to appreciate the skills among R&D staff. When researchers become firefighters whose creative and technical skills are no longer valued, innovation fatigue is imminent.

Fatigue and the Weakness of Corporate Strengths

One of the paradoxes of human life is that strengths can become weaknesses when they are not balanced or coupled with flexibility and openness to change and growth. When strengths lead to excessive pride or even blindness, a fall can occur. Witness Bobby Fischer, arguably the world's strongest chess player. His exclusive focus on chess, his strength, drove him to ignore many other dimensions of life that, in our opinion, crippled his life, and made him vulnerable to hostility and extremism. Just as individuals need to live broadly and be well rounded, so too do corporations need to have flexibility to develop competencies in multiple areas.

The paradox of weakness from strength has been addressed by a variety of writers. One contribution comes from Dorothy Leonard-Barton, who noted the relationship between core capabilities or competencies and "core rigidities" in businesses.[4] One of the problems she describes for a company with competency in one area involves the demotivating factors that may exist for those with other needed competencies. For example, in one company noted for the strength of its engineering design, marketers might feel that they have limited career opportunities, and strong marketers might wish to leave or not join in the first place. The problem is exacerbated by the "Pygmalion Effect" (from George Bernard Shaw's play *Pygmalion*, in which a professor wins a bet that he can teach a poor flower girl to behave and speak like an upper-class lady), also known as the Rosenthal Effect or the "teacher-expectancy effect," describing the phenomenon in which students who are expected to perform better than others are more likely to do so—a form of the self-fulfilling prophecy. In companies with great engineering prowess, the engineers may expect that marketers will have nothing valuable to contribute, and the marketers, with their confidence undermined by these negative expectations, may be more likely to live up to that expectation. In this case, the strength of engineering expertise can naturally lead to devaluation or deprecation of skills in other specialties, leading to weaknesses that can be traced to strengths. Leonard-Barton explains that non-dominant disciplines in corporations can easily fall into this problem.

Innovation, however valued in print, tends to be a non-dominant discipline ripe for deprecation. Not that innovation is a well-defined discipline, but the mindset and skills that lead to potential innovations are often found in non-dominant disciplines. The Pygmalion Effect can result in decreased prospects for their success, contributing to inventor devaluation.

Companies need to look for inequalities between disciplines and take steps to have dominant disciplines listen to and learn from the others. Those who do can find radical or disruptive innovation in the synergy that can emerge. It may require isolating a project from the normal corporate systems and cultures, as Leonard-Barton describes in several case studies. She encourages project managers to continually challenge the systems and values traditionally revered in the corporation, for those who do so "may cause a complete redefinition of core capabilities or initiate new ones." This is the path to a sustainable culture of innovation, and the kind of flexibility that can give disruptive innovations a chance.

Fatigue among Senior Innovators

Some senior employees feel less engaged and less valued by the time retirement is in sight. Fearful that they will be laid off, some take the easy path of trying to lay low and stay out of trouble, avoiding the risk of real innovation, in order to keep their job and sail into retirement quietly.

Senior innovators may succumb to innovation fatigue and largely check out at a time when they are most capable of making a difference. This is a tragic loss of human capital. Managers accept it as normal and some look at their most senior people as unwanted ballast. If these senior employees could be re-energized and offered the chance to be respected, involved, and needed, they have the potential to deliver radical benefits to the corporation. Energizing and engaging senior innovators must be a priority for corporations to retain their competitive edge.

The Young Are at Risk as Well

In 1945, Sir Alexander Fleming was honored with a Nobel Prize for one of the most significant pharmaceutical advances of the modern era, penicillin. His discovery came in 1928, 32 years after the antibiotic effect of penicillin was discovered and documented by Ernest Duchesne (1874–1912), a French physician. In the Military Health Service School of Lyon, France, Duchesne conducted research and submitted a doctoral thesis in 1897 dealing with the "antagonism between moulds and microbes." He may have been the first to explore the therapeutic anti-microbial power of molds. Interestingly, Arab immigrants played a role in this discovery. Duchesne observed that Arab stable boys at his hospital kept their saddles in a damp, dark room to promote mold growth. He inquired why and learned that the mold helped in the healing of saddle sores on horses. Duchesne applied a solution made from the mold and injected them into guinea pigs infected with typhoid, all of whom recovered. Duchesne studied *Penicillium glaucum,* a different strain than the one Fleming would later use (one ineffective against typhoid), but both strains produced forms of the drug today known as penicillin, a medicine that has saved many thousands of lives and led to further discoveries that have saved millions.

Perhaps even more lives could have been saved if Duchesne's discovery had not been ignored. The powerful Institut Pasteur in France ignored his work, not even acknowledging receipt of his dissertation, because he was too young. At age 23, he lacked the social standing needed in that day for his discovery to be seriously considered. Failure to identify the active agent from the mold may also have contributed to uncertainty about his discovery. Unfortunately, Duchesne's military service after receiving his degree prevented him from carrying out further research that might have gained the attention his work deserved.

Actually, many others before Duchesne found that various molds had therapeutic or antimicrobial effects.[5] Ancient and traditional medical practices from Greece, Serbia, India, Russia, and Sri Lanka point to relevant uses of molds, and a variety of European researchers found anti-bacterial effects from the penicillium fungus before Duchesne's independent discovery, but his demonstration may have come closest to being a game-changing innovation that could have greatly advanced medical practice—if only he had received a little encouragement. Sometimes the very young, like Philo Farnsworth, are immigrants of innovation in a land of the experienced and credentialed.

Thinking with an Accent: A Diversity Problem

Rigid corporate systems pose huge barriers for some creative types. Part of the problem is that such people tend to suffer from an ailment that is not welcome in some corporations: *diversity.* Not the diversity that comes from physical factors, but the sometimes more challenging diversity of thought. These immigrants think with a foreign accent.

While companies spend millions to exhibit their commitment to some forms of diversity, "diversity of thought" is a different matter.

Employees often quickly learn that it is important to "think like everyone else." Those who don't may be neglected or stifled. Sometimes the pressure to conform to corporate culture can be a subtle influence that unintentionally discourages innovative thinking. Sometimes the message is not so subtle. One bright Ph.D. from a major technology school joined a Fortune 100 company where, in his first meeting with his boss, was told to "hit the ground walking" and not try to do anything extraordinary. In such cases, innovation will be an uphill battle.

Sometimes formal performance management systems tend to reward those who follow the predominant culture and think in line with corporate culture. Those who think with an accent—the immigrants within a corporation of blueblood citizens—may remain discouraged and unrewarded.

Management must be able to handle the discomfort of employees who think differently in order to reap the rewards that maverick innovators can bring. While all employees need to build up the company and be supportive team members, there is a need for those who can respectfully challenge the status quo. Enlightened behavior from the mavericks is also needed. Mavericks, to be successful, require more than enlightened management: they need communication skills, tact, and patience with those who don't share their views. There are many with tales of persecution and woe, but there are two sides to these stories. Many times the real problem lies with the brusque or even intolerant behavior of alleged victims. Mutual respect is always needed for healthy communication. The challenge of innovation is influencing others to adopt that which is new, something not easily achieved by disrespecting corporate norms.

Sony co-founder Akio Morita in his book, *Made in Japan*,[6] describes an encounter with the chairman of Sony. He blatantly disagreed with the chairman in a conversation—normally a serious cultural error. Morita, however, told the chairman his reasons for his impudence, saying that if he didn't disagree, he would have nothing to learn from him and *visa versa*. This is a wise observation. We have seen many leaders surrounded by "yes men" who had little to offer in terms of new perspectives, while the sometimes annoying presence of truly diverse associates can bring strength and wisdom. Dare to listen to others who dare to disagree. In fact, leaders are wise to cultivate "loyal opposition."

In the scientific and engineering community, one rises in a culture of "improvement by disagreement" where knowledge is advanced in a process that encourages outside criticism and review. Graduate school in these disciplines trains students to think and challenge. It is a boot camp to build lifelong skills in disagreeing. What a pity that such skills should be squelched in some corporate environments. Learn to listen to, understand, and respect those who may disagree, if there is logic and reason behind it.

When those seeking innovation learn that their different ways of thinking are respected and their viewpoints solicited, they are energized. When the immigrants are treated like citizens who are welcome, human talent can be unleashed.

Culture Codes for Innovation and Corporate Innovators

Clotaire Rapaille's book, *The Culture Code*, reveals how we have imprints in our psyche that govern our emotional responses to the world around us.[7] Rapaille through his detailed surveys of responses to various culture-related concepts has identified a wide array of "culture codes." For example, the culture code for the American perception of food is "FUEL," describing our tendency to tank-up and focus on quantity to make sure we get the energy we need. In contrast, the French, whose culture code for food is "PLEASURE," focus on quality and taste over quantity. Other examples: The American culture code for money is "PROOF," describing how wealth is used to validate and show one's success to others. The American code for quality is "IT WORKS"—referring to our tendency to be satisfied with things that are "good enough." Numerous other codes are explored, but now we tentatively offer a few suggestions of our own.

In the consumer products industry and other mature or maturing industries, the culture code for "research and development" may range from "EXTRAVAGANCE" to "TAXES." In either case, it's something to avoid, when possible, although like taxes, it may be viewed as a necessary evil, with less being better. R&D in many corporations is funded as a tax on business units, a painful tax that they are constantly tempted to resist.

The R&D community of a corporation may often be tagged with the culture code of "HANDYMEN." They won't help you pick what car you drive or where you drive it, but when you need the oil changed, they can do it on demand. Their job is to make what others tell them to.

Sometimes we wonder if the culture code for innovators in some corporations is "CHILD." This code is unintentionally reinforced in typical brainstorming sessions with members of the technical community, where the managers or facilitators in charge feel a need to bring in loads of toys to help their Ph.D.s and others think. (Some of us kids enjoy them, of course.)

Finally, there is another culture code which may describe the status of prospective innovators in many corporations and in society in general: "IMMIGRANT." They are creative foreigners in a strange land where they may always be viewed with some suspicion and never quite fit in.

Promotion Systems, Performance Management Systems

The implicit culture codes for innovators within a company may be reflected in the consequences and operation of a performance review system. Following GE's lead, performance management systems have been implemented that use forced ranking to put a percentage of employees into various categories. Some companies, for example, mandate that 10% of employees in some groups will be given the lowest ranking (a "1" when "9" is the highest) and thus be largely slated for excision. That can work for a year or two to trim the "fat" (if fat is the problem), but if that becomes an ongoing system, it can lead to fatigue and other problems. What better way to tell innovators and other employees that they are easily replaced handymen in need of discipline (maybe the real culture code here should be "EXPENDABLE")? Many people in the middle levels will recognize that they will inevitably be forced down to the lower ranks unless they achieve more and more. The steady raising of the bar is generally done without a corresponding rise in compensation. Soon many who can leave do, and others become discouraged. It can be a truly terrible system.

In many cases, the criteria for performance evaluation may reflect the skills that upper management values in other managers. Thus, promotion may hinge on how one stacks up against vague criteria for "leadership" skills, often more reflective of personality or communication skills than they are of actual benefit delivered to the company. Technical skills may be largely ignored for those in the technical community, but excellence in PowerPoint presentations and mastery of jargon can keep you rising. When this fate befalls an organization, it faces innovation fatigue.

Of course, there is a whole series of problems that stem from the human tendency to reward and promote people for the wrong reasons. When a corporate performance management system frequently allows people to be promoted or punished based on factors other than performance, key contributors can easily be left behind and discouraged. Prospective innovators might not be interested in playing the games that work in decaying organizations, whether it be joining the boss's sports team or taking up the right hobbies. When performance management goes bad, the casualties can be enormous.

Performance management systems are expensive investments, so leaders may be unwilling to reconsider when trouble occurs. However, we feel it is vital that the impact of performance management system on the innovation community be carefully examined. This means that the inventors in the ranks need to be heard. Interviews to understand its impact would be helpful—and might send an energizing message to the "immigrants" that someone cares. Careful exit interviews of those who leave should include probing regarding the impact of the performance management system. New systems that affect employees must always be scrutinized for unintended consequences, including those on the innovation community.

Far more important than the system itself is the mindset of management in running the system and conducting performance reviews. There must be constant vigilance about the criteria used and messages sent. Sometimes the messages are surprisingly hostile to innovation, even when a corporation values it. For example, one respected senior employee at a major corporation was doing his job well. In addition, he was also contributing creative thoughts occasionally to another group. His strong technical background and creativity made him sought out by others for help in ideation. He would occasionally meet with other inventors at lunch or even after hours to collaborate. As a result, he became a co-inventor on a handful of patents. One might expect that his extra-mile efforts as a good corporate citizen and inventor would have been praised by management, but in his performance review, he was chastised for getting too many patent applications.

His manager told him that his growing number of applications—all in areas unrelated to his primary objectives—raised questions about his dedication to the project at hand, and that further efforts of that kind would be viewed negatively. In this case, the inventor felt punished for his innovative efforts and would soon apply his creative energy in pursuing outside innovations for his own business on the side. Innovation fatigue, in this case, was localized: it made an inventor weary of inventing for a company that punished innovation, but did not deter him from being innovative in other spheres. The company got what it wanted: less innovation. Such stories, unfortunately, are far too common among many corporations around the world.

Listen to the Voice of the Innovator

The phenomenon of listening to the wrong voices is inevitable when channels of communication prevent listening to others who have something valuable to share. Internal communication barriers in corporations are endemic and usually take vigorous, deliberate action of top leaders to overcome. Witness Kimberly-Clark's former CEO, Darwin Smith, the visionary leader featured in Jim Collins' famous book, *Good to Great*.[8] Darwin cut past spin and misinformation by going into the ranks of the corporation and talking to people about their work. He knew what was happening and was less subject to information doctoring than many leaders who rely solely on direct reports for their knowledge. He had the wisdom and the humility to listen.

Sadly, such efforts to communicate are rare and many prospective innovators feel muted. Without accurate information from the front lines, a general's decisions may be out of synch with reality. The results are illustrated by Intel's 2000 fiasco involving a DRAM product for the Pentium 4 platform.[9] Intel's philosophy of "disagree and commit"—meaning that employees who disagree with a decision were expected to simply accept it and carry it forward—failed when the "disagreers" had vital information that was neglected in decision making. Intel's engineers were upset that another company's product was forced upon them, in spite of their warnings of trouble. Rather than being heard, some of those pointing to problems were punished, but eventually proven right. Intel was hurt, careers were damaged, and trust was lost.

For an organization to be flexible enough to respond to the problems and opportunities identified by those in the know, it must have healthy internal ecosystems in which exchange of information is enabled and encouraged at many levels. It must have mechanisms to listen to "the voice of the innovator."

Learnings

- Maintaining the trust of the innovation community is absolutely vital for organizations wishing to innovate.
- Changes in the organization and its policies should be considered in light of impact on innovators, and "the voice of the innovator" should routinely be heard to ensure that innovation engines are healthy.
- Promotion systems and other corporate systems should be evaluated in light of impact on the innovation community. Is the will to share maintained? Is diversity of thought encouraged or at least allowed?

Notes

1. IBM, "Expanding the Innovation Horizon: The Global 2006 CEO Study," Armonk, New York, 2006, available online at www-935.ibm.com/services/us/gbs/bus/pdf/ceostudy.pdf via registration at www.ibm.com/ibm/ideas-fromibm/us/enterprise/mar27/ceo_study.html.
2. Margaret B.W. Graham and Alec T. Shuldiner, *Corning and the Craft of Innovation* (Oxford: Oxford Univ. Press, 2001), 369–371.
3. Ralph Messing, *Biotechnology Patent Digest*, p. 1968 (no year given), as cited by Graham and Shuldiner, *Corning*, 370.
4. Dorothy Leonard-Barton, "Core Capabilities and Core Rigidities: A Paradox in Managing New Product Development," *Strategic Management Journal* 13 (1992): 111–125.
5. Wikipedia contributors, "Discovery of Penicillin," *Wikipedia*, http://en.wikipedia.org/wiki/Discoveries_of_anti-bacterial_effects_of_penicillium_moulds_before_Fleming (or http://tinyurl.com/gyv6s) (accessed Nov. 5, 2008).
6. Akio Morita, *Made in Japan* (New York: Dutton, 1986).
7. Clotaire Rapaille, *The Culture Code: An Ingenious Way to Understand Why People Around the World Live and Buy as They Do* (New York: Broadway, 2006).
8. Jim Collins, *Good to Great: Why Some Companies Make the Leap . . . and Others Don't* (New York: HarperBusiness, 2001).
9. Steven Fyffe, "Culture Clash Erupts Inside Intel," *Electronic News*, Oct. 23, 2000, http://findarticles.com/p/articles/mi_m0EKF/is_43_46/ai_69237707/print (or http://tinyurl.com/intelclash) (accessed May 19, 2008).

8

Unintended Consequences

REINVENTING HP

Corporate policies and transformations need to be understood from the perspective of innovators if innovation is to be given encouragement. Anything less is an invitation for innovation fatigue.

An illustrative story comes from the Hewlett-Packard facilities in Boise, Idaho, where an engineer and inventor from their "golden era" has shared his story with us for this book. This engineer was attracted to HP by their impressive calculators that he used in high school and college, and resolved to work for them. He landed a job with HP and eventually worked for many years as an engineer at the Boise site where LaserJet® printers are designed.

The patent office in Boise encouraged invention disclosures in a variety of ways. Our engineer submitted numerous invention disclosures and had a healthy number of patent applications and patents. He also observed that HP not only relied on patents, but also had a significant number of defensive publications as well as trade secrets, all part of a sound approach to intellectual assets (IA). He was pleased with the innovative culture he was in and found excitement in his work.

So what was HP doing right? Incentives were a part of their approach, but there was more, such as obvious interest from management in innovation. Further, the IA system was responsive to inventors: they interacted with inventors, frequent training was provided that stressed the importance of IP and helped inventors know what was needed, inventors knew what happened to their disclosures, and inventors could request personal ownership of inventive concepts not of interest to the business. These little things contribute to a culture that makes inventors feel respected and appreciated.

Our engineer discusses the approach to IA he experienced in Boise:

> The leaders in Boise felt that many patentable ideas were being developed and put into products without proper protection, so in about 1998 they beefed up their incentive program. For every idea submitted, the submitter got $100, even before it was reviewed. Engineers are generally honest so there was very little abuse of that simple incentive. Most disclosures were good attempts and generally in line with HP's business, even if there was no applicable product for that idea at the time. For every idea that was made a trade secret or published as a defensive pub, HP paid $500. For each patent application filed, $1000. If a patent was granted, the inventor got a nice plaque. No additional money was given when the patent was issued because once it was filed, there was generally no more work that the inventor could do—it was in the hands of the U.S. patent office.
>
> To help with this process, the HP patent office trained engineers to be patent coordinators and to hold patent workshops. They explained what constitutes an invention and an inventor. They explained how they wanted to build up HP's patent portfolio to, among other things, help in patent litigation battles. They explained to the engineers to not worry whether it was patentable or if HP wanted it. Engineers were to turn in all ideas and let the patent team make that decision. Besides brainstorming at the patent workshops, engineers would get together in small groups over lunch to brainstorm, then go off and write up more disclosures.
>
> Most of management supported this effort, even though it occasionally took engineers away from their main jobs.
>
> During those few years, HP Boise was the top patent producing division in the company, leading HP to be one of the top in patents issued in the country. In 2003, for example, HP Boise produced 15 percent of HP's granted patents. The number of employees at the Boise site at that time was less than

3 percent (about 3500) of the whole company (about 125,000). Note that there would be a delay between when filed and when granted, so those awarded in 2003 were generally filed in the 1998–2002 timeframe. HP moved from 15th place in 2002 to 11th place in 2003 in overall patents issued.

While many engineers had a fun time getting paid to brain-storm, the HP patent office was getting overwhelmed with the number of disclosures running through the system. So they had to scale back some, and eventually would only give the $100 bonus if it passed their initial inspection. They also had to raise the bar as to which ones they would spend money on for preparation and patent application filings.

Engineers' ideas are not limited to their employer's line of business but HP claims they own all of the engineer's intellectual property. So HP Boise had procedures to allow an engineer to submit an idea for release to the engineer to go off and do on his or her own. Even something as far removed from HP's business such as cat food feeders was recommended to be approved. And HP was generally pretty good about releasing inventions when asked.

Other statistics bear out the productivity of the Boise division during that time. HP's issued U.S. patents from Idaho inventors (as of Sept. 25, 2008) based on applications filed per year are shown in Exhibit 8.1 for applications filed from 1993 to 2005. The percentage of HP patents with at least one Idaho inventor ranged from under 8 percent in 1996 to 16 percent in 2001, when HP filings peaked. That percentage took a steep dive a couple of years later.

In 1999, Carly Fiorina, former Senior VP of Lucent, became CEO of HP. She sought to "reinvent HP" and publicly emphasized the importance of innovation to the company, even going so far as to add the word "invent" to the HP logo. This was announced with much fanfare on Nov. 15, 1999, as part of the launch of a $200 million global brand campaign.

"Our brand is the strongest expression of who we are," said Fiorina. "We are a company founded by inventors, fueled by invention and adept at reinventing ourselves to track with new market opportunities. Our new brand will give us a clearer,

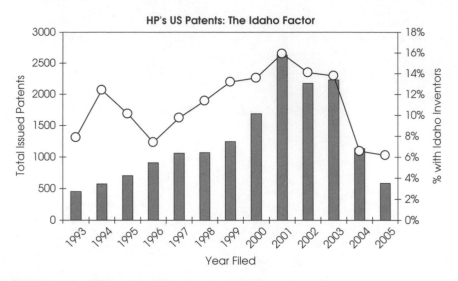

Exhibit 8.1   HP's patents for Idaho inventors over time

stronger voice in the marketplace, and the world will get a picture of us that reflects our true inventiveness. . . ."

"The message for employees is this: Remember your HP gene—the DNA to invent—that drew you to our company in the first place."[1]

With the bursting of the dot-com bubble and general economic malaise in the technology sector around 2001, she oversaw a layoff of about 7,000 jobs. HP's services business was losing market share to IBM, driving HP to increasingly depend on the profits from its printer division. But the market share and margins that enabled these profits arguably relied on the innovation culture in Boise, which was beginning to change under her leadership. The HP logo notwithstanding, inventors in Boise were already beginning to experience a few innovation fatigue factors.

> Right before HP bought Compaq, Carly had massive layoffs, eliminating people but not projects. Those who remained behind had to pick up the work of those who left. It is hard to brainstorm ideas when you don't have idle time to think. My own time spent inventing went down and my submission rate decreased.

Further fatigue factors came after the 2002 acquisition of Compaq.

> Carly started making changes to streamline everything by mak-
> ing everybody follow the same rules. She bought Compaq
> and had their intellectual property people lead the way. The
> Compaq people had a very different mindset regarding pat-
> ents. They had very few patents and, in some ways, discouraged
> patent applications. Compaq engineers with patents granted in
> their name were a small and privileged group.

Invention disclosures had to be submitted to a remote patent
department in Harris County, Texas, site of the former Compaq
Computer Corporation. From the perspective of Boise inventors,
inventions disclosures sent to Texas seemed to enter a black hole.
One subtlety may have had a surprisingly significant impact at the
emotional level: inventor requests to retain inventions unrelated
to the company were also generally denied, when they would have
been granted under the previous system in Boise. "Pretty soon
Boise engineers started whispering among themselves, 'if you have
an invention you want to do on your own, don't invent it until you
leave HP.'" Such sentiments were even expressed off the record by
significant voices other than the engineers themselves.

The new IA system was opaque, slow, and less responsive, when
viewed from Boise. Bonds of trust and mutual respect between
inventors and IA overseers eroded. "That led to a big decline in submissions and left many engineers/inventors disillusioned with the
process," our engineer told us.

Further discouragement came in the recognition given to HP
inventors. As part of "reinventing HP," the internal Web site would
often profile selected inventors, but the process may have been too
selective: "None of them that I saw were from Boise. Boise led the
way but was not recognized for its contributions."

Call it the shifting of continents or the redrawing of borders,
but in any case, at least some of HP's citizen inventors in Boise
now felt like new immigrants without having moved an inch. While
HP patent applications were declining, the relative contribution
of Boise was plummeting as well, falling from about 16 percent in
2001 to under 7 percent in 2005 (based on patents that had issued
by the end of 2008—the contribution of a tiny handful of additional

published HP applications does not change the picture with respect to Boise's IA impact).

Our engineer had learned that he loved inventing and contributing, but for him, HP had become a less inviting place for that activity. Our inventor would later accept a voluntary severance incentive aimed at workforce reduction. "A major reason for leaving was to allow me to freely invent." Now he is busy earning a living and raising a family, while also preparing to pursue a variety of inventions. We wish him the best of luck.

The changes that HP underwent all seem logical from the perspective of management. Common systems and streamlined practices are reasonable and even best practices. But the perspective of the innovator is often overlooked. Various incentives and disincentives, energizing factors and fatigue factors can move a company one individual at a time past a tipping point from a culture of innovation and cooperation to one of innovation fatigue. Perhaps simply being aware of what Boise inventors were feeling might have helped upper management better manage the transitions they felt were necessary.

Learnings

- Praiseworthy innovation goals can misfire when corporations are out of touch with the innovation community and neglect the voice of the innovator.
- In times of corporate change, leaders must not take their eyes off the innovator community. Special efforts may be needed to keep them motivated, maintain trust, and preserve the "will to share." The extra effort to communicate and listen effectively during change may be difficult, but is essential for the future.
- Timely feedback, responsiveness, and personal relationships with the innovation community can be crucial in good corporate IP systems.

Note

1. "HP CEO Carly Fiorina Launches New Brand, New Logo," *BusinessWire*, Nov. 15, 1999, http://findarticles.com/p/articles/mi_m0EIN/is_1999_Nov_15/ai_57571801 (or http://tinyurl.com/da3ryc) (accessed Sept. 24, 2008).

CHAPTER 9

Fatigue Factor #5

FUNDAMENTAL FLAWS IN DECISION MAKING AND VISION

Many great sports teams lose to weaker opponents by failing to execute the fundamentals. The same applies in innovation.

Leaders generally believe they have vision, but there are some symptoms when the vision is weak or lacking. One symptom is constant re-organization, or an emphasis on committee consensus and rigid processes to deliver results. Process without vision results in uncertainty and indecision. With sound vision and sound strategy, the corporation will naturally develop the flexibility needed to respond to the opportunities that innovation creates, as well as the external threats that may require response.

The Armada Effect: Fatigue Through Reshuffling

A few years ago in the beautiful coastal community of Nagshead, South Carolina, tourists looking for a cheap place to stay might have strayed into the Armada Inn. According to one local, it was once acquired from a major chain by an owner unwilling to invest in its upkeep. The stingy attitude was reflected in the very name of the hotel. Unable to decide on a new name, and unwilling to spend money for a new sign, the owner decided to simply reorganize the individual neon letters that made up the old sign. Thus, the

Armada Inn was created by reshuffling the letters of—you guessed it—the Ramada Inn. Recently upgraded, the hotel has apparently changed its name and its ownership. A similar story may be behind a former Armada Inn in another southern city.[1]

What we call "the Armada Effect" in the business world refers to the tendency of some leaders to create the appearance of change and progress by simply reshuffling the elements of the organization without making the changes that are really needed—changes that may require more significant investment and vision, not just revision.

Innovators within corporations often don't cope well with the Armada Effect. Fatigue can set in when groups are constantly reorganized and objects shift unnecessarily. It's amazing how R&D groups are reshuffled in some corporations. Two-to-three year cycles of dissolving and reorganizing R&D groups seem painfully common. During a single cycle, a researcher may report to two or three managers, who report to two or three different directors, who may report to two or three different vice presidents. The Armada Effect often means "layering" for inventors as new layers of management are added between them and the top, constantly increasing organizational entropy. Change can be energizing, but change without vision leads to confusion, disruption, and fatigue.

One of the greatest fatigue factors for the technical community undergoing Armada Effect changes is the lost relationship between management and researchers. The problem can be especially severe for leading contributors whose track records have led to healthy respect from management. A new manager may suddenly come in who has no idea who these arrogant inventors are. "I'm not interested in what you did in the past. What are you doing for me today?" An investment of years of effort into building a reputation and earning privileges may suddenly count for nothing.

"I don't know who you are, I don't know what you do," said one manager to a senior scientist at a major corporation, a scientist who had been there for 25 years and had helped bring in some of the most significant money-making technologies of that company. He was a scientist renowned among his peers for his creativity and vision. Suddenly, he was being asked to prove himself to a skeptical manager. This kind of change is particularly unhealthy, leading star performers to give up or retire early instead of offering their best work to the company at the time when they have the most experience, the broadest networks, and the most potential.

Leaders Listening to the Wrong Voices— Like Shareholders?

When vision and strategy are inadequate, there is a strong temptation to get guidance by listening to the wrong voices. This can be a particularly dangerous source of innovation fatigue.

"Our investors don't want a lot of innovation. They don't want rapid growth. They want safe, steady dividends based on our existing product lines, and that's what we are going to deliver." In several major corporations, this is the message that has been delivered from management to scientists, product developers, and other innovators. It's a logical message based on feedback from major investors and analysts. Yet it's a message based on fatally flawed assumptions.

One flawed assumption is that management should focus on keeping stockholders happy and listen to them carefully. In fact, this can put blinders on strategic vision that can harm a company. As Clayton Christensen has pointed out, the stockholders of most large corporations are dominated by institutional investors, who own any given stock for an average of about *10 months*[2] (in fact, hedge funds are typically in and out of a stock within *60 days*). With such a short time frame, they have little motivation to worry about the long-term welfare of a corporation or its brands, employees, and communities. Making decisions based on the short-term whims of those parties is no way to run a business—but it is often the only way for some executives.

Listening to mainstream customers can also provide the wrong guidance at times, as we discuss next.

The Foolishness of Crowds Revisited: iPod® Skepticism

The theory of disruptive innovation (see Chapter 19) explains why listening to some messages from mainstream customers can leave you blind to important strategic opportunities or threats. But if there are risks to listening too intently to mainstream customers and stockholders, who should get your ear? How about non-users?

Do you really understand why people aren't yet using a product or service? Or why they quit using it? Do you know their unmet needs and wants?

Fortunately, some leaders have enough vision to look past the pressure for incremental change to appease their current crowd of customers or stockholders. Instead, they pursue more promising innovation, sometimes over jeers. A case in point is the revolutionary iPod® from Apple. After years of adulation for Apple's genius in marketing the iPod®, many have forgotten the initial jeers Apple received when they first announced the product. Even serious Apple fans were skeptical or harshly critical. Why was their favorite computer company venturing into the unknown with a $400 music player that was little more than a 5GB hard drive for playing songs?[3] There were already MP3 players on the market. What could Apple bring to the party? Revolution, anyone?

MacRumors.com has a forum from 2001 showing the response of Apple devotees.[4] The iPod® responses in late 2001 reflected mostly negative opinions (173 negatives to 133 positives), and this was on a forum of Apple fans. That's surprisingly negative. MP3 players weren't new. Storage devices weren't new. So what was the revolution? It was a tool that could change lifestyles through its combinations of numerous innovations, not driven so much by technological advance as by a vision of what could be done for the consumer. The iPod® provided new convenience and usability not just through its elegant interface and software, but with rapid data transfer enabled by Firewire technology, with a battery that recharged rapidly when the iPod® was connected to a computer, with 20-minutes anti-skip protection, and a convenient scroll wheel. A few fans recognized this right away, though most didn't. The market didn't get it either, as Apple stock dropped significantly on the day of the announcement.

The story of the iPod®'s success in the face of great skepticism is incomplete without considering how other companies with bright inventors and marketers "almost" came up with the iPod®. Naturally, the incumbents in the world of portable music players were aware of the development of the iPod®. But consider what a new product manager in a multinational electronics company would face when given the charge to develop the "next generation portable music player." The options to explore would have been a product that was either new to the world, new to the company, or a major modification or revision of the existing player. Market research would have invariably indicated that smaller is better. So far so good. The other major market indicator was the price of these portable music players. None of the players sold for more than $60—selling a player for over $400 would seem ludicrous. Further, the core technical competency of incumbent music player companies involved rotating devices where a CD was constantly scanned by a laser beam. These factors would define the new product development track—namely, a smaller, inexpensive CD device selling CDs made by other companies—and would never let the company think on the same track as Apple. The music player incumbents could not think from the perspective of a computer company offering not just a convenient solid-state device, but a new business model with iTunes®.

Rewinding to 2001, we can see that there were clues pointing to the need for Apple's approach, but the incumbents lacked the understanding to appreciate them. These clues include the increasing importance of music in digital form, the explosion of Web-based media, and a digital lifestyle in general. Incumbents considered their competition to be limited to other incumbents, instead of considering a computer-selling company as a major threat. The price tag was the most blinding indicator: incumbents never thought that people would pay $400 for a portable music player. Incumbents could not think about creating an experience with their product. According to them, a portable music player depended upon a compact disc manufactured by someone else and recorded by music studios. On the contrary, Apple created user experience via iTunes® software.

Sometimes it pays to document rejected ideas during product development and archive them for later review. Old ideas stored in a "recycling bin" could become newly relevant and helpful at some point.[5] They may resonate with important new voices, if you are listening to them, such as the voices of non-users with unmet needs that you may address. Vision plus a willingness to listen to the right voices is what will give us the breakthrough innovations of the future.

Errant Metrics in Evaluating Innovation

Financial tools are essential in making decisions for a business, when these tools are improperly applied, innovation can become a casualty. We discuss the importance of sound financials and give recommendations for innovation metrics later (Chapter 22), but here we discuss how improper metrics can be a significant source of fatigue.

Exhibit 9.1 offers a tongue-in-cheek depiction of how errant metrics can misinform and deceive. Here metrics from a commercial apple grower show outstanding improvements in the business, with apples being harvested more productively than ever and costs for labor and ladders dropping at the same time. The reason for this boon, however, is that the trees have been felled, making the harvest easier than ever before—for a final season. If management is unaware of what is happening on the ground and views the business through errant metrics, a completely wrong understanding will be obtained. Unfortunately, some companies take a similar approach when it comes to innovation. Management may sometimes believe that innovation is thriving even while innovators are toppling or the will to share has been axed.

Metrics themselves can also be a barrier to innovation, hindering the decisions needed to give innovation a chance. In a 2008 *Harvard*

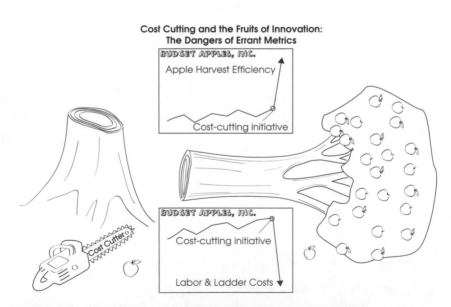

Exhibit 9.1   The apple harvesting metaphor for innovation productivity illustrates the danger of errant metrics and the need for management to be aware of what's happening at ground level

Business Review article, Clayton Christensen et al. point to three problems in this area:[6]

1. The use of discounted cash flow (DCF) and net present value (NPV) to evaluate investment opportunities obscures the real benefits of investment in innovation.
2. The way that fixed and sunk costs are considered when evaluating proposed investments hinders incumbent firms in responding to an attack by newcomers.
3. The focus on earnings per share as the primary driver of share price diverts resources from investments for future growth.

The first point is particularly relevant to innovation fatigue. Christensen et al. explain that those determining the NPV of innovation investments often assume a future baseline in which the present health of the company continues if no investment is made. In reality, a company usually faces declining returns without further investment. The fallacy of unrealistic future projections for the base case of doing nothing results in low estimated values for innovation investments. If more realistic assumptions were used, as shown in Exhibit 9.2, the financial case for investing in innovation would appear stronger. Using the typical assumptions in DCF analysis, the returns on innovation often appear too small to be justified, resulting in missed opportunities and often more fatigue for innovators.

The authors explain that methods used to estimate future values beyond a few years are often wildly inaccurate. Single terminal values are estimated to handle remote time periods (e.g., beyond three or five years) and are then discounted to future values. In the more remote time periods where terminal values are used, the likely

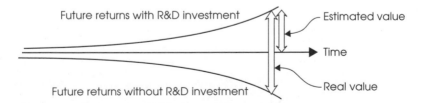

Exhibit 9.2   Graph showing the real and estimated future value of innovation as a function of which assumption is made for the "do nothing" scenario. Adapted from Christensen et al. (2008)

decline of the business without investment in innovation tends to be accelerating, yet is not accounted for in the computations.

The uncertainty of future returns in innovation, especially for radical or disruptive innovations, further compounds the anti-innovation bias of many financial computations. It is relatively easy to make reasonable projections of returns for an incremental innovation in a known market. Use of the popular stage-gate process requires financial justification for each stage in development of an innovation, and teams familiar with the criteria can easily tweak the assumptions in the financial modeling to make the incremental innovation meet the criteria for going forward. Less certain innovations are more difficult to quantify and can easily be challenged or even killed in the stage-gate process, especially when pitted against seemingly safe incremental innovation projects.

The stage-gate system may be inadequate for assessing innovations aimed at building new growth businesses, but it remains widely used for that purpose. Unfortunately, numerous promising innovations may be rejected because credible estimates of future returns cannot be generated, in contrast to safe incremental innovations. We have seen several leading companies striving to innovate, while the innovators within face innovation fatigue driven by improper use of metrics and rigorous application of the stage-gate system.

Baruch Lev also discusses the challenge of accounting procedures that fail to recognize the high value of intangibles. Their neglect in accounting can result in greatly undervaluing investment in R&D.

Current accounting regulations require that R&D projects in the development process and certain other tangible and intangible assets must be completely and immediately expensed by the acquiring company. Thus, when IBM acquired Lotus Development Corp. with an estimated $1.84 billion value (60 percent of the price for Lotus) in its "in-process R&D," IBM expensed that and reported a massive $538 million loss in the third quarter of 1995, whereas the previous year's third quarter showed a $710 million profit. Shouldn't executives demand a change in the rules that depress earnings? Lev explains why they don't:

> One would expect corporate executives to rebel against [this] accounting rule. . . . In fact, however, when the FASB announced in 1999 its intention to change the in-process R&D

expensing rule, it encountered such strong opposition by mangers that it backtracked. Why the opposition to a change of a clearly inappropriate procedure—expensing asset values acquired in arm's length acquisitions? Enter the politics of intangible's disclosure.

The GAAP-mandated expensing of practically all investments in intangibles—both internally developed (R&D, customer acquisition costs) and acquired from others—is a recipe for inflating future reported profitability and growth and, in addition, serves to protect managers against embarrassments. When IBM expenses almost 60 percent of the Lotus acquisition and when Cisco writes off almost 80 percent of the value of its acquisitions, they guarantee that future revenues and earnings derived from these acquisitions will be reported unencumbered by the major expense item: the amortization of acquisition costs.[7]

The expensing of intangibles also inflates reported return on equity and return on assets since the expensed part of the acquisitions does not get included in the denominator. Even the impact of a failed acquisition can be largely hidden from investors. Meanwhile, investors tend to accept these write-offs as one-offs. The net result, as Lev puts it, is "the best of all worlds . . . : no price hit at the time of expensing and a significant boost to future reported profitability."[8]

Thus, current accounting procedures allow companies to keep the public in the dark about the value of intangibles and the impact of acquisitions. Other intangible aspects of a business are also not visible in accounting, including the preservation of trademarks and brands. The resulting undervaluation of intangibles can decrease the incentives for companies to make needed investments in R&D—ultimately a source of innovation fatigue for corporate innovators.

We offer recommendations for improved metrics later in Chapter 22, where we address the general topic of financials.

The Danger of Focusing on Cost Alone: Dismembering the Ecosystem

Sometimes leaders with the wrong vision, listening to the wrong voices, can achieve short term success as they utterly destroy the long-term capabilities of a company. This destruction can be in the form of dismemberment of a once-healthy business ecosystem (the network of relationships and connections that give life to an organization). When leaders only focus on the tangibles and the immediate bottom line, the value of intricate flows of intangibles may be missed. Huge portions of a vital ecosystem may be destroyed without recognizing how much loss is occurring. Pursuit of short-term goals that destroy future capabilities is a common pitfall—one we expressed earlier in Exhibit 9.1 with the metaphor of the apple harvest.

One executive we interviewed pointed to the downfall of General Motors as a herald of this phenomenon, pointing to their purchasing policies in the 1980s that some vendors saw as ruthless. General Motors allegedly pressured partners to deliver the lowest possible price or lose the business. Prices came down, but relationships and critical ecosystems eroded. Losing access to the numerous intangibles—knowledge, tips, market insights, best practices—that flow from healthy, mutually beneficial and respectful relationships arguably destroyed part of GM's competitive advantage and ability to innovate. Today GM is a tiny fraction of what it once was. It is improper to pin all the blame on the cost-cutting steps that GM took, but one can only wonder how much healthier the company would have been if it had a healthier ecosystem to support innovation when it was most needed. On the other hand, Toyota sends their engineers to actively work with suppliers in their plants and transfer the best practices from Toyota so that everyone benefits.[9]

Learnings

The impact of flaws in decision making and vision on innovation fatigue could be the subject of an entire book, but here we have only touched upon a few highlights. Key recommendations to leaders include:

- Do not let your attention to process get in the way of innovation success. Likewise, do not let organizational change impede innovation.
- Understand what is happening at the root level in your innovation community.
- Do not be deceived by questionable metrics or by cost factors alone. Understand that innovation is essential for future success.
- Learn to listen to the right voices. Naturally, this includes the voice of the innovator.

Notes

1. "Armada Inn: Traveler Reviews," *TripAdvisor.com*, www.tripadvisor.com/Show UserReviews-g60898-d86245-r4974996-Armada_Inn-Atlanta_Georgia.html (or http://tinyurl.com/bkduea) (accessed July 19, 2008).
2. Clayton M. Christensen, Stephen P. Kaufman, and Willy C. Shih, "Innovation Killers: How Financial Tools Destroy Your Capacity to Do New Things," *Harvard Business Review*, Jan. 2008, 98–105.
3. "Apple's New Thing (iPod)," *MacRumors.com*, www.macrumors.com/2001/10/23/apples-new-thing-ipod/ (accessed Nov. 3, 2008).
4. Comments on "Apple's New Thing (iPod)," *MacRumors.com*, http://forums .macrumors.com/showthread.php?t=500 (accessed Nov. 3, 2008).
5. Mukund Karanjikar, "Managing failed ideas—Could this have been the next iPod®?," *PDMA Visions*, Sept. 2007, www.pdma.org/visions/sept07/npd-trend2 .php (accessed Dec. 27, 2007).
6. Christensen et al., "Innovation Killers."
7. Baruch Lev, *Intangibles: Management, Measurement, and Reporting* (Washington, D.C.: Brookings Institute Press, 2001), 88–89.
8. Ibid., p. 89.
9. J. Liker and T. Choy, "Building Deep Supplier Relationships," *Harvard Business Review*, December 2004, 104–112.

CHAPTER

Fatigue Factor #6

OPEN INNOVATION FATIGUE

Open innovation is the practice of reaching beyond corporate borders and opening corporate gates to bring in capabilities and solutions (e.g., products, technologies, and services) from others to strengthen innovation within the corporation. Open innovation is an essential best practice for modern companies, as eloquently taught by Henry Chesbrough in *Open Innovation*[1] and *Open Business Models*.[2] Unfortunately, external immigrants of innovation are shunned by some companies, not just through the flaws of some individuals that we discussed in the context of NIH Syndrome, but from deliberately crafted strategies and systems, which we address here.

A simple example of such problems involves the formal offices some companies have for receiving external invention submissions. When inventors contact companies on their own, they are typically directed to a single contact point that handles unsolicited requests. Many inventors imagine that the forms they submit to these offices will be carefully reviewed and shared with people in the corporation who might be most interested in the invention. This is a naïve point of view. For some companies, the purpose of these official portals for unsolicited requests often is to keep outside ideas away from the "right" people, preventing them from being "contaminated" with the external invention. They are actually more like sealed barriers than gates. (See Exhibit 10.1.)

Exhibit 10.1   Corporate barriers to external innovation are a source of innovation fatigue

Inventors can lose precious time trying to work through such channels. They may be astonished to learn that these official channels generate so little interest in what they feel should be a great fit. This strange behavior is entirely rational when viewed through the lens of risk. A corporation does not want to face the risk of lone inventors claiming that they are the source for a new product concept that the company might be working on already. Thus steps are taken to prevent "contamination" of key people with unsolicited outside ideas. But when someone knows the company's needs, and knows the people inside, it can be possible to quickly identify if the outside invention might be of interest and—when it's clear that contamination is not a threat—arrange for a meeting in which the external innovation can be seriously considered by the company. Relationships, coupled with good timing and a compelling reason to believe are essential for this process.

In one case, we recommended that a client's invention should go to a particular Fortune 500 company for consideration. The inventor said he had already taken his invention to that company and could assure us that they were completely familiar with it and simply not interested. When we went to our contact there—a VP charged with bringing outside innovations into the company—we learned that he had never heard of the invention and was intensely interested in it. The inventor was surprised, but we weren't. The inventor had been working through "official" channels that weren't necessarily designed to get outside inventions in front of decision makers. Some people, perhaps more focused on the risk of contamination than on business growth and competitive advantage, have every motivation to decline the innovation. Through their lens of risk, every outside idea is a threat in need of aggressive antibodies to protect the corporation.

At the Management Roundtable's CoDev 2008 conference on open innovation, Steve Goers of Kraft Foods spoke about the history of the Bagel-fuls® innovation, a refrigerated bagel that has a cream cheese filling built in. A third-generation bagelmaker developed the concept and wanted to expand by licensing the product to Kraft Foods. Not having direct contacts with the company, the inventor did some research, made some calls, and identified several people at the company who might be interested in the product and possibly able to do something about it. A case of the product was sent to each person on the list. Most ignored the opportunity, but one person had an "aha" moment and recognized that this could fit Kraft Foods' needs. It would mean extra work and risk, but it was an opportunity that shouldn't be missed.

It took about 18 months from that point to move through licensing and manufacturing issues, but today Bagel-fuls® are a popular product seen in grocery stores around the U.S. If the inventor had been less persistent, it might still be a relatively unknown product today. Fortunately, Kraft Foods recently strengthened its approach to open innovation, including re-launching the InnovateWithKraft .com Web site to help those with unsolicited innovations. Now external innovators can receive a lot more guidance and don't have to guess where they should send samples. We expect many more successes to follow.

"The Statement We Read to People Like You"

One of our partners contacted the corporate headquarters of a major sportswear company to find how best to present an innovative product to them. The employee was perplexed as to why anyone outside the company would want to bring a product concept to them, and said, "Wait just a minute while I get the statement I'm supposed to read to people like you." She then read a lengthy and dull statement about how this company does not accept unsolicited ideas and new product concepts. Amazing! The company's stock was at a five-year low at that moment (before the 2008 crash). With that attitude toward external innovation, its future prospects may not be all that bright.

Perhaps we should create a mutual fund based on shorting publicly traded companies with similar policies toward external innovation.

In a related effort to share an innovative clothing concept with a major clothing company, we ran into an interesting Idea Submission Policy. Here is the email we received:

> [Our company] and its affiliated companies and employees are unable to accept or consider unsolicited ideas, including ideas for new or improved products, technologies, product enhance-ments, advertising campaigns, promotions, marketing plans, product names, etc. Therefore, we kindly decline your offer to submit an idea.
>
> The reason for this policy is simple . . . we wish to avoid any misunderstanding that might arise should your idea appear similar to one that [the company] is already considering, has developed for use or has used in the past. . . .
>
> If you send [us] your ideas, despite our policy, then the fol-lowing terms shall apply to your idea submission, regardless of what you may state in your submission: (1) your idea will automatically become the property of [the company], without any compensation to you; (2) [We] will have no obligation to return your idea to you or respond to you in any way; (3) [We] will have no obligation to keep your idea confidential; and (4) [We] may use your idea for any purpose whatsoever, including giving your idea to others.[3]

"Your idea will automatically become the property of [our company], without any compensation to you." There's a chilling message to greet would-be innovation partners.

One can argue that some industries such as the clothing and apparel industries face intense competitive pressures that make the risk of contamination especially severe. But the intense competitive pressures also greatly increase the risk of not exploiting open inno-vation. As an example of how a company in this area can effectively manage open innovation while also containing contamination, we recently dealt with one sportswear company that, unlike many of its competitors, allowed outside inventors to submit inventions for consideration. Their policies required that the invention be the subject of a patent or a pending utility patent application (a provisional application would not be accepted). The patent had to be included in the submission on a non-confidential basis. The patent provides protection for the submitter, who also must certify that they are submitting non-confidential information and recognize that the company may already be developing similar concepts on their own. A fine line was walked through this process, which is currently under internal review and may soon be modified. Systems for receiving external innovations can be demanding and may require review and revision, but we feel a process that permits it is far healthier than a "Keep Away" sign at the front gate.

Competitive OI and Connecting with a Personal Touch

While some companies build resilient barriers against external innovations, other companies with real vision are accelerating their OI efforts, even using highly publicized competitions and contests to bring inventors their way. One example is Cisco, which recently announced a competition intended to draw thousands of contestants from around the globe.[4] The competition for the Cisco I-Prize—aimed at finding a concept that could be the basis of a new business unit—received over 1,000 pitches from 104 countries. Similar competitions have multiplied rapidly in recent years, making the contest a key tool in some OI efforts. It shouldn't be the only tool, but can generate publicity and interest. Meanwhile, other less dramatic channels are needed.

One of the best examples we've seen of a company with a solid OI system and culture is Procter and Gamble. In our dealings with them, they have stood out and defined standards of excellence that we feel others should emulate. While P&G has received much attention for their Connect and Develop system, what many people don't realize is how effective they have been in building personal relationships—networks of intangible transactions—that encourage open innovation.

In our experience taking some of our clients' concepts to P&G, we found cheerful, positive people in the various groups we interacted with. We did not encounter layers of Kafkaesque bureaucracy or people unsure about how to move forward or what to do, as we have seen in other companies. We did not have lengthy statements read to us about why they weren't interested in outside innovation.

After initial contact with some business leaders, we were asked to submit the concept through the Connect and Develop Web site at PG.com, a process expected of everybody to help the company track external innovations. We let our contacts know the case number the concept received so they could make sure they had their hands on the submitted information to guide it through the proper channels. After some email correspondence, we were pleased to get a phone call from the head of their External Business Development group who simply wanted to make sure we understood who they were, how they operated, and how we could work with them most effectively. The fact that P&G would make a personal relationship-building call to a small firm who had just submitted their first concept speaks volumes about their attention to the human side of innovation. After the 20-minute phone conversation, we better understood what they were looking for and felt highly motivated to bring several other inventions from our clients to them. We understood that we would receive rapid feedback, that our concepts would get personal attention, and that the concepts would quickly be brought before the right people.

This kind of response is so rare among the major corporations of the world, yet makes such good business sense that we must point to this as a best practice and encourage other companies to add this kind of sound external outreach program. P&G's system and the personal attention they provide have a tremendous encouraging impact—a healthy step toward alleviating OI fatigue and energizing the world of inventors. We wish more companies would follow their lead.

Lessons from the British Navy: Why the Cure for Scurvy Took 200 Years to Be Implemented

Organizational barriers to innovation can be fatal, as we learn from the tragic history of scurvy in the British Navy and the navies of other seafaring nations. With thousands of sailors dying from this disease, it was one of the most serious challenges the Navy faced. On lengthy voyages, 30% or more of the crew might die from scurvy. Though confusion and error among learned men about the cause of scurvy and its cure would persist into the 20th century, there was credible medical information in the early 1600s pointing to citrus fruits as a helpful aid in preventing and curing the disease.[5] Physicians on land and at sea would later provide strong evidence in the mid-1700s that citrus or other fresh fruits and vegetables reduced the risk of scurvy, but this knowledge was not only ignored or resisted by those in the Navy, it was resisted by the mainstream European medical community. The medical thought leaders of the day perpetrated a form of "strategy fatigue" by making a general understanding of the nature of disease their primary quest. They were simply uninterested in the "merely empirical" work aimed at curing any given disease. For example, the work in the 1730s of physician John Bachstrom in Holland pointing to fresh fruits and vegetables as the decisive cure for scurvy was dismissed by the medical community of his day, for he was "a mere empirick" in the eyes of his elite peers.[6]

The adoption of the innovation of citrus fruit in treating scurvy took more than compelling evidence. It took someone with powerful connections to champion the innovation. This man was the prominent Scottish physician, Sir Gilbert Blane, who was only 4 years old when a detailed study on the cure for scurvy was published by James Lind in 1753[7]—only to be ignored for decades. (To be accurate, the information from Lind and others was obscured by terrible confusion about physiology and disease, and continued to point to the dangers of various "airs" and climatic factors as key contributors to scurvy, obscuring the fact that it was a nutritional deficiency.)

In London, Blane became the private physician to Lord Rodney and sailed with him to the West Indies in 1779. Blane's efforts to keep sailors healthy were increasingly successful, and through his connections to Rodney and other naval leaders, Blane was able to give lectures to senior leaders and gain support for improved practices across the entire navy. Drawing upon past work and a further demonstration of his own, he would introduce compelling evidence to naval leaders that lime juice prevented scurvy, leading the Navy to adopt lime juice in its global operations beginning in 1795.[8] For nearly two centuries, the British Navy had been closed to a safe, inexpensive innovation from outsiders that solved what may have been its most vexing and costly problem. The citrus "sales pitch" fell on deaf ears until someone with the right connections to senior management could deliver it. It's a tragic lesson of the dangers of closed innovation, of organizational rigidity, of devaluing the work of innovators, of listening to the wrong voices, of "not invented here," and the importance of delivering the story of an innovation to the right people, through those who have the right contacts. It doesn't need to be this way, but it often is. Thousands of needless deaths over centuries: these are some of the fruits of innovation fatigue.

Incidentally, innovation-related lessons from scurvy continued long after 1795. Though citrus juice was adopted in the British Navy, the nature of the disease and the reason for the cure were still unknown. Without careful efforts to preserve knowledge and best practices, erosion can quickly occur. Thus when the Royal Navy undertook arctic expeditions in the 19th century, the leaders took with them a belief that good hygiene, good morale, and regular exercise prevented scurvy. Not surprisingly, scurvy was a recurring problem in these voyages. In the 20th century, when Robert Scott trekked into the Antarctic, tainted canned food was believed to be a cause of scurvy. The connection between vitamin C and scurvy was not discovered until 1932. Likewise, we have seen many organizations lose best practices, healthy processes, and even technical capabilities and knowledge when efforts weren't taken to preserve and pass on what they had.

Learnings

- Seeking and welcoming innovation from outside an organization's boundaries is essential for success. The key to your future may be in someone else's lab or garage right now.
- The risk of contamination from external sources can be managed with proper systems.
- Companies wishing to pursue open innovation should communicate in word and deed that they are open to partnership and external innovation.

Notes

1. Henry Chesbrough, *Open Innovation: The New Imperative for Creating and Profiting from Technology* (Boston: Harvard Business School Press, 2003).
2. Henry Chesbrough, *Open Business Models: How to Thrive in the New Innovation Landscape* (Boston: Harvard Business School Press, 2003).
3. Email to Meliah Lindsay from a major clothing company whose name we would rather withhold, received Aug. 22, 2008.

4. Rachael King, "Cisco Pays Big for New Ideas," *BusinessWeek*, June 2, 2008, www .businessweek.com/technology/content/may2008/tc20080529_968185.htm (or http://tinyurl.com/bsg9r7) (accessed July 21, 2008).
5. Stephen R. Brown, *SCURVY: How a Surgeon, a Mariner and a Gentleman Solved the Greatest Medical Mystery of the Age of Sail* (New York: St. Martin's Press, 2003).
6. Kenneth J. Carpenter, *The History of Scurvy and Vitamin C* (Cambridge, UK: Cambridge University Press, 1988), 44–45.
7. James Lind, *A Treatise of the Scurvy. In Three Parts. Containing an Inquiry Into the Nature, Causes and Cure, of that Disease. Together with a Critical and Chronological View of What Has Been Published on the Subject* (Edinburgh: Sands, Murray and Cochran for A. Kincaid and A. Donaldson, 1753). Portions of the original reproduced online by the James Lind Library at www.jameslindlibrary.org/ trial_records/17th_18th_Century/lind/lind_tp.html (or http://tinyurl.com/ bk9yyo). Also see Carpenter, *History of Scurvy*, 51–52.
8. David Nash Ford, "Biographies: Sir Gilbert Blane (1749–1834)," *Royal Berkshire History*,www.berkshirehistory.com,2005,www.berkshirehistory.com/bios/gblane .html (accessed Oct. 9, 2008).

11

Case Study on Overcoming Fatigue

HI-TECH GEMS FROM THE "LOW-TECH" PAPER INDUSTRY

Even when corporate culture truly supports innovation, the challenge can be enormous. No matter what corporate leaders do to enable innovation, it still comes down to the need to have the right people in the right places, with a dogged determination to push forward to success. The "right people" are those with the "right skills" to innovate—not necessarily subject matter experts (SMEs). In fact, relying on SMEs can sometimes propagate the status quo. Sometimes the most important skills aren't technical expertise or experience in a field, but creativity, persistence, the ability to learn, the ability to forge new connections, the ability to see what might be possible, and the determination to bring the vision to life.

In this case study, we explore the rise of a suite of innovations and a successful new start-up in a high-tech area that emerged from the least likely of places, driven by a combination of visionary leaders and a group of people willing to do whatever it took to find the right opportunity and deliver.

If you've ever walked through the damp, noisy heart of a paper mill, you've seen the massive machinery processing wet fiber slurries, complex pathways of fabrics carrying wide wet webs at high speed, and giant rolls of paper. You might be surprised that this old smokestack industry could have been the breeding grounds for a high-tech startup that is bringing sophisticated electronic solutions to trendy industries like women's fashion.

The rise of Vue Technology from MeadWestvaco Paper is a valuable story of determined inventors—aided by visionary leaders—who overcame innovation fatigue factors from multiple sources.

Vue Technology is a hot Orange County startup, filled with talented professionals from southern California's vibrant start-up community. As this book was being finalized, Vue was acquired by Tyco International a confirmation of their success. Vue has been working to realize the promise of RFID—radio-frequency identification, in which microchips attached to small antennas in tags have unique ID codes that can be read remotely with radio signals. The antennae in the tags receive the signals, energizing a circuit that interacts with the chip, and then re-radiates a signal conveying the ID code on the chip back to a remote reader. (See Exhibit 11.1.)

The promise of widespread RFID at the "item level" has been hindered for decades by cost. Now that tag costs are coming down, system architecture remains a barrier. For example, tracking an RFID-tagged product on a shelf is simple: have a tag on the object and an RFID reader nearby. Doing this for thousands of objects in a store becomes much more difficult and expensive. Are hundreds of

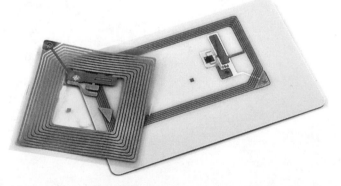

Exhibit 11.1   Sample RFID tags. Will printed versions of these devices be a common part of paper packaging in the future?

readers with power supplies and coaxial cables needed? How does one manage the constant readings coming in from thousands of objects? The system architecture and software systems need to be simple and inexpensive. That's where Vue Technology comes in.

Vue Technology has been building the dream of simple "plug-and-play" devices that can let retailers know exactly what is on the shelves, where items are, and what is available in inventory. In one demonstration conducted for Best Buy in Apple Valley, Minnesota, a unique "smart shelf" was demonstrated with a clever, patented antenna design that allowed a single reader to work with a network of antennas to activate just one antenna at a time to read nearby RFID tags.[1] This foundation for practical in-store item-level RFID has been buttressed by additional innovations in software systems and intelligent antennae networks. These advances did not come from a crack team of electrical engineers at MIT or an electronics company like Texas Instruments. It began in an old paper company, Westvaco, originally the West Virginia Paper Company established in 1888 along the Potomac River in what is now Luke, Maryland. This mature company carried one of the few single-letter tickers on the New York Stock Exchange, "W," before merging with Mead Corp. in 2002. (MeadWestvaco's NYSE ticker is MWV.)

The rise of Vue Technology is a story of overcoming barriers, filled with lessons for innovators and business leaders, as we learned when we interviewed Dr. Paul Rasband,[2] cofounder of Vue Technology and co-inventor on many of Vue's patents.

"Go Find Out"

When Paul Rasband received his Ph.D. in chemical engineering from Cornell University in 1996, many industries were in a downturn, but not the paper industry. It was an especially active year for Westvaco, which would later merge with Mead Corporation in 2002 and become MeadWestvaco.

Shortly after joining, Paul was given the challenge of developing materials and processes for printable electronics. Paul was delighted but confused: "What are printable electronics?" he asked. "I don't know," said his new manager. "*Go find out.*"

Westvaco's interest in "disposable electronics" as Paul would call it, can be attributed to vision at the top. Westvaco's leaders recognized the potential of that emerging technology and asked the company to pursue it long before it became sexy.

Not only was Westvaco willing to pursue potentially radical technologies at an early stage, they also exemplified the spirit of open innovation before it became popular. In 1998, Laura Pingle, a capital projects engineer was given a personal sabbatical to pursue a research project with Lucent Technologies, one of the first major companies to explore printing digital electronics. This brought new ideas to Westvaco, inspiring VP John Glomb to launch the project that created the new opportunity for Paul.

"None of us knew much about the possibilities—all of us were naive and uncomfortable with the electronics nature of the thing." Paul now explains to his own children that productivity in radical innovation often requires "being comfortable with being uncomfortable," learning from mistakes, and constantly revising and challenging assumptions.

Comfort with uncertainty partly came from Westvaco's supportive culture. Scientists knew the company was committed to growth and innovation to sustain its long-term business plan with value-added products involving paper, plastics, and polymer films. That gave them the courage to be part of such a risky project. After all, what right to win did this inexperienced team in a paper company have?

Paul's first project involved finding a way to print antennas for anti-theft tags similar to those produced by Checkpoint Systems, Inc. one of the two major EAS (electronic article surveillance) companies in the world. This proved to be a catalyst in several ways. During this time of exploration and strategic consideration, Paul and his team learned much about the opportunities in the marketplace and also honed their approach to patent strategy. They also considered new business models. Checkpoint had been charging a premium for their patent-protected EAS tags, following Gillette's "razor and blades" model. The tags were Checkpoint's blades, and the detectors were the razors. Could disposable electronics become a blade for Westvaco?

18 Months of Solving the Wrong Problem—And Paul's Conversion on the Road to . . . Cambridge

Printed electronics on packaging to make low cost anti-theft tags sounds like a great idea, but it's still mostly a dream today. That dream was Paul's assignment. He and his team had exerted themselves to overcome the disadvantage of little formal training in that area.

The night he received the new assignment, Paul retrieved his old Electrical Engineering 101 textbook from his undergraduate days at Brigham Young University and began studying it with new passion, reading it cover to cover in 3 days. "That's when I started to really love my job, when I was learning new things under pressure."

However, after 18 months of intense effort, Paul recognized that he was solving the wrong problem by pursuing a printable anti-theft tag. Even if printable electronics could be manufactured, the company could not afford to retrofit their numerous packaging lines to add anti-theft features. Paul and his peers also worried that anti-theft tags might become irrelevant as RFID promised to do much more than just carry the "off/on" single bit of data in EAS tags. The many bits of data in an RFID tag allow each tag to have a unique serial code, allowing individual items to be tracked.

The pursuit of printable anti-theft tags now appeared to be a mistake. Paul felt that he had done things in the reverse order, starting with a cool technology rather than first understanding what problem needed to be solved. But this path introduced them to passive RFID—low-cost tags that don't have a battery, but get the energy they need to broadcast a signal from the radio signal sent out by a reader. Paul realized he needed to switch gears and learning about RFID. He was soon on the road to Cambridge, Massachusetts, where he attended MIT's SmartWorld symposium. He heard speakers from Motorola, Microsoft, Ericsson, and Nokia talk about their work and vision, and heard professors discuss the future of a data-rich world with tools like RFID fueling information flow at new levels. It was an experience which Paul describes as "quasi-spiritual." In fact, he refers to this as his "conversion"—a conversion to the future that Westvaco could help build.

The new convert returned and instead of writing traditional engineering reports, he began writing internal epistles in a new style, more as a futurist with "fluffy, touchy-feely memos" explaining the need for cutting-edge products and showing why RFID could help fulfill Westvaco's business goals.

Skepticism, Uncertainty, and Encouragement

At that crucial time, Paul's boss, Chris Parks, respected him enough to allow him to try to influence higher-ups in the corporation, coaching him in how to deal with the realities of bringing change.

Paul faced skepticism and even outright opposition from some mid-level managers. Some questioned his sanity and may have been insulted at the prospect of this young engineer trying to convince a venerable paper company to pursue a wild goose chase where the company had no expertise. Some who knew and accepted the original objective of Paul's project were frustrated that he wanted to change course toward RFID, which would not involve printed electronics at all. Some critics felt he should return to printed EAS tags and start making winning products ASAP. Why wasn't Paul doing his duty instead of writing fuzzy papers about vision? The concerns were understandable, driven by a desire to make something happen. Paul had a different perspective. He had spent 18 months climbing a technological ladder that was leaning against the wrong wall. "We needed to figure out WHY we were doing something before we did it." Realizing that had transformed him from a technologist into a strategist overnight. On the road to Cambridge, the vision Paul encountered made him not so much a convert to RFID as a convert to thoughtful strategy development.

Another positive internal change at Westvaco helped Paul build momentum with RFID. Two engineers, Rick Spedden and Laura Pingle, interested in radical innovation and corporate ventures, had studied the writings of various thought leaders and felt it was time for Westvaco to do more. With management support, particularly that of VP Ronnie Hise, they formed a group called Radical Innovation and Venture Capital Activities (RIVCA). Their goal was to create opportunities that could lead to new businesses and external venture opportunities. Paul got involved unofficially, crossing organizational lines apparently with the implicit blessing of top management (an attribute of an innovative culture). Paul, Rick, and Laura were occasionally invited to headquarters to review their work with CEO John Luke—a highly motivating expression of support from the top, though there would still be painful setbacks when some projects lost funding or faced other challenges from mid-level managers and vice presidents from various units who didn't understand the project. That gap was understandable, for the RFID was being kept largely secret until the team had obtained real evidence and developed prototypes that could convince others. "Better to stay quiet until we had the goods," adds Paul.

Laura and Rick in RIVCA were not his formal managers, but he was coordinating with them and virtually taking orders from them, while he belonged officially to R&D. This was a problem. Paul says he only "got away with it" because his boss knew how much the CEO wanted RIVCA to succeed. Paul, after two years of study, was Westvaco's only RFID expert at that time and RIVCA needed his help. Naturally, a young upstart who suddenly gets special treatment and CEO support in "breaking the rules" is likely to get some flack. If Paul were to do it over, he believes he would be more sensitive to some of the political issues and work harder to smooth things over.

Standing His Ground

While Paul and the others inside the blossoming Intelligent Systems group plunged forward with RFID, possibly stepping on some toes, competitive threats were mounting. International Paper issued press releases announcing that they were giving birth to the dream of smart packaging with plans to put Motorola's Bistatix® RFID tags on packages. Paul pondered his audacity in thinking that he, with so little training and experience, could have led his small company to make a name for themselves in the increasingly crowded world of RFID, dominated by big boys with big companies. Nevertheless, Paul and Westvaco chose to press on. Westvaco quickly joined the AutoID Center at MIT, the epicenter of RFID-related thinking in the United States.

Paul was excited to attend the meetings of thought leaders and technical experts, but this inexperienced chemical engineer from a relatively small paper company faced a variety of barriers—potential fatigue factors that could have hindered his efforts to gain the knowledge he needed. In many meetings Paul was over his head, sitting in advanced electronics technology meetings with experts who had studied RFID for many years, with vast experience in various deep technical aspects. Sometimes, Paul found himself pretending to understand things he knew little about in order to avoid looking foolish. Paul has this word of advice to others entering new fields: "*You must never be intimidated by what you don't know.* If you need to be there, go there, and don't wait until you know enough. Jump in now and begin, and make sure you do what it takes to learn really fast."

Some AutoID Center meetings of experts were by invitation only. Paul had the audacity to recognize that he needed to be there, and simply went. His lack of credentials was overlooked a couple of times, but eventually a leader at the Center asked him and a few other "low-tech guys" to not attend. "Only RFID engineers and IC engineers need attend," the meeting announcement had clearly indicated. He held his ground as he spoke to the leader: "We paid our money to join, and we should have the right to learn from these meetings. If you want to kick me out, you'll need to use physical force to remove me." Paul has no remorse for standing his ground, and feels that the attempts to keep him out of technology meetings were completely wrong. The immigrant of innovation prevailed.

By this time, Westvaco's success depended on Paul learning all he could about RFID to help guide the corporation with the right strategy, to know the right problem to solve. He realized that he needed to build competencies in new areas and aggressively pursued them. His conversion to strategy only increased his appreciation of sound knowledge and ceaseless learning, an important lesson for innovators and strategists everywhere. He was still looking for the right business application to define what technical problems they should solve. The logical approach seemed to involve Westvaco making low-cost RFID tags for packaging. They were already pursuing products such as RFID-enhanced smart packaging for medical products. He started writing business plans, strategy papers, and road maps for a start-up company to be spun out of Westvaco. A new division was formed, MeadWestvaco Intelligent Systems (after Mead and Westvaco merged in 2002). Paul was the technology director, but the strategy was not yet complete.

Certifiably Nuts: Finding the Right Problem to Solve

Paul values frequent discussion and even debate with others as a way to refine his approach and learn from others. Paul credits Rick Spedden with an important insight offered in a heated discussion: "We don't want to make tags—they are going to be a commodity. We want to make the infrastructure." When Paul realized that Rick was thinking about smart shelves and RFID readers, the hardware that could enable RFID tags on packages to be read, he thought Rick was "certifiably nuts." However, within a few days, Paul had shifted his thinking and saw the wisdom of Rick's view. The opportunity was in infrastructure. As tags fell in price and became ubiquitous, the people making the money would be the ones helping stores to read and manage RFID data.

Paul and his peers began a project to build a smart cabinet with RFID readers that could read and track the position of DVD cases with RFID tags. This is when Intelligent Systems began some of their most important inventing. Paul recognized that a smart shelf or cabinet capable of tracking the location of items would be clunky using existing technology. A different reader with its own cabling and power supply for each zone on a shelf would result in a monstrosity of cables, expensive installation, and excessive consumption of space. What was needed was a smarter smart shelf.

Drawing upon all they had learned about antennas, RFID readers, signal transmission, and RFID tags, the team pondered the problem. One day at lunch, Paul and two others, Rich Campero and Don Bauer, began penciling different smart shelf systems on a napkin. "Rich did all of the writing and about 80 percent of the thinking, but Don and I helped a bit. It was one of those epiphanies that engineers get a few times in their career—good ideas just flowed. We kept that napkin for a long time." They were attempting to solve a problem that some of the experts at the AutoID Center would tell him couldn't be solved. Perhaps he, too, was certifiably nuts. But the answer came swiftly as the three collaborated, and a major portion of what would become a foundational patent for Vue Technology was hammered out that afternoon. Others would strengthen the invention in a group effort, but there was a flash of genius that day, based on many months of preparation and, perhaps most important of all, strategy. This time, Paul recognized that he was solving the right problem. The ladder was against the right wall. Now it was time to climb.

Connections for Success—and Disappointment

The innovative smart cabinet with its clever patent-pending smart shelf would be demonstrated to a variety of companies, such as Tesco, Best Buy, and Office Depot. It was crude proof of concept, not yet a product.

Paul felt they had the beginning of a breakthrough with tremendous value for retailers. Some retailers were enthusiastic and welcomed trials, while others were incredulous or uninterested and wanted to know nothing more. Based on Paul's disappointments with the response of some companies, he recognizes that companies go through different phases, and sometimes, no matter how

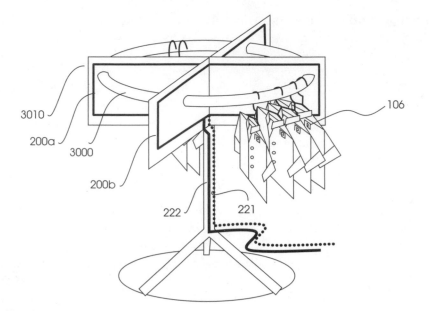

Exhibit 11.2   "Intelligent shelf" with RFID antenna system integrated into a circular clothing rack. From Vue Technology's U.S. Pat. No. 7,084,769.[3]

good the fit might seem, they just "aren't in the mood" for a major innovation. When that mood reflects the whims of an individual, it may change quickly, but sometimes it reflects a corporate culture that won't change for years.

In early marketing of smart packaging technologies, Paul found that their long-standing handicap was actually an advantage. They were neither an electronics firm, nor a team of world-class scientists with a clever technology looking for an application. However, they could look their customers in the eye and say, "We live on the same street you do. We understand low-cost, high-volume manufacturing from our packaging business. Packaging for us is not an afterthought. Our smart packaging is built from the ground-up with low-cost functionality in mind. We already make the materials for that, and now we add the electronics with low-cost as the primary requirement from the beginning. When they learned what our products cost, they knew we were serious—vastly less expensive than those of the competitors."

This attitude, understanding how apparent weaknesses might actually be positioned as strengths, continued to guide the Intelligent

Systems team as they took his business forward and helped found Vue Technology. Much remained to be done. They realized that the software for RFID infrastructure would be critical.

The crude prototype would soon be enhanced with software tools to help local retailers know when items were misplaced, when inventories were low, or when theft was in progress (e.g., detecting that five copies of "Batman Returns" were just removed from the shelf). The software tools could also integrate smart shelf data with Vendor Managed Inventory (VMI) systems, allowing vendors to know when to replenish inventories. Antenna networks would come later. (See Exhibits 11.2 and 11.3.)

The vital software aspects of their smart shelving solutions were found in collaboration with an outside software contract developer. Elario, a small Orange County software firm, had the skills Intelligent Systems needed. MeadWestvaco decided to bring Elario's competency in house, with the software development team remaining in California rather than relocating to the East Coast (reducing the risk of lost talent). When Intelligent Systems was spun off as Vue Technology, the Intelligent Systems employees were the ones who relocated, joining the vibrant entrepreneurial environment in the area.

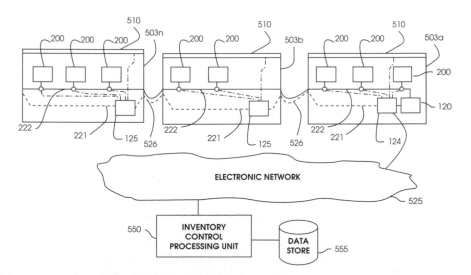

Exhibit 11.3   Schematic of an intelligent shelf station for efficiently tracking RFID tags. From Vue Technology's U.S. Pat. No. 7,084,769.[4]

Labor Pains: Birth is Just the Beginning

Paul cautions entrepreneurs to know their limitations. "You may have skills that are good enough to get your venture moving forward in the early stages, but whatever skills were vital to your success at that stage are likely to be inadequate for the company to move forward. Your job in a startup is to make your company successful enough that you can hire someone else to do your job better than you." Vue has hired world-class people for almost every role that Paul played during the rise of MeadWestvaco Intelligent Systems. The strategy and overall leadership is handled by CEO Robert Lock. Others lead sales and financial management. The Chief Technical Officer is his former co-inventor, Rich Campero, who Paul credits as an absolute expert and brilliant inventor who has built their technology from the ground up.

Most recently, Paul has focused on patents, competitive intelligence, elements of long-term strategy, and special projects for the CEO. "I have had a dozen jobs inside the company, and now I have come full-circle, doing what I was initially doing for MeadWestvaco."

The spin-off to form Vue Technology was just the beginning. Paul has been amazed at how many challenges one must face in moving a start-up forward. He says finding success in a startup requires facing a series of challenges each requiring new skills and involving new pains. "It's like crossing a desert, followed by climbing a mountain, and then swimming across an ocean. Many entrepreneurs climb the mountain, only to drown in the sea. You need to almost start from scratch with each new stage of company evolution." Numerous challenges crop up—relationships with customers, financial burdens, setbacks with personnel, competitive threats, regulatory burdens, on and on the list goes. Dogged determination and a focus on the vision to be achieved is needed by everyone involved to overcome the challenges.

On Oct. 7, 2008, Sensormatic Electronics Corporation, a division of Tyco International company, announced the acquisition of Vue Technology. The press release stated that the "Vue's item-level RFID technology includes a full software platform, RFID readpoints and RF networking devices to track inventory on a real-time basis. Simplifying the inventory process, Vue's software platform enables efficient and effective inventory cycle counts to ensure accuracy." Intended benefits of the acquisition include enabling retailers to deploy RFID "to gain better control, security and visibility into their inventories and increase operational efficiencies."[5] And to think that it began in an old paper company and a young chemical engineer whose first task was reviewing his old textbook for Electrical Engineering 101. Even old paper companies can surprise the world if they nurture a culture of innovation.

Learnings

- Successful innovation requires the right people with the right skills in the right place.
- Sometimes the key to innovation is challenging assumptions and finding the right problem to solve.
- Courage is at the heart of innovation: courage to tackle the unknown, courage to develop new skills, courage to stand one's ground, and courage to do what it takes to deliver.
- Even mature companies with low-tech products can become engines of impressive innovation when strong vision and strategy is in place, coupled with a culture that encourages innovation.
- "Never be intimidated by what you don't know."—Paul Rasband.

Notes

1. D.G. Bauer, E.R. Buiel, R.J. Campero, W.J. Carpenter, S.P. Metzler, R.E. Nordgren, P.B. Rasband, M.A. Taylor, and H.E. Wood, Jr., "Intelligent Station Using Multiple RF Antennae and Inventory Control System and Method Incorporating Same," U.S. Pat. No. 7,084,769, issued Aug. 1, 2006.
2. Interview with Jeff Lindsay, Sept. 2008.
3. Bauer et al., "Intelligent Station.".
4. Ibid.
5. Tyco Intl., "Sensormatic Strengthens Technology Platform for Retailers Through Acquisition of Vue Technology," Press Release, Oct. 7, 2008, http://investors.tyco.com/phoenix.zhtml?c=112348&p=irol-newsArticle&ID=1206336&highlight= (or http://tinyurl.com/7gxd8m) (accessed Oct. 16, 2008).

PART IV

EXTERNAL FATIGUE FACTORS

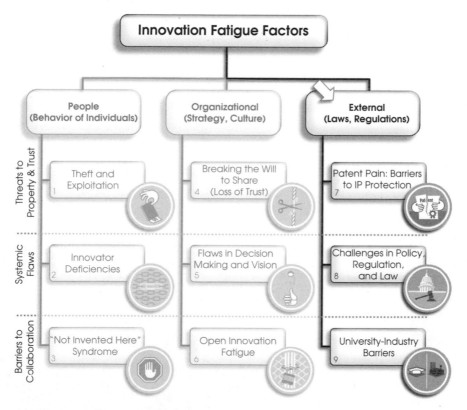

Exhibit 12.1   External fatigue factors

CHAPTER

Fatigue Factor #7

PATENT PAIN: BARRIERS TO INTELLECTUAL PROPERTY PROTECTION

Even experienced innovators with a track record of success can be hindered by external fatigue factors. External fatigue factors beyond the control of a company or inventor can add delays or sometimes quash an opportunity. The challenges can be bewildering and costly. Understanding how to cope with external fatigue is essential for prospective innovators. We also hope that policy makers, regulators, and others might understand how their domains impact innovators. We begin by exploring some of the challenges from IP practice and policy.

"The ability of an inventor to obtain a United States patent which fully covers his or her invention is at an all-time low." So wrote patent attorney and IP columnist Steven Ludwig in 2007,[1] referring to recent changes in patent law and practice in the United States. He urged Congress, the judiciary, and others to recognize the importance of innovation and do more to encourage it—something that China and other nations are doing. Recent events in the United States may pose some new challenges for some inventors, but there are also positive developments and many opportunities for informed inventors to receive fair protection.

Judicial and PTO Hurdles to Protecting Good Inventions

Among the three greatest invention and discoveries in world history, Abraham Lincoln included "the introduction of Patent Laws" in his list (also the arts of writing and printing, and the discovery of America). Patents themselves are a brilliant innovation, one that solves the problem of how to encourage the sharing of knowledge without undue risk of theft. Patent laws stand as a social compact in which an inventor is encouraged to tell the world secrets of knowledge in exchange for a limited monopoly over the invention. For a fixed period of time, the inventor can prevent others from making, selling, using, or importing the invention, in exchange for a detailed description of the invention. Once the time period for exclusive rights expires, the world can benefit more fully from that knowledge. It is a brilliant system that has fueled technological advance. However, when the system is defective or even hostile to inventors, the benefits may be lost. When the "will to share" via patents is lost, innovation fatigue may be at hand.

"Patent fatigue" occurs when IP rights become unnecessarily difficult to obtain, decelerating the engine of innovation. Uncertainty, delays, shifting laws, and increasing costs can all add to patent pain. In the United States, recent changes in patent law, particularly from judicial practice, sometimes reflect an anti-patent attitude that has discouraged some inventors. Congress has also been advancing a variety of patent reforms that many experts worry could further weaken U.S. patents. There are healthy sides to some recent and proposed reforms, but understanding the potential impact on innovation is important.

If out of touch with the "voice of the innovator," politicians can take actions that have unintended consequences on innovation. For example, Congress's hunger for spending money has long resulted in the diversion of fees submitted by patentees to the United States Patent and Trademark Office (USPTO). For a while, roughly $100 million a year was siphoned from PTO fees to spend elsewhere, meaning that the PTO had fewer resources available for patent prosecution. This was essentially a tax on innovation, and while it has been reduced with recent changes in fees, the tax continues. The impact of resource limitations at the PTO are felt by patent applicants in the form of delays in prosecution that can discourage inventors and decrease the value of the patents. Meanwhile, the patent allowance rate reported by the PTO has been dropping sharply in recent years, as shown in Exhibit 12.2. This is consistent with the increasing difficulties many patent practitioners are experiencing in prosecuting and obtaining patents.

On an international scale, the World Trade Organization in 2003 crafted an agreement in which poor nations can force the owners of patents for medicines to license the manufacturing to a local company. If there is not a suitable manufacturer in the country, it can import the drugs from other countries like India. The compulsory licenses are subject to several restrictions, including a prohibition against exporting the low-cost drug made under a compulsory license to developed countries. However, given the track record of some governments in ignoring or even encouraging the theft of foreign intellectual property, this arrangement might ultimately result in more foreign drugs being slipped into the supply chains of developed nations,[2] resulting in erosion of income to patent holders and disincentives to take on the risks of developing drugs. Many companies accept the concept of two-tiered pricing systems to make their product affordably available in emerging nations, while still retaining benefit from their IP and are willing to make painful compromises. But actions that eradicate patent

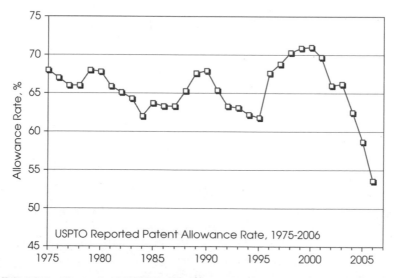

Exhibit 12.2   Reported USPTO allowance rates from 1975–2006 for all patents[3]

rights in the name of social justice may not do justice to anybody in the long run.

Enforcement Fatigue

For many companies, large and small, the value of intellectual property and the value of one's unique invention can be eroded when intellectual property rights are not enforced by a government. In some cases, a nation unilaterally decrees that a company's patents (typically a foreign company) will not be respected. This taking of IP is justified in the name of advancing the public good, but the act becomes a disincentive for companies to bring their products to that nation, or to develop new products at all.

Hot Property by Pat Choate[4] documents some of the numerous abuses of intellectual property rights in many nations. Taiwan, for example, in spite of an advanced IP system and a reputation for enforcing IP rights, has organizations financing pirating operations in multiple nations. Such challenges can be extremely difficult to root out. Impact? Over 40 percent of all movies and electronic games sold there are pirated, costing the United States $300 billion annually and driving some legitimate producers into bankruptcy.[5] Equally or more severe problems with pirating and counterfeiting exist in several other nations. Hundreds of billions of dollars of lost revenues to IP owners, and vast disincentives to innovation at many levels, are the fruits of the massive intellectual property theft that occurs globally. Just in the area of textiles and apparels, illegal counterfeits cost American companies $20 billion annually. Counterfeit clothing and shoes make up roughly 25 percent of the U.S. market.

Failure to adequately enforce IP law is not a problem unique to emerging nations, but also occurs far too often in the U.S. For example, the Customs Office is tasked with preventing known counterfeit goods from entering the United States, but this has become a relatively low priority for this agency. With an estimated $250 billion of counterfeit goods entering this nation annually, the Customs Office manages to capture less than 1 percent of this, partly because of inadequate staffing and also because they are tasked with enforcing over 400 laws from 40 federal agencies, with intellectual property law apparently having become a low priority.[6] Many painful stories can be told of inventors and entrepreneurs who are largely shut down when officials choose to turn a blind eye to piracy and theft of their work.

We urge officials to recognize the dramatic scope of intellectual property theft that occurs globally and in this nation. We urge these officials to step up their efforts to protect the engines of innovation and business growth that are being jeopardized by pirates and thieves globally.

KSR: A Potential Fatigue Factor from the Supreme Court

On April 30, 2007, the Supreme Court issued a decision, *KSR v. Teleflex*,[7] which will significantly affect U.S. patent law on the issue of "obviousness." In subsequent patent cases, it has become clear that this decision will limit the scope and validity of many patents, arguably eroding the value of many patents.

"Obviousness" is one of the most challenging aspects of patent law. Section 103 of the U.S. Patent Act specifies that a patent cannot be obtained "if the differences between the subject matter sought to be patented and the prior art are such that the subject matter as a whole would have been obvious at the time the invention was made to a person having ordinary skill in the art to which said subject matter pertains."

But what does "obvious" mean? Courts in past decades—particularly the Court of Appeals for the Federal Circuit (CAFC)—have held that a combination of previously known inventions brought together in a new way could be denied patentability due to obviousness if there were some "teaching, suggestion, or motivation" (TSM) to combine the various parts together. Thus, in the prosecution of a patent, if the examiner cited two references from different technology areas that, when combined, could result in the invention in question, the applicants could respond by showing that there was no written hint in references that might motivate one to combine them. Challenging the motivation to combine was a standard shield, but that defense has become more limited. Now the examiner can point to "common sense" or other factors, suggesting that an inventor faced with the problem at hand would naturally look to other areas to find technologies that could be used or tried, thus allowing the combination of references to stand in spite of their being of no clear teaching or suggestion in the art to motivate their combination.

KSR has been applied in several ensuing cases, often with unpleasant results for the patent holder. In discussing the recent

Translogic case where *KSR* was cited in invalidating a patent—after five years of prosecution in which a district court had already issued an injunction order in favor of the patentee—the law firm Robins, Kaplan, Miller, and Ciresi offered this observation:

> Patent holders navigating an obviousness-based validity challenge face a rocky road. . . . As we predicted when *KSR* first issued, alleged infringers have freer reign to string together disparate inferences from different fields of endeavor to show that all elements of an invention existed in prior art references. . . . Patent litigation has become a much riskier undertaking.[8]

Indeed, it is more important than ever to carefully craft a patent and the ensuing prosecution efforts with the implications of *KSR* in mind.

One way to overcome obviousness rejections for inventions based on new combinations of known elements is to show that there are teachings in the art that speak against the inventive combination, or that provide motivation not to try to pursue the combination. When appropriate, we feel that the application should also be drafted to highlight the inventive *story*, showing why the claimed invention involves more than straightforward, predictable work to solve a known problem with known tools. "Story telling" rather than dry recital of technical facts alone may become an important part of patent strategy in the future. Further approaches that patent applications can take to deal with *KSR* and related issues will be an ongoing topic on our blog at *InnovationFatigue.com*, where we will also offer tips on innovation, business strategy, and other aspects of conquering innovation fatigue.

Fatigue and Weak Property Rights

The barriers and systems that can grind down the will of inventors are as old as civilization. The systems of guilds in the Middle Ages grew from the lack of IP rights in the law, requiring great lengths to keep details of inventions secret. While the trade secrets of the guild system still provided means for inventors to benefit personally, thereby providing incentives for individual invention not unlike those in a patent system, there were still many limitations in terms of social benefit and the diffusion of knowledge.[9] The rise of the first patent in Florence (1421) and the first written patent law in Venice (1474)[10] marked significant steps for the sciences.

A brilliant compact between government and inventors was evolving. Ultimately, inventors would be rewarded for sharing their secrets with the public by being given a limited monopoly for the claimed invention, if it met certain criteria such as being novel, non-obvious or inventive, and useful. Respect for the IP rights of inventors provided motivation to accept the risk of publishing the invention for all the world to see. Indeed, the strength of the American patent system has been touted as a primary factor in America's economic rise in the past two centuries. The strength of patent systems in many other nations has played a role in their prosperity. However, there are many downfalls for inventors mining for gold in the hills of patent law.

The patent system has long provided many opportunities to wear out inventors. Such phenomena are not recent results of an overburdened PTO or of declining respect for patent rights globally. Since the early 19th century and beyond, some inventors have worn themselves out and depleted their resources in their ongoing quest for protection. John Steinbeck captures the phenomenon in a passage from *East of Eden* (1952):

> Meanwhile Samuel got no richer. He developed a very bad patent habit, a disease many men suffer from. He invented a part of a threshing machine, better, cheaper, and more efficient than any in existence. The patent attorney ate up his little profit for the year. Samuel sent his models to a manufacturer, who promptly rejected the plans and used the method. The next few years were kept lean by the suing, and the drain stopped only when he lost the suit . . . But he had caught the patent fever, and year after year the money made by threshing and by smithing was drained off in patents. The Hamilton children went barefoot, and their overalls were patched and food was sometimes scarce, to pay for the crisp blueprints with cogs and planes and elevations.

The way of the individual patent holder has long been a hard one, often with little chance of winning suits from larger infringers equipped with deep pockets and excellent lawyers. The playing field was somewhat leveled in 1984 with the creation of the Court of Appeals for the Federal Circuit, resulting in a court that understood patents and gave their legitimate holders a reasonable chance of enforcing them. This time period corresponds with rapid escalation in the stock market, attributed to the increasing value of companies due to their intangibles—especially intellectual property.

The greatest fatigue of the inventor is experienced in countries where corruption or poorly developed legal systems result in little IP protection. So argues Hernando de Soto, a Peruvian economist and winner of many awards such as the 2006 Innovation Award from *The Economist* magazine for the promotion of property rights and economic development.[11] De Soto has shown that lack of property rights has been a key factor in keeping poor nations poor. It is respect of property rights that creates the means for men to be equal in opportunity. The lone inventor can stand, patent in hand, before the giant corporation and declare, "This is my property, and you have no right to take it as your own for free." It's not easy, but IP gives the inventor a chance.

Remove the protection of IP rights, and innovators quickly experience the fatigue induced by theft.

There seem to be currents of decreasing respect for IP in some nations. These are currents that must be carefully navigated and, we hope, reversed, to provide the protection and motivation inventors need to take on the risk of innovation. Innovation needs liberal encouragement for the welfare of each nation.

Business Method Fatigue

Traditionally, patents have been directed to tangible objects and the methods of making them. It was some time before it became clear that various aspects of software could also be patented. In fact, it wasn't until about 1998 that U.S. court cases clarified that "business methods" could be patented, reversing a prior USPTO policy. 1998 was the year the Court of Appeals for the Federal Circuit decided *State Street Bank & Trust Co. v. Signature Financial Group*,[12] confirming that it was possible to get a patent on a computer-aided method of managing financial data. The monumental changes introduced by that decision may be partially reversed by a new case, *In re Bilski*,[13] decided by the Federal Circuit on Oct. 31, 2008, which rejects part of the *State Street* decision and limits the scope of "business method" and software patents.

The poorly defined category of "business method patents" has been the subject of much controversy and public backlash, for some patentees have obtained patents on practices that were viewed by the public as obvious, trivial, or simply computerized forms of well-known practices. The term "business method patents" often refers to patents that involve manipulation of data in some way, often with computer assistance, and is commonly associated with U.S. Class 705,[14] though other classes have also been involved in the debate.

For Europe, the European Patent Convention declares that "Schemes, rules, and methods for . . . doing business" are not patentable,[15] but if a new method solves a "technical" rather than a purely administrative problem, it may indeed be patentable. Business method patents are expected to be difficult to obtain in most other nations as well. Japan, on the other hand, accepts business method patents, and they may be possible in Australia. They generally cannot be obtained in Canada, unless claimed in a way that focuses on an apparatus rather than the business method.

Where business methods are patentable, a problem is that the most relevant prior art is rarely contained in patents—the traditional resource searched by examiners as they consider novelty and obviousness or "inventive step." Extensive patent archives in business methods simply do not yet exist because practitioners in the past understood that such topics were not patentable subject matter and did not pursue patent applications. While examiners have long turned to other archives to supplement their searching, patents generally are the first and sometimes only resource to be explored. Many business method concepts are not written up in detail, and when they are, the sources where relevant articles may exist are extremely diverse and often use inconsistent terms that are likely to be unfamiliar to patent examiners. The result is that the explosion of business method patent applications in the dot-com era, fueled by excitement in the wake of the U.S. court cases that clarified the opportunity for business methods, resulted in some patents that arguably never should have been issued.

"Business method patents" soon became the subject of public backlash as the press featured a series of stories lampooning the PTO for allowing "ridiculous" business method patents. A particularly influential article was "Patently Absurd" by James Gleick in *New York Times Magazine*.[16] Gleick listed several patents that soon became widely cited as examples of the foolishness of "business method patents." One example was the widely lampooned "Method of Exercising a Cat."[17] However, Robert Yoches and Erika Arner have pointed out the irony of Gleick's influential essay, for none of the patents discussed are in U.S. category 705, nor are any of them what most practitioners would consider "business method patents." Even so, "business method patents" would become the whipping boy for alleged slackness by the PTO.[18] Many other writers have followed suit, including editorial writers in major media sources such as the *Los Angeles Times.*[19]

In response to the backlash, the PTO imposed strict new rules. Since 2000, applications in Class 705 require two layers of review, with no justification for this requirement other than "a marked increase in public attention" to Class 705 applications.[20] Such "quality initiatives" have made it extremely difficult to obtain patent protection in this category. The allowance rate of applications in Class 705 dropped from 45 percent in 2000 to 11 percent in 2005, with nearly 44 months of pendency required before an application in this class will receive a first office action from the PTO—roughly twice as long as required in most other classes. The allowance rates have since risen to about 20 percent, still about half the typical allowance rate. For those seeking protection in this area, the added barriers may be a source of innovation fatigue. As Yoches and Arner put it, "The USPTO has thus effectively overruled the Federal Circuit's establishment of e-commerce patents by rendering them nearly impossible and impractical to obtain. Moreover, in so doing, it delegated to itself the authority Congress has to determine the reach of the patent laws."[21] With the recent *In re Bilski* decision, business method and software patents may be more difficult to obtain. The decision adds a new test for patentability requiring that the invention (1) is tied to a particular machine or apparatus, or (2) transforms a particular article into a different state or thing. The impact of this decision remains to be seen, with some forecasting a drastic reduction in business method patents and others seeing the impact to be primarily in the drafting of claims since most business method and software patents tend to involve machines or apparatus in some way.

For those unwilling to face the challenges of "business method patents" in the United States, there are other strategies to consider. First, protection for a business model can often be obtained by pursuit of claims that don't fall directly into Class 705. Careful review of the various novel aspects of a business model may sometimes be used to identify aspects that can be claimed outside of Class 705, emphasizing technology and tangible items when possible. In some cases, two or more related applications may be drafted that take different approaches in structure, language, and focus in hopes of at least one evading Class 705.

One important opportunity for software-related and business method applications is found in the new Peer to Patent pilot program, available at PeerToPatent.org. The brainchild of Professor Beth Noveck, Professor of Law at New York Law School and Director of the Institute for Information Law and Policy, this program seeks to tap the "wisdom of crowds" in finding the best prior art for pending applications. U.S. applications in Technology Center 2100 (Computer Architecture, Software and Information Security) and Technology Center 3600 Class 705 (Data Processing: Financial, Business Practice, Management, or Cost/Price Determination) can be submitted for consideration in this program. Once in the program, a pending application will be exposed for review by the world, typically before it publishes. Anyone can submit prior art and comments for pending applications in the program. Based on input from the community, the best prior art for each case will be submitted to the USPTO with the comments, a process that can greatly simplify the difficult task of finding material art in business method cases.

This process would normally be anathema to most applicants and patent attorneys, who don't want the world searching for art and making potentially harmful discoveries related to their patent applications. However, an important benefit is offered by the PTO: a first office action is promised within one year—far less than the current 44 month average. If a patent does issue, it will likely be much more valuable, having already been subjected to scrutiny by those who may have various reasons to invalidate it. Many inventors who believe their inventions are valid and already well searched may be willing to have added scrutiny during prosecution to ensure that whatever issues—if anything—is more likely to be valid and strong. Intrigued by this opportunity, one of our own "business method" applications successfully went through the Peer To Patent program and has received a first office action, exactly as promised, within one year.[22] We found it to be an exciting value-added activity whose benefits outweighed the risks, at least in this case.

The challenges with business method patents in the United States represent just one more aspect of what some see as increasing hostility toward IP in the Federal Government. We suggest that true quality can be obtained in the U.S. as well as other nations

Jeff's Experience with Peer to Patent

In July 2007, I met Beth Noveck and heard her speak at a conference on business method patents in New York. I had just filed a patent of my own for a security system that, among other things, includes tools to let users customize security rules for various password-protected accounts and assets. Special uses of passwords and hidden ways of conveying information about credentials are included. When I learned that business method and software patents could be eligible for the Peer To Patent program, I was excited. The prospect of shaving years of prosecution time and having a better prior art search to perhaps strengthen patent validity was exciting. I applied for the program and soon had my application available at PeerToPatent. org for the world to criticize. I later looked at the art that multiple users had cited, and filed a new Information Disclosure Statement to submit those references to the PTO, an action that may have been redundant but probably required by the legal "duty of candor" regarding disclosure of material prior art known to the applicant.

When the office action came, I was elated. It had only taken a year in the system, and I was pleased with the results. In my interactions with the PTO, I found them also supportive of the system. I am excited by the prospects of this system and hope that it will be expanded. It has the promise to improve the scope of prior art searching for higher quality patents, while also rewarding inventors with accelerated examination.

without excessive taxation of patentees, punishment of applicants in targeted classes, or excessive delays and uncertainty. However, without innovation-friendly reforms and public pressure for protection of property rights, further erosion will likely continue, exacerbating innovation fatigue and jeopardizing the economic strength of the affected nations.

Global Fatigue: The Demise and Rise of International Intellectual Property Rights

The protection of intellectual property rights in the U.S. has arguably been a key factor in the explosive rise of the American economy in the few short decades since its founding. The U.S. Constitution itself is the basis for this protection. Article 1, Section 8 stipulates that "Congress shall have Power . . . To promote the Progress of

Science and useful Arts, by securing for limited Times to Authors and Inventors the exclusive Right to their respective Writings and Discoveries." It is the inventors—not those who first file a patent application—who should have the exclusive right to their inventions for limited times, reflecting the important concept of property rights. When property rights are protected, people are motivated to invest time and effort in developing that property, whether it is land, a business, or an invention. When such rights are not secured, when others can simply take what you build or invent, then the motivation to develop and invent is removed. When the only way to protect an invention is to keep it secret, then progress is stymied and we return to the Dark Ages, when inventions were not made public but hidden within the protections of archaic guilds, requiring years of apprentice work before one could be trusted with the secrets of technology. Such a system keeps nearly everyone in the dark and hinders scientific progress.

The beauty of the U.S. patent system is that inventors are offered exclusive rights for a limited time, if they will share their secrets with the whole world in the form of an enabling disclosure in the specification of a patent. Once their limited period of exclusivity expires (currently 20 years from the date of filing), the monopoly is over. Inventors are motivated to invent and to share their knowledge, and progress can be incredibly rapid. However, that motivation disappears when property rights are denied.

Sadly, intellectual property rights are not recognized or adequately protected in many parts of the world. Significant innovation fatigue can be experienced where corruption or poorly developed legal systems result in little or no protection for intellectual property. Around the globe there are increasing challenges to protecting inventions, as Bruce Lehman has observed.[23] These challenges include pressure for weaker IP rights in developing nations, where those with patents are often viewed as having unfair power. Further, trade diplomats rather than patent experts are the representatives for many developing nations in international efforts to harmonize patent laws. Understandably, their motivation is to obtain trade concessions in these talks, not to advance intellectual property systems.

In discussing several dimensions of the "assault on the international IP system," Lehman observes that "while the financial press is full of stories emphasizing the importance of global markets and developing economies to corporate growth, few corporate leaders today seem to be responding to these assaults on the system that protects their shareholders' intellectual property rights in these very same markets." He calls for senior management of global corporations to "become more engaged, proactively working with their own governments and sending the message that strong IP protection and enforcement is worth fighting for."[24] We agree with his call for action. Weakening intellectual property rights around the world bodes poorly for innovation and prosperity, while raising the specter of increased "innovation fatigue" for prospective inventors, who only need a little recognition and protection for their creations in order to benefit us all.

On the other hand, some nations are moving toward strengthened intellectual property rights and may therefore be preparing for rapid growth in innovation. China, once criticized for inadequate concern for intellectual property, has made massive strives in the past decade. At a recent intellectual property conference, Jeff spoke with Dr. Lulin Gao, founder of China's intellectual property system and currently Chairman of East IP in Beijing. Dr. Gao was Commissioner of the Chinese Patent Office and the founding Commissioner of State Intellectual Property Office of China. He was a senior advisor to the World Intellectual Property Organization (WIPO) in Geneva for two years and is currently the President of All-China Patent Agents Association (ACPAA). Dr. Gao helped implement the patent system based on the "Patent Law of the People's Republic of China" that went into effect in 1985. Significant advances came in later years as the system was revised to further strengthen it and bring it in harmony with practices in other nations with many generations of experience in patent law.

Dr. Gao shared an impressive vision for strengthening China in the community of nations and creating a climate where both domestic and foreign business could prosper with improving protection of intellectual property rights. There are still weaknesses to overcome and many barriers to the level of protection that Western nations would prefer, but profound progress has been made in only a few years.

The impact of the rising intellectual property system in China is borne out by a variety of statistics:[25]

In 2007 there were 245,161 20-year patent applications filed in China, of which more than 62.4 percent were domestic applications. The year-on-year increase in the filing of domestic 20-year patent applications was 25.1 percent, whereas that of foreign filings was only 4.5 percent.

This shows that Chinese companies are increasingly recognizing the value of pursuing Chinese patents.

As of 2008, China is the world's 3rd largest patent jurisdiction, receiving more patent applications than the European Patent Office, second only to the U.S. and Japan. Leading Chinese corporations filing patents include Huawei Technologies, leading the way with 5,593 20-year patent applications, followed by ZTE Corporation, Hon Hai Precision Industry Co., Hong Fu Jin Precision Industry (Shenzhen) Co. Ltd. and Zhejiang University.[26] Discussions with businessmen and researchers involved with China confirm a growing increase in patent protection among the Chinese, both in China and elsewhere. China still faces the stigma from its many counterfeiters and pirates, but companies are increasingly recognizing the trend of strengthening IP law in China. China is also experiencing an explosion in IP litigation, on its way to surpassing the United States in terms of the number of cases being handled. Patent-related lawsuits involving international companies have increased dramatically, with 268 cases in 2005 involving at least one non-Chinese party. The No. 1 Intermediate People's Court of Beijing reports that foreign parties won 60 percent of these cases, suggesting that at least some of the barriers for foreign parties protecting their rights have come down.[27]

Increasing incentives, including the protection offered by the rise of China's intellectual property system, are removing fatigue factors for many inventors within large and small corporations as well as universities.

With India and other nations in Asia also working to strengthen intellectual property systems,[28] we expect to see many more inventions with origins in Asia.

Learnings

- Changes in intellectual property law and practice can affect the value of intellectual property rights. Corporations and innovators seeking IP protection should make sure that these changes are taken into consideration and that proactive efforts are made in response.

- Innovators should consider a variety of approaches in protecting their intellectual assets, including broad and proactive strategies in crafting patent applications. (See Chapter 18 for related guidance.)

Notes

1. Steven Ludwig, "Never Give In," *IP Today,* 14, no. 10 (2007): 10–11, www.iptoday .com/articles/2007-10-ludwig.asp (accessed Jan. 15, 2008).
2. Pat Choate, *Hot Property* (New York: Alfred A. Knopf, 2005), 85.
3. Based on a chart in United States Patent and Trademark Office, "Fiscal Year 2006: A Record-Breaking Year for the USPTO," Dec. 22, 2006, www.uspto.gov/ web/offices/com/speeches/06-73.htm (accessed Dec. 28, 2008).
4. Ibid.
5. Ibid., 87.
6. Ibid., 86.
7. The decision is available at www.supremecourtus.gov/opinions/06pdf/04-1350. pdf(accessed Nov. 3, 2008).
8. Robins, Kaplan, Miller and Ciresi, LLP, "Side-Swiped," Advanced Patent Trial Strategies (APaTS®) series, Nov. 19, 2007, http://groups.rkmc.com/apats/ archive/2007/11/19/side-swiped.aspx (accessed Jan. 6, 2008).
9. Robert P. Merges, "From Medieval Guilds to Open Source Software: Informal Norms, Appropriability Institutions, and Innovation," Conference on the Legal History of Intellectual Property, Nov. 13, 2004, Madison, Wisconsin, http://papers.ssrn.com/sol3/Delivery.cfm/SSRN_ID661543_code403341 .pdf?abstractid=661543&mirid=2 (or http://tinyurl.com/merges2 — see also http://papers.ssrn.com/sol3/papers.cfm?abstract_id=661543) (accessed July 9, 2008).
10. Michael A. Gollin, *Driving Innovation: Intellectual Property Strategies for a Dynamic World* (Cambridge, UK: Cambridge University Press, 2008), 31.
11. "And the Winners Are . . . ," *The Economist* 381, no 8506 (December 2, 2006): 16.
12. 149 F.3d 1368 (Fed. Cir. 1998).
13. *In re Bilski,* ___ F.3d ___ (Fed. Cir. 2008), www.cafc.uscourts.gov/opinions/ 07-1130.pdf
14. Gregory A. Stobbs, *Business Method Patents* (New York: Aspen Law & Business, 2002.
15. Article 52(2)(c) and (3) of the European Patent Convention.
16. James Gleick, "Patently Absurd," *New York Times Magazine,* March 12, 2000, 44–49.
17. K.T. Amiss, and M.H. Abbott, "Method of Exercising a Cat," US Pat. No. 5,443,036, issued Aug. 22, 1995.
18. E. Robert Yoches, and Erika Harmon Arner, "Recent Developments of E-Commerce Patents: The Ever Precarious Nature of E-Commerce Patent Protection in the U.S.," *Global Intellectual Property Asset Management Report,* August 2007, www.finnegan.com/publications/news-popup.cfm?id= 2166&type= article (accessed March 28, 2008).

19. Los Angeles Times Editorial Staff, "Patently Obvious: the Internet Has Fueled an Unhealthy Demand for Dubious Patents Covering Common Business Practices," *Los Angeles Times*, October 30, 2006, A–20.
20. United States Patent and Trademark Office, "USPTO White Paper on Automated Financial or Management Data Processing Methods (Business Methods)," 2000, http://uspto.gov/web/menu/busmethp/, as viewed March 27, 2008.
21. Yoches and Arner, "Recent Developments."
22. Jeffrey D. Lindsay, "Security Systems for Protecting an Asset," U.S. Patent Publication 20070250920, published Oct. 25, 2007. The application is based on work with security systems done outside of work with employers and was filed independently with written approval from his employer at the time. It is part of a business model currently being developed for commercialization.
23. Bruce Lehman, "Global IP in Crisis: The Threat to Shareholder Value," in *Making Innovation Pay*, ed. Bruce Berman (New York: John Wiley & Sons, 2006), 125–139.
24. Ibid,. 131–132.
25. Evaluserve, "Patenting Landscape in China: History, Growth and Utility Model," May 22, 2008, available online with registration at www.evalueserve.com/Media-And-Reports/WhitePapers.aspx (accessed Sept. 10, 2008).
26. Ibid.
27. Ibid.
28. Evaluserve, "Patenting Landscape in India," May 23, 2008, available online with registration at www.evalueserve.com/Media-And-Reports/WhitePapers.aspx (accessed Sept. 10, 2008).

When Questionable Patents Are Allowed to Sprout

ANOTHER FORM OF PATENT FATIGUE

While obstacles to obtaining patents can be a serious source of innovation fatigue, there is another side to this story—one that may justify further efforts to strengthen the quality of issued patents. For every innovator who was has been frustrated by the patent process, there may be other innovators discouraged by overly broad or seemingly invalid patents used to hinder their own enterprise.

Patents can cause great pain to those against whom they are used. Imagine the pain of Kodak executives who, after ignoring Polaroid's many patents, invested hundreds of millions of dollars and hired many employees to produce a product falling squarely under Polaroid's patents. When they lost the battle in court, it was a few weeks before Christmas. They had to lay off hundreds and pay a giant fine, shutting down an entire business unit. That is painful, but the pain may have been self-inflicted by ignoring the property rights of others.

It's a different story when pain is brought on by patents that never should have been issued. Let's explore one such story from the field of agriculture.

"We Didn't Know Where to Turn": A Patent Battle over Sprouts

Frank Crikelair of Neenah, Wisconsin, knows the pain that a questionable patent can inflict. Frank is an entrepreneur who long ago recognized the healthy benefits of sprouts. He spent years crafting a business model based on providing a variety of sprouts to grocery stores and restaurants, allowing them to offer safe, fresh, and highly nutritious products to their customers at a reasonable price. Unfortunately, his business would eventually come close to destruction because of some questionable patents from a large and respected university.

"How can someone get a patent on a plant that has been cultivated and eaten for thousands of years? A patent that offers no improvement, no change in the plant, just an alleged discovery that the sprout is good for you?" These questions had been spinning in Frank's head since the day he and his wife received the notice that Johns Hopkins University was suing them for selling broccoli sprouts based on the University's patents related to that ancient plant.[1]

"We didn't know where to turn. Where do you find a patent attorney in a small town like Neenah?" Frank had to turn somewhere for help and eventually found an experienced patent litigator, Joe Kromholz, in Milwaukee. They met and discussed the details, the prospects, and the costs.

Frank took a deep breath, pushed aside the papers in front of him, and looked the Milwaukee litigator in the eye. "Yes, I know this will cost a lot. More than I have. But I give you my word that I will pay every penny that it takes to fight this." With those words, Frank began a five-year battle that would end in victory, vindication, and more pain and stress than Frank ever imagined. He had just begun putting his daughter through college—not the best time to take on a legal battle, but it had to be done.

It was the darkest hour for Sunrise Farms, Frank Crikelair's business of 20 years. Years earlier in California, Frank had been ahead of his time in recognizing the value of raw, wholesome foods. When he came to Wisconsin, he joined his brother Dan, already an entrepreneur in the health food industry, in launching Sunrise Farms, a business aimed at providing fresh, healthy, safe sprouts. They began with a $400 investment and put every dime back into the business for the next two and a half years.

When they started in 1978, sprouts were unknown and growth was slow. Marketing began with numerous local deliveries of small quantities of sprouts. The brothers soon realized they needed to go to wholesale distributors to reach the potential consumer base. After securing some major accounts, the company experienced 30 percent to 40 percent annual growth rates in those early years.

Innovating for Quality

Frank's commitment to quality and innovation led to advanced systems and methods that put a moat of competitive advantage around his business. "It looks easy," Frank explains, "but it's very hard." The quality control demands are enormous and require extensive attention to detail. Sprout producers now must be licensed food processors operating according to FDA guidelines.

"There is no handbook for sprout farmers that tells you how to set up and run your operation. We developed most of our processes and systems, and our equipment was built and installed piece by piece over the years. Many details are our own developments." In spite of the proprietary nature of Frank's operation, he has always shared tips with other sprout farmers in his network, especially tips that advance safety. "My business is only as secure as the worst sprout processor out there, because if a grower in Arizona or Illinois has an outbreak of bacteria, it scares the public across the country and directly hurts my business. So we all need to work together to ensure the highest standards for safety are met." Frank is on the board of the International Sprout Growers Association, which encourages the exchange of information among sprout growers and commercial suppliers internationally.

In terms of safety, sprouts may be unique among processed foods. At Sunrise Farms, 100 percent of the products are tested for safety. The effluent from every batch of sprouts is tested with advanced techniques, including PCR, for the presence of *E. coli* or salmonella bacteria. Before any sprouting occurs, the seeds for each batch are completely sanitized using an FDA-recommended process. For green-leaf sprouts like broccoli sprouts, special rotating chambers are used to sanitize the seeds. The seeds are then grown untouched for 4 or 5 days, provided with irrigation water and air carefully controlled by computerized equipment. It is the effluent from these chambers that is tested—every chamber, every batch.

While Sunrise Farms and other sprout growers are routinely inspected by the FDA, to further strengthen their approach, Frank voluntarily pays a third party to conduct additional safety audits to ensure that they are operating at the highest possible standards.

This approach to quality and innovation is nothing new for Sunrise Farms. In 1983, when Frank realized the need for an expanded dedicated facility for sprout farming, he designed it by anticipating strict standards that weren't even on the radar screen at the time. He had seen the evolution of strict standards for the dairy and meat processing industries, and looked to them for guidance in preparing for the future. At a time when regulations were relatively lax, his visionary anticipation of strict government standards for his product gave him a tremendous head start in quality and compliance.

Among his many innovations over the years, Frank developed a unique processing system for his sprouts. These innovative processes greatly extend the shelf life and produce a better tasting sprout. Many innovations seem minor on their own, but each add up to a system of quality and safety.

The Lawsuit

Just as things were looking most promising, the lawsuit was served. Johns Hopkins and Brassica, the company that had licensed the patent, wanted triple damages for every case of broccoli sprouts Frank had sold since the patent was issued. The royalty they demanded for their licensed growers was roughly 100 percent of the wholesale price of the product: about $4 of royalty per case of sprouts. Multiply that by three for all the infringing sprouts Frank had sold, and Frank was facing disaster. To make matters worse, he wasn't being offered a license to continue selling his sprouts. He would simply have to stop. In this small market, grocers and suppliers didn't want to have to deal with multiple growers to get different varieties of sprouts. Frank figured he would have been shut out of the sprout business completely. There was also a very real possibility that the entire sprout market would have been taken over and controlled.

Frank couldn't understand why the plaintiffs dared to tell him to stop his business. Was he using an exotic genetically modified species that had been developed by and stolen from Johns Hopkins? Was he using unique equipment that had been stolen from the university or its partner? No. He was using standard equipment and standard broccoli seeds to produce the same kind of sprouts that had been raised and eaten by others long before the research that led to the Johns Hopkins patent. Frank might be doing it more efficiently and more safely, but the sprouts he was selling—the ones that allegedly infringed the patent of a famous university—were normal sprouts. How could they be the subject of a patent?

An arsenal of three patents had been launched against a number of sprout farmers. The patents stemmed from the notable work of two professors who helped the public realize that broccoli sprouts and some other sprouts had very high concentrations of compounds that could have cancer-preventing effects. Publicity surrounding their scientific work led to increased demand for sprouts and improved business opportunities for sprout farmers like Frank Crikelair. Now, however, the sprout farmers had to face the impact of the patents.

The first of the three is U.S. Pat. No. 5,725,895, "Method of Preparing a Food from Cruciferous Seeds," issued on March 10, 1998 to two professors in the Johns Hopkins University School of Medicine. The patent offers this as claim 1:

> A method of preparing a food product rich in glucosinolates, comprising germinating cruciferous seeds, with the exception of cabbage, cress, mustard and radish seeds, and harvesting sprouts prior to the 2-leaf stage, to form a food product comprising a plurality of sprouts.

In other words, harvesting sprouts of cruciferous plants such as broccoli would "read on" (be covered by) claim 1 (one of seven claims in this patent that were at issue in the lawsuit). Nothing unusual had been done to the sprouts or their DNA. The legal battle also involved eight claims from U.S. Pat. No. 5,968,567, "Method of Preparing a Food Product from Cruciferous Sprouts," issued Oct. 19, 1999, which describes naturally occurring chemical components in certain sprouts and claims "a method of preparing a human food product" comprising cruciferous sprouts high in such chemicals. The method involves identifying certain seeds, germinating them, and harvesting them to form a food product. The third patent in this arsenal was U.S. Pat. No. 5,968,505, "Cancer Chemoprotective Food Products," also issued Oct. 19, 1999 (claims 1 and 9 were at issue). Claim 1 describes a method of increasing the amount of certain enzymes in a mammal by "identifying" certain seeds which produce cruciferous sprouts, then germinating, harvesting, and administering them in a food product to the mammal.

The lawsuit against Frank and four other companies was filed by Johns Hopkins University and Brassica Protection Products LLC, a company formed in 1997 after the patents were filed. Its stated purpose is to develop and market "cancer-protective foods, functional foods, nutriceuticals, and pharmaceuticals."[2]

Frank understood that Brassica had taken its patents to several other sprout farmers and told them that if they wanted to continue selling broccoli sprouts, they would need to sign a marketing agreement with Brassica and pay a substantial royalty. Frank believed that the goal of Brassica was to create a limited set of distributors who would only sell through Brassica. Others, like Frank, would be excluded from making the sprouts.

"I didn't know where to turn." As a small businessman in the little town of Neenah, Wisconsin, Frank wondered how he could possibly fight a giant like Johns Hopkins and their team of Washington lawyers. However, the more he studied the patent, the more he felt an obligation to fight. Although he appreciated the work that the professors had done in highlighting some of the benefits of sprouts, something had gone wrong with the system. Did discovering an added benefit of an existing plant mean that the plant could be patented? To grant the University a patent on natural sprouts that people had been growing and eating long before the research was conducted seemed like a terrible mistake. If he failed to overcome the patent battle with one of the nation's most respected universities, he would lose everything he had. His business would be shut down and a precedent would be set that could threaten agricultural businesses across the country. Frank chose to fight.

It seemed like it should be easy to show that the sprouts claimed in the patents had been used and eaten as food for years before the Johns Hopkins work. However, Frank's education in litigation would teach him that the process can be painfully slow and expensive. Johns Hopkins, for example, received a ruling that the hearings would be held in Maryland, convenient for their lawyers, but it meant that Frank would have to pay not just for him but also for his attorney to travel, greatly adding to his expenses.

As a hint that his defense might not be easy, Frank knew of another defendant in Delaware that had fought back, challenging the validity of the patent—and lost. A request for re-examination of the first patent had been filed on October 11, 1999, in which Johns Hopkins asked the PTO to consider some additional prior art and see if the patent was still valid. The PTO initially rejected many claims, but then after Johns Hopkins' response, the PTO let the claims stand (July 10, 2000). This result might seem to suggest that the patent was on solid ground. On the other hand, it could also mean that the right art had not yet been considered, or that the one-sided nature of the debate in the re-examination process did not adequately address the real issues.

If they wanted to prevail, Frank learned from his experienced attorney, Joe Kromholz, that nothing could be left to chance. If something was well known in the prior art and seemed like common sense, it would not be enough to simply say that. Extensive, even excessive documentation was needed to absolutely nail down the case. To cut down on the normal expense of patent litigation, Frank and another defendant, Robert Rust of International Specialty Supply, joined forces in conducting extensive literature reviews, digging through hundreds of books, articles, reports, and Web sites, in order to document the use of cruciferous sprouts and other sprouts prior to the Johns Hopkins patent filings and prior to the research of the named inventors. Their findings were reviewed and distilled by their lawyer, and used in his arguments and briefs. By the time the case was over, Frank had a stack of documents over three feet high for this case.

Frank's search for prior art included calls to researchers at many universities to gain more information. He learned, according to some scientists he had spoken with, that many allegedly new aspects of the Johns Hopkins work were actually old, including the methods they used to extract chemical components of the plants. Some university researchers expressed outrage at the patents. (We recognize, of course, that thorough prior art searches are difficult and expensive, and not required by law. Even when a serious search has been done, it is far too easy to miss the most relevant art that might invalidate patent claims. If anything, this case is a reminder of the importance of more thorough prior art searches to reduce the chance that an issued patent is invalid.)

Eventually, on Aug. 8, 2001, a decision was received from the U.S. District Court in Maryland[3] granting *summary judgment* that the Johns Hopkins patents were invalid because they were anticipated by the prior art—the very thing that was claimed was already present in the prior art (such as the high concentrations of healthy compounds in sprouts). Summary judgment means that the facts were clear enough that no jury trial was needed—a most favorable ruling. Judge William M. Nickerson quickly got to the heart of the matter:

> As defendants succinctly present the question before the Court: "Can a plant (broccoli sprouts), long well known in nature and cultivated and eaten by humans for decades, be patented merely on the basis of recent realization that the plant has always had some heretofore unknown but naturally occurring beneficial feature?" For the reasons that follow, the Court finds the answer to that question must be "no."

"Wonderful!" Frank thought. Their hard work had paid off. However, because of appeals, the process would continue, with more hearings, motions, meetings, briefs, etc., but finally, on August 21, 2002, the U.S. Court of Appeals for the Federal Circuit handed down its ruling.[4] The previous summary judgment of invalidity for the claims in question from the three patents was affirmed, making Frank and his co-defendants the victors. The decision would be appealed again, this time to the Supreme Court, but the Court chose not to take this case. At last in 2003, it was completely over. Frank still had his business.

The Federal Circuit (CAFC) ruling clarified the issues nicely:

> Brassica has done nothing more than recognize properties inherent in certain prior art sprouts. . . . While Brassica may have recognized something quite interesting about those sprouts, it simply has not invented anything new.
>
> Brassica nevertheless argues that its claims are not anticipated because the prior art does not disclose selecting the particular seeds that will germinate as sprouts rich in glucosinolates and high in Phase 2 enzyme-inducing potential (as opposed to selecting other kinds of seeds to sprout) in order to form a food product. We disagree. The prior art teaches sprouting and harvesting the very same seeds that the patents recognize as producing sprouts rich in glucosinolates and having high Phase 2 enzyme-inducing potential. . . .
>
> In summary, the prior art inherently contains the claim limitations that Brassica relies upon to distinguish its claims from the prior art. While Brassica may have recognized something

about sprouts that was not known before, Brassica's claims do not describe a new method.

CONCLUSION

For the foregoing reasons, we affirm the district court's summary judgment that the claims at issue are anticipated by the prior art. The prior art indisputably includes growing, harvesting, and eating particular sprouts which Brassica has recognized as being rich in glucosinolates and high in Phase 2 enzyme-inducing potential. But the glucosinolate content and Phase 2 enzyme-inducing potential of these sprouts are inherent properties of the sprouts put there by nature, not by Brassica. Brassica simply has not claimed anything that is new and its claims are therefore invalid.

The decision then cited multiple examples from the prior art references Frank and Robert Rust had found.

Frank came to the brink of ruin, but prevailed. Today Sunrise Farms is thriving and rich with innovation. Frank's case was a relatively easy one. The issues were so clear-cut that no jury trial was needed: a judge could simply make a summary judgment, but it took five years, a good part of Frank's retirement funds, and enormous physical and emotional stress. Being threatened with a questionable patent is more than just a lengthy distraction. It's a major fatigue factor that could have ruined Frank's 20-year investment. Everything he had learned about sprouts, all the innovations he had brought to his business, would have been wiped out if he had not prevailed in court.

Aftermath

In spite of the invalidity ruling, Frank understands that many sprout growers are still under contract to Brassica. Frank's connections in the sprout community have told him that the Brassica contracts were structured as marketing partnerships as opposed to an explicit license of Brassica's patents. Although the patents were obviously a motivation to sign the marketing contract, the contract allegedly did not depend on the patents or their validity.

Of course, there are always two sides to legal battles. One can imagine the frustration of the researchers who, through the publicity from their work, created a surge in demand for a product that previously was largely unappreciated. Their work had resulted in patents. Then, when new prior art was identified, the PTO considered it but still granted the patents. Shouldn't they realize value from their work that had transformed the sprout market? We answer yes, absolutely, but not through patent claims lacking novelty. Broccoli sprouts were known, though not popular before their work. Fortunately for the inventors, Brassica appears to be flourishing in spite of the disappointment of having several claims in their patents found invalid. At least as of April 19, 2008, Brassica's Web site contains this declaration:

> Brassica Protection Products is the exclusive licensee of Johns Hopkins's patents to grow and sell broccoli sprouts rich in sulforaphane glucosinolate (SGS). Brassica's broccoli sprouts are available in the fresh produce departments in supermarkets throughout the United States under the brand name BroccoSprouts®.[5]

Learnings

Several lessons can be learned from Frank's experience, as shown in Exhibit 13.1. To conquer external fatigue factors, innovators should prepare with vision, always anticipating stricter standards and demand for higher quality in the future. When adversity strikes, innovators must have the courage to stand for what is right and press forward, knowing that success is possible, even for underdogs.

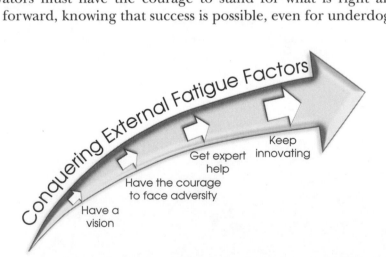

Conquering External Fatigue Factors

Have a vision

Have the courage to face adversity

Get expert help

Keep innovating

Exhibit 13.1   Lessons from Sunrise Farms: Conquering external fatigue

Crucially, innovators must find the right help. When it comes to patents, solid expertise is needed, even when a case might seem easy. Further, successful innovators should never stop innovating.

Unfortunately, even when a business has a solid patent clearance position, unexpected patents may arise that threaten it. It's one of the inherent risks of doing business.

A final lesson involves the value of invalid patents. Even a patent that seems clearly invalid can cause much pain for a competitor. In this case, it cost Frank Crikelair part of his retirement and almost cost him his business. To reduce the risk of invalid patents issuing, we recommend to many of our clients and partners that they consider frequent low-cost defensive publications at services such as IP.com in order to make information readily available to patent examiners and the public.

Notes

1. Broccoli was a favorite among the ancient Romans, according to Pliny the Elder. They received broccoli from the Etruscans, who moved into the Tuscany area from Asia Minor (modern Turkey) around the 8th century BCE. See "Broccoli, the Crown Jewel of Nutrition," www.vegparadise.com/highestperch44.html, as viewed April 20, 2008.
2. Brassica Protection Products LLC, "Company Background and History," www.brassica.com/coinfo/background.htm (accessed April 19, 2008).
3. William M. Nickerson, District Judge, *In Re Cruciferous Sprout Patent Litigation*, U.S. District Court for the District of Maryland, MDL Docket No. 1388, Aug. 8, 2001.
4. Brassica Protection Products LLC and Johns Hopkins University vs. Sunrise Farms, Becky Crickelair, and Frank Crickelair, et al., *In Re Cruciferous Sprout Litigation*, U.S. Court of Appeals for the Federal Circuit, 02-1031, Aug. 21, 2002, www.ll.georgetown.edu/federal/judicial/fed/opinions/02opinions/02-1031.html (accessed April 19, 2008).
5. Brassica, "Company Background."

Fatigue Factor #8

REGULATORY PAIN: CHALLENGES IN POLICY, REGULATION, AND LAW

Regulatory burdens are complex and ever-changing. Restrictions on what can and can't be done can sometimes hinder extremely valuable innovations, while modest adjustments may open doors of opportunity that benefit millions. As an example, consider Vanguard Mutual Funds.

Now widely celebrated as one of the great innovations in financial services, Vanguard Mutual Funds allow users to gain access to numerous market areas through indexed funds at remarkably low cost. As sensible and beneficial as that innovation seems today, it was nearly killed by regulatory burdens when it began. Founder and innovator John C. Bogle explains that his enterprise was in a precarious position at first, operating only under a temporary SEC order permitting their novel mutual fund structure. Three years after that temporary approval, disaster struck:

> [T]he SEC reversed its ruling, leaving us in a no-man's-land that I never contemplated. Aghast, for I knew we were doing what was right for our shareholders, we mounted a vigorous appeal. Finally, in 1981, after a struggle that had lasted four long years, the SEC did an about-face, approving our plan. . . .[1]

How many innovations of similar potential have been killed or bludgeoned by regulatory excesses or the unintended consequences of well-intended law?

Politicians frequently assume that new regulations will stir innovation due to the pressures and incentives found in the law. For example, environmental regulation can be a powerful stimulus for investment in improving processes and developing environmentally friendly technologies, as James Foster, Mikael Hilden, and Niclas Alder argue in their analysis of the pulp and paper industry.[2] What is often not considered is whether a given law will impair innovation elsewhere. In the business world, we hear frequent discussion of the barriers and excessive costs created by regulations. Even there, the impact of these barriers and costs on innovation is often overlooked. We suggest that regulation can have unintended consequences on the future competitiveness of an industry or even a nation, and recommend that "the Voice of the Innovator" be considered in considering new legislation as well as in reviewing the effects of what is already in place. Sometimes the impact of tighter regulation is broader than simply diverting resources that might have been used to innovate in another area in order to meet the needs of the new regulation. Sometimes the impact can be of dangerous delay in areas of great importance to public and national welfare.

Safety Regulations and the Dangers of Risk Aversion

When the drug Vioxx® began showing unanticipated risks, the FDA learned a lesson: be much tougher on the pharmaceutical industry and reduce the risk of harmful drugs being released. In terms of the risk factors FDA officials face, this seems entirely logical. Unfortunately, the risk factors that the FDA responds to are usually weighted in favor of keeping drugs off the market to avoid the risk of visible harm, while overlooking the risk of "invisible harm" when beneficial drugs are held back. It's easy to raise alarms about a handful of people who suffer from the use of a drug, while ignoring the hundreds or thousands who could have been helped had a drug been available.

From 1980 to 2006, the U.S. pharmaceutical industry ramped up R&D from $2 billion to $43 billion. However, the number of drugs being approved annual by the FDA in 2006 was about the same as in 1980.[3] Based on these numbers alone, one could argue that the impact of increasing regulatory burdens has dramatically decreased R&D productivity.

In June 2008, *The Wall Street Journal* carried a front-page story by Avery Johnson and Ron Winslow on the regulatory pains felt by the pharmaceutical industry.[4] Several observers believe that in order to avoid criticism for approving drugs with potentially deleterious side effects, the FDA has raised the safety standards to such high levels that drug development has been greatly depressed. Schering-Plough, for example, ceased two drug-development projects that they felt had big potential, and may scrap another.

> The reason: Mr. Hassan [the CEO] believes an intensifying focus on safety and a diminished tolerance for side effects at the Food and Drug Administration have dramatically lowered the odds that the drugs would make it to market—at least not without a lot of extra time and money.

Hassan explained that they simply don't know what it will take to get approval for new drugs.

Johnson and Avery show that new drug approvals by the FDA are tapering off. Only 19 new medicines were approved in 2007, the lowest in 24 years. The agency also announced 75 new or revised "blackbox" warnings about potential side effects—twice the number from 2004. The increasingly conservative approach of the FDA is said by some to be a response to the criticism it received for its role in the Vioxx® debacle.

The problem is that no drug is completely safe. While even rare problems for those using a drug can be highly visible and broadly publicized, there is essentially no visibility for the many who suffer or die because they are denied access to drugs that could have helped. Drug manufacturers and FDA officials are routinely grilled by Congress when something goes wrong with a drug, but those who delay the approval of helpful drugs rarely face such scrutiny.[5] The U.S. has the most severe drug approval regulations in the world, resulting in valuable drugs being kept out of the market for years while they are available in many other nations.

In some cases, it's not simply a delay. Novartis, for example, has stopped trying to gain FDA approval for its diabetes drug Galvus®, even though it is already available in Europe. Sanofi-Aventis, which markets the new weight-loss drug Acomplia® in Europe, has also given up on gaining U.S. approval after an FDA panel demanded further costly studies to explore possible psychiatric side effects.[6] Other drug companies are withdrawing their U.S. applications or never filing them in the first place because the barriers seem too high. The fatigue of regulatory delay can be especially severe when coupled with weakened intellectual property protection. For example, instead of the former patent lifetime of seventeen years from the date a patent is granted, drug makers now face a 20-year clock that begins ticking upon filing the patent application. It can take many years before approval is finally granted, resulting in ever shorter effective patent lifetimes. Then there are the risks of compulsory licensing of drugs at low cost in some nations—another regulatory fatigue factor—and rampant counterfeiting of successful medications. All told, the long-term viability of biotech may be in serious jeopardy.

The regulatory and IP burdens are exacerbated by the hostility of many politicians who grandstand by blaming pharmaceutical companies for the high price of drugs. They show little concern for the high cost of development, patenting, and litigation. It may only be a matter of time before additional crippling laws are passed that will further tax the innovators in biotech. Innovation fatigue in biotech jeopardizes the healthcare of the world and must be overcome. We implore legislators to recognize that many of their actions intended to reduce prices and help consumers may have unintended consequences such as stifling innovation, creating scarcity, and facilitating the introduction of dangerous counterfeit drugs into the market.

Medication is filled with risk. There is a risk that any drug or medical procedure may not work for some patients and could possibly even be fatal. However, the backlash of politicians and regulators rarely involves a true cost-benefit analysis. Vast unseen harm can occur from well-intended actions.

The pain of antiquated or excessive regulatory burdens extends to many areas besides pharmaceuticals. Consider the regulations faced by innovators in the field of food and nutrition. After extensive research, many experts in the industry are aware of significant health benefits that some foods can bring to those seeking help with various illnesses. Unfortunately, it is exceedingly difficult to legally share that information in product labeling due to federal regulations. As a telling example, simply marking citrus fruit with "helps treat scurvy" is an illegal act in the U.S. A vendor might be able to say that lemons provide nutrients that can reduce your risk of developing scurvy, but to state that it can treat a disease violates federal law. As we learned in interviews with leaders at a major food corporation, the inability for food providers to discuss the benefits of special ingredients in their foods is a burden on food innovation. Many food companies feel stymied by FDA regulations in this area, and it is a discouragement to some potentially valuable innovation.

One of the often ignored consequences of tight safety regulations on drugs is not just the drop in industry productivity, but also the drop in personal productivity for researchers. When an ambitious scientist can spend decades in pursuing novel drugs and have zero of them get anywhere close to the market, the yearning to make a difference is stymied and the motivation to keep innovating can perish. While the corporation as a whole may experience success, innovation fatigue can be daunting for those at the bench, the heart of the innovation engine for pharmaceutical industry. Will scientists of the future be willing to take on the emotional risk of such a career? Or will the industry face chronic fatigue due to lack of talent?

Sarbanes-Oxley: the Dangers of Averting Financial Risk

Among the many well-intentioned legislative efforts that have brought unintended negative consequences, the Sarbanes-Oxley Act is one that places extreme burdens on American business not faced by companies overseas. It was passed in 2002 to prevent the excesses and corruption we saw with Enron's collapse and other accounting scandals. The undesirable result is that many companies are increasingly fleeing to other nations, resulting in lost jobs and opportunities in the U.S. The burden is especially great on small companies that generally have the greatest potential for growth. For example, in 2005, Calavo Growers (NYSE: CVGW), a small cap producer of avocados and other produce with a market cap of about $200 million, reported a loss after many quarters of good profits. The sudden loss was due to the millions they had to spend to comply with Sarbanes-Oxley. The process hurt them in the following quarter as well. Sales were still good, but the investment required for compliance with the bureaucratic demands of the new legislation imposed grievous costs on the company. They are not alone. The average annual cost for Sarbanes-Oxley compliance for firms with market caps under $100 million is a whopping 2.55 percent of revenue, while firms between $100 million and $500 million suffer a hit of only 0.53 percent, and the relative burden is lighter still for larger companies.[7]

U.S. Senator Kay Bailey Hutchinson of Texas has warned that Sarbanes-Oxley can jeopardize America's competitiveness through overregulation. Citing the American Enterprise Institute's estimate of the exorbitant costs, Hutchinson argues that Sarbanes-Oxley is in effect an 8 percent or 9 percent tax on every good and service, and that is driving companies to relist overseas.

> In the past few years, the statistical evidence for this capital flight has become undeniable. In 2001, the year before Sarbanes-Oxley was passed, half of the dollars raised in global IPOs were raised on a U.S. exchange. By 2005, that amount had shrunk to only 5 percent. During the same year, the New York Stock Exchange had only six new foreign listings, but the London Stock Exchange had a whopping 129.[8]

Regulation is clearly needed to prevent financial fraud. But sometimes regulatory efforts have unintended consequences that harm rather than help the economy. We urge Congress to evaluate the impact of regulatory approaches to understand and mitigate unintended consequences. Creating an economic environment that encourages innovation and growth requires that government leaders exercise great caution and wisdom regarding regulatory burdens, taxation, monetary policy, and other factors that can contribute to external fatigue, especially in times of financial distress.

Sometimes It's Not Enough to Be Innocent

Several innovators have been stopped in their tracks by misguided charges raised by regulatory agencies. Even when they have been cleared of all charges in the end, the negative publicity alone can destroy a business or product, not to mention the impact of legal fees and years of delay. Preston Tucker and his amazing automobile, the Tucker '48, may have fallen into that category. After World War II, Tucker took advantage of government auctions of surplus manufacturing facilities to pursue his dream of producing a new car. Praised as "the first really new car in 50 years," Tucker's vehicle featured many advances that gave it high safety, excellent performance, and advanced styling. His air-cooled, flat-six rear engine with fuel injection was an advanced concept. The windshield could pop out for safety. A movable third headlight on the front changed direction during turns to provide better illumination. The frame of the vehicle enclosed and protected the passengers. The car had tremendous market potential, and in spite of engineering challenges in production, may have succeeded, if it were not for the heavy hand of regulation. Its 1947 premiere was greeted with enthusiasm and the future looked bright for Tucker Corporation.

The problem was that Tucker's innovations went beyond engineering and design into financing. The SEC accused him of fraud for his creative method of raising money by pre-selling accessories. While all charges would be dropped eventually, the negative publicity destroyed the company. In an open letter, Tucker claimed that the actions against him were the result of influence from competitors.[9] Only 51 Tuckers were produced, 47 of which are still in existence. Tucker's story is told in a movie, the 1988 Francis Ford Coppola film, *Tucker: The Man and His Dream.*

A possible lesson from Tucker: innovate with technology, but not with other people's money. When there are powerful competitors, caution must be exercised at many levels. For example, Tucker might not have sought the right help in dealing with his challenges.

Related stories are numerous and often far less publicized. One innovator we spoke with had spent years bringing a controversial health-related service to market. While there are voices on both sides of the debate about the efficacy of the treatment, she had worked closely with the appropriate government agency to ensure that her work was acceptable, but one day was raided by a different division of that agency. The agency seized all computers, client records, and more, bringing the business to a complete halt. News of negative allegations from the agency was broadcast widely. After a lengthy investigation, the agency simply closed the case with no charges filed. Without even an apology, the agency called one day to say the case was closed and she had 24 hours to pick up her equipment or it would be thrown away. By then, the business had been destroyed. There was no media coverage when the charges were dropped.

Crimes of Omission: When Regulations Aren't Enforced

Some of the most severe fatigue factors tied to regulation come when regulations aren't enforced, especially those meant to protect property rights. This takes us back to Fatigue Factor #1, theft, but the theft can be of an entire business. In the U.S., for example, some small companies have complained of manipulation of their stock price after they go public. A corrupt practice known as "naked short selling" has been blamed, though for years regulators and major players in finance denied that it was a problem. That changed in 2008, when the CEO of Bear Stearns, the great financial banking institution whose stock imploded, blamed illegal naked short selling for the collapse and drew significant media attention to the practice.

The SEC finally launched an investigation into naked short selling. This practice refers to firms who take advantage of mysterious loopholes in trading regulations and in effect sell "naked" shares that they don't own and haven't actually borrowed (borrowing real shares to sell and eventually buy back is legal short selling). Naked shorting in essence creates phantom shares that drive the price down. Regulations specify that borrowed shares in short selling need to be delivered within three days of the sale to show that the seller really has borrowed shares, but a loophole allows the equivalent of IOUs to be offered in some cases. Dr. Patrick Byrne, CEO and founder of Overstock.com, has documented shares from naked shorting of his company's stock that stayed on the market for 3 years, contributing to the artificially inflated supply of shares that moved prices lower. Regarding the hedge funds and institutions that are big enough to do this, Byrne explains that "if they pick the right company, they can make it disappear and may never have to pay off the IOUs."[10]

If the charges concerning naked short selling are true, then it is a regulatory failure that adds heavily to the burdens borne by some entrepreneurs when they go public (small companies are especially vulnerable). We hope that the investigation of this practice will proceed aggressively and honestly.

Failure to enforce intellectual property laws is an issue we have previously addressed. We urge policy makers in all nations to protect intellectual property rights, while also ensuring that quality patent examinations are conducted to reduce fatigue factors from questionable patents.

Recommendations to Innovators

Dealing with regulatory burdens often requires experienced, professional help. Generally, we suggest that you don't try this on your own. In some cases, it also requires political savvy. For example, when dealing with a judge or public agency, additional steps may be needed to build credibility.

The impact of regulatory burdens often depends on the details of your business model. Re-evaluate some of the assumptions you have made and explore alternatives. Are there government programs that can help you? Is a change of venue going to help? Do you have contingency plans to deal with unfavorable or even favorable changes in policy and law? Do you have a wide variety of claims in your pending patents to increase the chances of surviving new twists in patent case law? Flexibility and keeping options alive is the rule.

The following chapter considers a success story in conquering innovation fatigue, where a truly green energy-saving company overcame a variety of fatigue factors, including regulatory and legal issues, on its path to success.

Notes

1. John C. Bogle, "Vanguard—Child of Princeton," Princeton Entrepreneurs' Network 5th Annual Conference, Princeton, New Jersey, May 28, 2004, www .vanguard.com/bogle_site/sp20040528.htm (accessed Oct. 14, 2008).
2. James Foster, Mikael Hilden, and Niclas Alder, "Can Regulations Induce Environmental Innovations? An Analysis of the Role of Regulations in the Pulp and Paper Industry in Selected Industrialized Countries," in *Innovation, Science, and Institutional Change: A Research Handbook*, ed. Jerald Hage, and Marius Meeus (Oxford: Oxford University Press, 2006), 122–140.
3. Jean-Pierre Garnier, "Rebuilding the R&D Engine in Big Pharma," *Harvard Business Review* 86, no 5 (May 2008): 68–76; see p. 70.
4. Avery Johnson, and Ron Winslow, "Drug Makers Say FDA Safety Focus Is Slowing New-Medicine Pipeline," *Wall Street Journal*, June 30, 2008, A1, A10.
5. In the 1970s, Congressional hearings did explore whether the FDA was hindering approval for valuable drugs treating high blood pressure. Several such drugs that had been used successfully in Europe were subsequently approved. See Johnson and Winslow, "Drug Makers," A10.
6. Johnson and Winslow, "Drug Makers," A10.

7. Council on Competitiveness, "The Competitiveness Index: Where America Stands," Washington, D.C., February 2007, www.compete.org/images/uploads/File/PDF%20Files/Competitiveness_Index_Where_America_Stands_March_2007.pdf (or http://tinyurl.com/7k3vnu) (accessed Nov. 11, 2008).

8. Senator Kay Bailey Hutchinson, "Sarbanes-Oxley Is Outsourcing U.S. Leadership," *Investors Business Daily*, April 10, 2007, A17, also at www.senate.gov/~hutchison/opedsox.html (accessed April 11, 2008).

9. Preston Tucker, "An Open Letter from Preston Tucker," printed in many newspapers on June 15, 1948, www.tuckerclub.org/html/openletter.html (accessed Oct. 7, 2008).

10. Patrick Byrne, quoted by Anna Mason, "Taking Stock," *Equities* 57, no 6 (Sept. 2008): 38–40.

CHAPTER

Orion Energy Systems

CREATIVE SOLUTIONS TO EXTERNAL FATIGUE

W hen vision and sound strategy are in place, courageous innovators and leaders can navigate around innovation fatigue factors
and reach success. One example with many lessons comes from the
journey of an intriguing innovator, Neal Verfuerth, and his company in northeastern Wisconsin.

Bemis Manufacturing in Sheboygan Falls, Wisconsin is the
largest toilet seat manufacturer in the world. After meeting with
Neal Verfuerth, President of Orion Energy Systems in Sheboygan,
Wisconsin, Bemis Manufacturing agreed on an unusual project.
Industry-standard high-intensity discharge lighting in the plant
would be ripped out and Orion's new proprietary system would be
installed to provide better, brighter lighting for this early adopter.
When the project was finished and the new lighting system was in
place, hundreds of employees began enjoying brighter, more com-
fortable lighting. But there is much more to this story. Over at the
local utility company, alarms were being triggered. Operators were
shocked. Eight percent of the entire power load for the city of
Sheboygan Falls (population 6800) had been taken out overnight.
Pinpointing the source of the change, the meters showed that
Bemis Manufacturing suddenly was using 50 percent less energy.
They knew the plant wasn't closed, so the dramatic drop in power

consumption pointed to one troubling possibility: someone was stealing electricity. Was there a thief working for Bemis?

Since that day, Bemis Manufacturing has saved hundreds of thousands of dollars in electrical bills not though thievery, but through innovations in lighting from Orion Energy Systems. Even with greatly reduced energy use, the plant is a brighter, better place to work.

Neal Verfuerth is a true leader of innovation who combines the best of environmental stewardship and capitalism to achieve solutions once thought impossible. Can a building be made brighter while using half the electricity? Can significant electrical power be added to a grid during times of peak demand without building new power plants? Can environmental advances be made in ways that also help businesses and utilities? Can improved technology replace antiquated lighting systems without creating any waste? In Neal's world, the answers are all "yes!" Neal's experiences highlight many wise behaviors for an innovator wishing to overcome innovation fatigue at all the levels considered in this book.

On a cold Wisconsin day in January 2008, the heat of innovation seemed feverish inside Orion's 200,000 square foot Manitowoc facility during a two-hour tour kindly conducted by Neal for Jeff Lindsay, just one month after Orion went public (Nasdaq: OESX). We also were assisted by Steve Heins, Vice President—Communications & Government Affairs, and Linda Diedrich, Director—Corporate Communications. They offered us a review of what persistent, directed innovation can do as innovators overcome fatigue factors and complete their "circuit of innovation" (see Chapter 18).

Orion provides specialized fluorescent lighting systems that use far less power than traditional fluorescent lighting, and offers higher efficiency than the LED lights that are often viewed as the standard for efficiency. Orion makes it possible to be even greener than LEDs and more cost effective, without having to rewire a building. Plants that previously installed high-pressure sodium, high-intensity discharge or metal halide lamps (often at the cost of employees unhappy with the color or noise) are now finding more significant energy savings with more pleasant lighting and longer life after switching to Orion's systems. Customers like the *Milwaukee Journal Sentinel* newspaper, who replaced their high-intensity discharge system, are achieving a return on their investment in about one year.[1]

Based on years of experience across the full supply chain in lighting, Neal has identified numerous gaps in prior systems and found solutions. For example, the reflectors behind fluorescent lights are far more important than previously realized. The details of the reflector shape control how effectively light is distributed below. By properly and uniformly distributing light, work areas can be made brighter with less power. For high bays with a 50-foot ceiling, the ideal reflector may be a deep, narrow valley, but for a 12-foot ceiling, a broader curved profile with a novel dimple in the middle gives the broad stream of light needed. Orion also uses a special aluminum alloy that gives outstanding heat distribution for ballast longevity and offers superior reflectivity. To make the ideal shape for low-bay reflectors, Neal found that existing equipment was inadequate. Neal and his team actually invented a machine, one of a kind in the world with a series of rollers that turn a flat alloy panel into a beautifully curved reflector panel.

Neal also found that the design of popular high-intensity discharge systems resulted in half the energy wasted as heat and vibration. By separating the ballast from the lamp and using a highly-conductive alloy frame to cool the lamp, energy use is reduced and ballast life increased. The performance of Orion's high-intensity fluorescent system is surprising: more light with half the energy—so surprising that many prospective clients simply refused to believe it. But Neal did not let skepticism and the difficulty of making sales slow him down. He saw a need for further innovation to provide a compelling reason to believe. Thus Neal invented and patented a meter that is installed with the lights and helps clients see the dollars being saved. It was a technological invention, but one aimed at supporting a business model.

Clients still refused to believe that such significant savings were possible—after all, how could the massive electrical lighting industry have missed this opportunity after all these years? Undaunted, Neal added another twist to his business methods. He would install the new lighting system for free, accepting payments based on the savings he was delivering in the clients' lighting bills. When the contract expired, clients would own the lights. It took 18 months of homework to ensure that this approach would not need to be mentioned in SEC filings of his clients,[2] an example of the many regulatory barriers he had to deal with. There were challenges at every

Lesson from Orion: When faced with doubt, innovate to create reasons to believe!

When prospective clients wouldn't believe the energy savings Orion's lighting systems offered, President Neal Verfuerth created and patented a meter that helped clients see how much energy was being saved. When that didn't break down the skepticism, he added a business model innovation: installing the new systems for free, and taking payment based on the measured savings clients experienced. Sometimes a great invention is not enough to deal with the social aspects of innovation. Further creativity is often needed to help customers change their behavior and try something new.

turn, but through added innovation, persistence, and homework, Neal pressed forward.

The manufacturing process is filled with further innovation. Neal found that the painting of ballast boxes affected performance and installed his own advanced electrostatic powder coating system using energy from an efficient Capstone Turbine microturbine generator. Energy in the hot gases is recovered to help dry the paint.

Part of Orion's suite of solutions includes light pipes that, characteristically, offer innovations in design giving them an edge over traditional skylights. Further benefits come from Orion's wireless control systems that provide a desired level of lighting automatically by sensing the light from the light pipes and turning off unneeded fluorescent lights.

Continuing Orion's theme of profitable sustainability, partners have been found to recycle every component of old lighting fixtures that are sent back to Orion. Plastic lenses, ballasts, wiring, and reflectors are all recycled with the help of partners. Orion even developed specialty bandsaws for cutting the transformers that are received, facilitating their recycling.

Advanced robotics also play a role at Orion. The synchronized beauty of Finn Power robotic machining units preparing large sheet metal for transformation into ballast packs was an impressive sight. The payoff has been excellent. That success depended on properly programming the robotics. Neal said that he hired "a young guy who likes Nintendo video games and made him the robot programmer. His superb videogame skills gave him the edge we needed to achieve outstanding performance with the robots."

Lesson from Orion: Consider Every Aspect of the Supply Chain for Innovation

By considering every aspect of the lighting business, from the design of individual components to system-wide performance, from installation challenges to uses for discarded components, Orion has found numerous innovation opportunities. Detailed knowledge of the business, the technology, and customer needs at every level gave Neal Verfuerth and his team a competitive advantage.

Neal has faced his share of opposition. Skeptics have said he was crazy, that it couldn't be done, and asked how he could compete against the giants of the industry who surely knew more than he did about lighting. Neal faced barriers in finance, in law, and in other areas that would have stopped most people, but Neal had a vision and persevered to find a way. A key to his success was that he actually knew what he was doing and was familiar in detail with the barriers to efficiency that had been accepted through decades of tradition in the industry. Sometimes the long-held assumptions of the experts in an industry are the greatest barrier to progress.

Innovation in Business Methods

Orion Energy Systems has been diligent in creating intellectual assets to protect their business. This includes seeking business method patents that go beyond traditional patents for products and manufacturing methods. For example, Orion is pursuing patents on their "Virtual Power Plant" business model, in which multiple participating companies can respond to surging power demand by cutting back on lighting, using automated management systems from Orion communicating across the Internet, and collectively selling saved power to a broker for a profit. (See Exhibit 15.1.) Financial rewards from returning power are shared among the participants. Orion's remote control systems and other tools come into play here.

Their business method innovations extend to some of the hottest topics in energy. "We've been working on the notion of monetizing emissions through efficiency for three years," Neal said. They monetized their first emissions trade in 2007. VP Steve Heins explains that Orion's membership in the Chicago Climate Exchange and Environmental Markets Association helps keep them involved

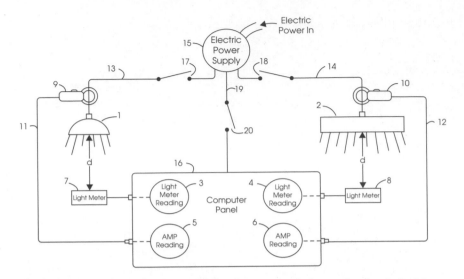

Exhibit 15.1   Figure from an Orion Energy Systems patent related to their virtual power plant concept[3]

in the growing markets for emission reduction credits. Neal and Steve believe that once the door opens on market trades based on energy efficiency, there will be a transformation in our sense of how much it will cost to reduce emissions. Neal said, "We're going to take energy efficiency and change it from being a social program to one that makes economic sense."

Orion even started a non-profit foundation called E4, whose charter is to bridge the gap between environmentalism and capitalism. With the help of E4, the State of Wisconsin was able to recognize the future importance of emission credits when they structured a deal between Florida Power and Light and WE Energies of Wisconsin, in which Wisconsin's Point Beach Nuclear Power Plant was sold. The original deal would have overlooked the value of emission credits entirely, but thanks to the efforts of E4, that value will be retained for the taxpayers of Wisconsin. WE Energy kept the rights to possible emission credits from the plant, preserving a benefit that may be worth up to $200 million a year.

A governmental fatigue factor was creatively conquered in this process. When the original proposal was made by Orion, a suspicious Wisconsin judge threw out the request and chastised the company for allegedly being self-serving and greedy. Rather than giving up, Orion sought to understand and allay the cause for suspicion. They openly and publicly repositioned their effort through a new non-profit foundation. No deception was involved—the relationship of the E4 to Orion Energy System was made clear, and the same person then made the same pitch to the same judge, but this time with the added clarity provided by their non-profit status. Now the judge could see the opportunity more clearly, and told the representative he once chastised that the plan was pure genius. Orion was acting in the interests of the public, but sometimes those who don't understand the nature of corporations can't see past their assumptions, so repositioning was a smart move. Sometimes people need a little help in overcoming their own biases. (Remember: when faced with doubt, innovate to create reasons to believe.)

Business method innovations from Orion also include development of their own ERP (Enterprise Resource Planning) software. Neal found that existing ERP systems didn't fit Orion. He tried two different commercial ERP systems, and after months and hundreds of thousands of dollars, determined that he would rather not have to change the way he did business to meet the demands of rigid software. Instead, his team developed a custom tool for the way they needed to manage sales and manufacturing. The tool Neal envisioned would be intuitive and easy to use for people on the shop floor and people in the field, one that revolved around the work people needed to do, not around the needs of accountants. "I didn't want the IT guys to be only ones who could make it work." Some said they were crazy to develop their own enterprise software, but the system has proven to be successful and cost effective. Their proprietary TaskMaster system, which we have seen in operation, is a model of what corporate software systems should be.

Part of Orion's leadership in business methods was expressed in their efforts to help Wisconsin benefit from carbon credits associated with the use of nuclear power. When Wisconsin was selling the management of its nuclear power plants to a third party, Neal recognized that the carbon credit benefits from Wisconsin's nuclear power plants should be treated as a valuable future asset that should be retained by the state. Without his intervention, Wisconsin would have lost the value of those carbon credits. Early recognition of their future value allowed Neal to save millions for the State, though it took significant efforts on his part to make it happen. It's just one more example of the innovations in business models that Neal brings to the table—a table sometimes freely shared with many.

Orion Asset Management

Orion Asset Management refers to Orion's suite of business method innovations that help clients generate revenue from their capital expenditures around lighting and other sources of power consumption. Energy consumption is monitored in real time with Orion's Intelite™ control system. Documented energy savings are aggregated with Orion technology and sold back to an energy broker. The Intelite™ control system communicates over the Internet to integrate local control with macro opportunities and needs. Users can remotely access data about their power usage, create budget reports, explore alternate usage and procurement scenarios, and implement load shedding strategies. The local control system can automatically turn lights off in areas that are not occupied. It can integrate information from fans, heating systems, cooling systems, lighting, etc., all of which can be controlled and can communicate with other components. The fans can respond to information from the lighting grid, for example, to optimize building performance. With this system, power can be reduced, emissions harvested, and multiple customers aggregated to sell power back to the grid, allowing the Virtual Power Plant to make money for participants.

As Orion works to provide the benefits of future emissions credits to their customers (a topic we discuss later in this book), Orion and its allies will be devising new ways of looking at how energy is used, how energy is procured, and even how energy issues are legislated. Steve Heins explains that "instead of 'greenwashing,' we are taking something that is measurable and verifiable, and ensuring that our customers get credit for what they are doing for their communities. In fact, our customers already have received more than 400 environmental stewardship awards."

Neal had more to say about this vision: "I've testified at the State Senate and Assembly. Everyone wants to beat their chest about energy issues, but not many are standing up to say 'I have a solution, it's cost-effective, here's how it will be paid for, and here are the benefits.' We can do that, and offer trickle-down economic effects and help for the environment."

That's what innovation is all about: *believable* real solutions to real problems that make life better for real people.

More Lessons from Orion

Growth has meant constantly seeking opportunity. In 2002, on a sales call to a manufacturing facility in Manitowoc, Wisconsin, Neal could see the signs of trouble there. "I could smell death in the air." Two years later, when he was ready to expand, he was able to negotiate a favorable deal for the facility, netting him a 265,000 square-foot facility on 30 acres of land. *Looking for opportunities in the midst of down markets is a key trait of many successful leaders and entrepreneurs.*

With a few negative experiences with vendors behind him, Neal has been careful to seek out and build relationships with partners he can trust. He knows that vendors get beat up by their customers, constantly being hammered down in price and being pressured to make concessions. When Neal finds good vendors, he makes it a point to keep them happy and build healthy relationships. "I tell them this: I want you to make money with us and to want to work with us, so that when we call, you'll be glad to answer instead of worrying about how much we're going to try to beat out of you now." Neal understands that building a mutually beneficial relationship of trust with vendors and other partners may mean some missed cost savings in the short term, but results in much more profitable business in the long term. This basic lesson is lost to many business leaders these days—relearning it could overcome several unintended but real barriers to success in relationships.

The importance of understanding end users is another lesson from Neal. For example, in the dairy industry, Neal knows that dairy farmers get higher productivity when the lighting is right. Using "long day lighting" can result in 8 percent more milk production. Neal is devising an entire product category for dairy farming, developed with the help of a dairy scientist. That's an example of another energizing factor for innovation: *turning to the right experts in a field to give you the insights to fuel further innovation.*

A customer-centric approach is shown in the Orion Energy Systems "org chart" that Neal uses. (See Exhibit 15.2.)

His approach to business recognizes that when a customer has a problem such as a warehouse with a section in the dark, they aren't interested in whose fault it is. They want the problem fixed. "When there's a mistake, we simply fix it rather than blaming others.

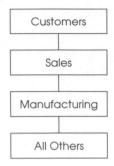

Exhibit 15.2   Orion's "org chart"

It's amazing how far this goes to build a relationship with a customer."
Coupled with this is Neal's conservative approach to commitments:
"We will not over-promise and under-deliver. We will always strive to
do the opposite." That's another great tip for building relationships
of trust.

Leading Others to Innovate

Neal's credibility as a serial inventor and the visionary behind the
success of Orion Energy Systems motivates others to listen and
accept his challenge to find further innovations. Indeed, Neal
expects his employees to be innovators, too. "I want MacGyvers
here," Neal said, alluding to the ABC television show of the same
name about a resourceful secret agent, Angus MacGyver, which ran
from 1985 to 1992. The hero in MacGyver was famous for finding
clever ways, based on scientific and engineering knowledge, to use
available materials to solve complex problems in fighting crime or
escaping danger. In a sense, Orion's MacGyvers are like the modern
"Da Vincis in the Boardroom" we call for in Chapter 21. Orion's
innovators are routinely challenged, brought together to innovate,
and encouraged to achieve a common vision: "Energy savings without compromise." The "compromise" part must be left behind if an
innovation is to become fully adopted, for people stick with what
works, according to Neal: "If an alleged energy-savings approach
solution makes a facility darker and less productive, people won't
stay with it. People want more for less. That's our heritage. That's
how we innovate."

Notes

1. Paul Studebaker, "Back to the Future: Facilities Engineers Say They Enjoy Upgrading to New-Generation Fluorescent Lighting," *Plant Services,* Feb. 2005.
2. Arlene Weintraub and Michael Arndt, "A Bright Idea," *BusinessWeek SmallBiz,* Spring 2005.
3. Neal Verfuerth and Michael Potts, "Apparatus and Method for Comparison of Electric Power Efficiency of Lighting Sources," U.S. Pat. No. 6,774 ,619, issued Aug. 10, 2004.

CHAPTER

Fatigue Factor #9

UNIVERSITY-INDUSTRY BARRIERS

As war was spreading across Europe in 1940, James Bryant Conant, president of Harvard, was approached by Vannevar Bush of the Carnegie Institution of Washington and encouraged to enter into research contracts to advance the war effort. As Timothy Atkinson of the University of Arkansas puts it, "a new relationship between the government and the nation's universities was established as a result of wartime needs."[1] The administration of organized research began to emerge, negotiating contracts for wartime research "according to the principle of no-loss and no-gain. Universities were reimbursed for costs they incurred and also given some allowance for overhead."[2] Today, research contracts with government or industry are routinely handled by central offices, and indirect costs are part of the contract. However, the paradigm of "no-gain" has been replaced with the recognition that intellectual property from a university can have great value that needs to be extracted. Some universities have seen revenues of hundreds of millions of dollars for some of their patents, driving some to hope that their university will offer the next Gatorade®.

Skipping School Again: Driving Companies Away from U.S. Universities

"Stay away from the universities." This surprising advice came in an interview with a respected Midwest businessman, thought leader, and inventor with many years of experience in advancing industry. It reflects some unfortunate experiences with a few large universities where he had sought a partnership to introduce agricultural inventions into their channels. From his perspective, the universities wanted the advances to belong solely to them and proved to be unacceptable partners. Part of this barrier may have been fueled by the demands of—or misapplications of—the Bayh-Dole Act, which drives universities to seek ownership for concepts to which they contribute and brings IP ownership to the forefront in negotiations about sponsored research and collaboration. Some universities have found ways to respect the law and be good partners in R&D, but this is one area where fatigue factors exist that need to be addressed.

The world of universities is central to American technology. So many startups and great products have their origins in university research (Google, Web browsers, numerous pharmaceuticals, biotech companies like Genentech, and so on). Today, however, the innovation potential between industry and universities is showing signs of fatigue.

"Forget about the universities" strikes us as an unfortunate viewpoint, but that voice is not alone among businessmen. There are genuine problems in need of reform.

The Bayh-Dole Act

The Patent and Trademark Law Amendments Act[3] (the "Bayh-Dole Act"), signed into law December 12, 1980, was intended to strengthen university-industry cooperation. One of its provisions permits the university to own and license patents based on work done with federal grants. Previously, there were inconsistent policies among government agencies regarding IP, making it difficult for industry to take advantage of patents obtained through federally funded institutions. The inability of businesses to retain title to inventions developed under federally-funded research programs was a barrier to commercialization, especially in the biomedical area. The Act also makes it possible for professors to receive a portion of the royalties from patents they help develop, adding a strong incentive to not only invent, but to also pursue IP. We have seen many exciting inventions and start-ups rise that appear to have been aided by the Bayh-Dole Act. However, as so often happens, well-intentioned regulations can have unintended consequences.

University personnel tend to focus on positive outcomes associated with the Act, such as significant increases in licensing revenues, an explosion in university efforts to license products, and hundreds of commercial products that originated in universities since the Bayh-Dole Act, contributing billions to the U.S. economy.[4] Would similar trends have been realized without the Act? The Act came as a "golden era" of intellectual property was beginning, with improved patent laws and a strengthened judicial system that led to an eruption in patent activity and value. It came before most companies began to pursue open innovation. Did the Bayh-Dole Act produce the observed changes? Has its effect been entirely positive?

Companies dealing with universities often find that the Bayh-Dole Act is used as justification for the university's requirement that it own the intellectual property arising from privately-funded research. Those familiar with the Act and its origins might be puzzled by this since the intent was to promote commercialization of inventions from federally funded research, and the Act makes an exception for privately-funded research (Section 401.1).[5]

Dr. Susan Butts, Senior Director of External Science & Technology Programs for Dow Chemical and Vice President of the University Industry Demonstration Partnership (UIDP, Washington, D.C.) has noted that many universities interpret the Act to apply as long as "one federal dollar touches" a privately-sponsored project.[6,7] Therefore, they claim a statutory right to own and control inventions and their patents that arise from privately funded research. In fact, companies are sometimes expected to pay the patenting costs but will receive no more than an option to negotiate a non-exclusive license.

According to Dr. Butts, the strained interpretation can lessen the attractiveness of universities as partners for R&D. As a result, many corporate leaders feel that IP issues are an impediment to working with universities, and some companies have at times chosen to work with foreign universities instead of U.S. universities to obtain better IP terms. It is typically easier to maintain sole ownership of IP rights when working with foreign schools, or some U.S. private universities where more flexible terms are often available. We are aware of a major European firm that has abandoned its relationships with several public universities in the U.S. in favor of a private university in the U.S. where much more flexible IP rights are available.

The National Institutes of Health even rebuked U.S. universities in 1998 for profit-motivated activities that could jeopardize scientific advances. As Jennifer Washburn summarizes, the NIH expressed dismay that universities commonly impose onerous legal conditions ("material transfer agreements") on scientific research tools created through public funding.[8] These were causing delays and barriers in technology transfer. Under these agreements, some universities may demand ownership of all future discoveries that stem from use of university materials and impose restrictions on what kinds of research can be pursued with the materials. Even simple sharing of data between scientists can now require lengthy legal review. The NIH complained about the increasingly profit-oriented operation of universities and stated that "It hardly seems consistent with the purposes of Bayh-Dole to impose proprietary restrictions on research tools that would be widely utilized if freely disseminated. Technology transfer need not be a revenue source to be successful."[9]

Some have also wondered if the increased emphasis universities now have on patents as a tool for technology transfer may be diverting university attention from technology transfer through publications, conferences, and academic training—the public routes that have historically been and continue to be recognized as the most significant and valuable technology transfer tools of universities.[10]

We suggest that these problems are not inherent to Bayh-Dole *per se.* Indeed, like the benefits attributed to Bayh-Dole, some of the harms may have crept into the system on their own even in the absence of that specific legislation. As with most fatigue factors, some aspect of human nature is often at play. We expect improved university-industry relationships will follow from the freedom that companies have to shop elsewhere and from a variety of efforts currently underway to improve relationships. As always, we urge future legislators around the globe to carefully consider the potential for unintended consequences in dealing with innovation.

Tax-Free Bonds and the University: Additional Barriers to Collaboration

While Bayh-Dole presents some well-known challenges, many overlook a potentially more serious regulatory barrier to industry-university partnerships: IRS tax regulations, specifically the policies known as Rev. Proc. 1997-14[11] and Rev. Proc. 2007-47.[12] These rules deal with the possible loss of tax-free status of public facilities. Under Rev. Proc. 97-14, for example, the tax-exempt status of a bond (the typical tool used to fund university buildings) is at risk if privately funded research for "private benefit" exceeds a mere 5 or 10 percent of the research being conducted. Susan Butts has pointed out that "this barrier is unique to the U.S. and is a competitive disadvantage."[13] These statements are not tax law, but are conservative safe harbor guidelines. Not surprisingly, universities tend to interpret Rev. Proc. 97-14 broadly to give them a further advantage in negotiating. The IRS guidelines may be applied in ways that leave companies uncertain of their future ability to use the technology they develop with a university.

There are many cases where the difficulties related to tax regulations have delayed negotiations with industry from six months to two years.[14] Some of these difficulties are incorrectly blamed on the Bayh-Dole Act.

Misaligned Incentives

We learned more about barriers to effective university-industry relationships from Dr. Merrilea Mayo,[15] Director of Future of Learning Initiatives at the Ewing Marion Kauffman Foundation and former Director of the Government-University-Industry Research Roundtable (GUIRR) at The National Academies. Dr. Mayo noted that reward systems in universities can be at odds with effective technology transfer. The incentives for each of the players in university-industry relationships are often out of alignment. For example, self-funded tech transfer offices are motivated to hold out for the highest possible returns and may take aggressive positions relative to IP rights and royalties. Leaders responsible for funded research are motivated to obtain big agreements ($50 million or above) and may have little incentive to pursue smaller projects with industry, though their support is usually necessary. The tenure system for professors rewards publications but not patents, inventions, companies started, royalties generated, or other manifestations of effective innovation. Professors may wish to simply get a project started as quickly as possible to provide needed R&D funds, without significant concern for commercialization and IP. These conflicting interests can lead to delay and confusion in the messages conveyed to prospective partners.

Technology transfer can be most effective when incentives have been crafted to align the interests of various parties at a systematic level. Establishing common metrics to motivate behaviors is one healthy approach. Many leading universities have recognized the need for improvement and are making significant gains. The University of California-Berkeley, for example, instituted significant changes under the leadership of Beth Burnside, the recently retired Vice Chancellor for Research. University-industry relationships were simplified and various interests aligned while complying with restraints and expectations across the system. The result was a doubling in industrial funds for R&D at Berkeley, followed by BP selecting Berkeley to lead a $500 million energy research consortium to focus on biofuels. MIT, long a leader in university-industry partnerships, has aligned interests at many levels and has provided strong programs to promote partnerships. For example, MIT's Industrial Liaison Program (ILP), established in 1948 as the first formal program designed to nurture university/industry collaboration, allows industry to gain access to professors by becoming affiliates with the university. Many other universities have followed suit with related programs.

Dr. Mayo noted that even when professors are motivated to pursue innovation, they often lack the appropriate social networks and expertise to succeed. They need help to find the support infrastructure they need—fabricators, machinists, accountants, lawyers, source of capital, etc. Some universities like the University of California-San Diego are working to help make these resources accessible. It's exactly the sort of encouragement that can make the most of a nation's investment in education.

Other Barriers

In addition to the impact of the Bayh-Dole act and tax regulations, there are other barriers that hinder successful transfer of technology from universities to business. On the corporate side, there is the barrier of "Open Innovation Fatigue" (Chapter 10)—the attitudes, processes and policies that often make it difficult to turn to outside entities. There may also be personnel changes that radically change the relationship, a mistrust of universities, and a failure to understand university perspectives, such as the importance of publications.

On the university side, other problems include inflated expectations regarding the value of the invention, pride that results in devaluation of the input and skills of industry, failure to consider the "lens of risk" from the corporate perspective, and failure to appreciate the challenges of commercializing a technology.

For the corporation, it helps to have a "champion of open innovation" who is well connected with business groups, but who also has an academic background or is at least close to academia. They should understand the life of professors and the pressures and expectations within the university. For the university, it helps when the technology transfer office has experience in industry, ideally in running start-ups as well as working in major corporations. It helps when representatives of industry and universities know a little something about the shoes the other partner wears.

Fatigue in Universities

Several fatigue factors affect the innovators within the ranks of academia as well. The challenges of policies, politics, funding, publication pressures, and other factors can make the innovator's life a difficult one in academia. Commercializing research work and pursuit of patents were even frowned upon in the past. In recent decades universities have become more aggressive in encouraging such things, although there are still fatigue factors which keep many from reaching their potential.

Theft of university inventions is becoming less common now that many universities have strengthened their approach to intellectual property, but it is still the subject of allegations and significant lawsuits. Some fatigue factors in universities have unique academic twists, such as rivalries within a department, underhanded tactics in the peer review process to limit rivals, the politics of federal funding, competition for students and resources, the burden of writing proposals and spending so much time seeking funds that real inventive work becomes difficult, the challenges of dealing with technology transfer offices, and the problems of inventorship when teams of students, post-doctoral researchers, and faculty may be involved (or uninvolved) to various degrees.

Fortunately, there are important energizing factors that can help. The financial incentives that many universities offer (30–60 percent of royalties for patents going to the inventors in many cases) can be a great stimulus for innovation. Recognition and other incentives keep professors performing at levels often far beyond what someone in industry might expect for the pay they are receiving. Also, the freedom many professors have to use their technology for launching a business can help.

Global Perspective

We have focused on the challenges in the United States, where many corporations complain of difficulty. Globally, university-industry partnerships are growing rapidly, with many benefits to both partners and to local economies. We find many nations such as China, Singapore, France, and Ireland actively working to promote university-industry collaboration. For example, among the successful "industrial clusters" in the French system, the Grenoble area with its "Minalogic" cluster for nanotechnology and miniature intelligent solutions benefits from alliances between several large enterprises, many start-ups, and local universities and laboratories.[16] Tax credits for participating enterprises also strengthen the appeal. Nations actively promoting innovation alliances will have a competitive advantage and added access to rich innovation engines.

India offers an example of proactive efforts to harness the power of innovation, as we learned in an interview with Dr. A.S. Rao (Aynampudi Subbarao), Adviser in India's Ministry of Science & Technology.[17] India is reaping the benefits of rapid innovation and world-class capabilities in the IT area, with thousands of programmers and web designers creating new technologies, services, and businesses for customers worldwide. However, the government of India recognizes the need to foster innovation in other areas. The Ministry of Science & Technology has launched initiatives to assist inventors and entrepreneurs, particularly those spinning off from universities or involving partnerships between universities and industry. Over 100 centers have been established to foster innovation, and legal resources and other support has been made available to help innovators gain domestic and foreign patent protection.

Some of the appeal that universities outside the United States offer to global corporations may be due to currently lax national requirements about IP arising from the partnership—a factor likely to change. Universities and governments worldwide would be wise to look to the future and ensure that actions taken to strengthen IP ownership for universities do not hinder beneficial partnerships with industry. University-industry partnership committees, similar to the UIDP in the United States, may be useful forums to proactively address issues that are likely to emerge in the future.

Having reviewed a wide variety of fatigue factors, we next consider innovation fatigue in the pulp and paper industry as a special case where several lessons can be learned.

Notes

1. Timothy N. Atkinson, "The Institutional Construction and Transformation of University Research Administration," *Research Management Review* 12, no 2 (Winter/Spring 2002), www.ncura.edu/content/news/rmr/docs/v12n2.pdf (or http://tinyurl.com/ncura2) (accessed April 11, 2008).
2. Roger L. Geiger, *Research and Relevant Knowledge: American Research Universities Since World War II* (New York: Oxford University Press, 1993), as cited by Atkinson, *Institutional Construction*.
3. P.L. 96-517, codified at 35 USC § 200 et seq.
4. Michael S. Lenetsky, "Technology Transfer Developments in University–Start-up Interaction: Modeling the Relationships," *Research Management Review* 12, no 2 (Winter/Spring 2002), www.ncura.edu/content/news/rmr/docs/v12n2 .pdf (or http://tinyurl.com/ncura2) (accessed April 11, 2008).
5. 37CFR401.1, Code of Federal Regulations, Title 37, Volume 1, U.S. Government Printing Office, Washington, DC, revised as of July 1, 2002, pp. 609–610, http://edocket.access.gpo.gov/cfr_2002/julqtr/37cfr401.1.htm.
6. Susan Butts, "Federal Investment in Research: Implications for U.S. Competitiveness–An Industry Perspective," PCAST Meeting, Aug,. 24, 2007, slide 7, slides available online at www.erc-assoc.org/annmtg/2007_meeting_ files/ILO_Susan%20Butts.pdf (or http://tinyurl.com/cvejk2) (accessed April 10, 2008).
7. Susan Butts, "Testimony Before the Subcommittee on Technology and Innovation, Committee on Science and Technology, U.S. House of Representatives: Bayh-Dole—The Next 25 Years," July 17, 2007, Washington, DC, http://democrats.science.house.gov/Media/File/Commdocs/hearings/ 2007/tech/17jul/butts_testimony.pdf (or http://tinyurl.com/bgxw7g) (accessed March 7, 2009).
8. Jennifer Washburn, *University, Inc: The Corporate Corruption of American Higher Education* (New York: Basic Books, 2005), 145–146.
9. National Institutes of Health, "Report of the National Institutes of Health (NIH) Working Group on Research Tools," presented to the Advisory Committee to the Director, June 4, 1998, www.nih.gov/news/researchtools/ (accessed Sept. 27, 2008).
10. Washburn, *University, Inc.*,143–145.
11. Revenue Procedure 1997-14, Internal Revenue Service, 1997, available online at www.unclefed.com/Tax-Bulls/1997/Rp97-14.pdf (accessed April 10, 2008).
12. Revenue Procedure 2007-47, Internal Revenue Service, 2007, www.irs.gov/ pub/irs-drop/rp-07-47.pdf (accessed April 10, 2008).

13. Butts, "Federal Investment," slide 8.
14. Merrilea Mayo, interview with Jeff Lindsay and Mukund Karanjikar, Nov. 6, 2008.
15. Ibid.
16. Jean-Louis Armand, "University-Industry Cooperation: The French Perspective in the European Perspective," *Journal of Industry-Academia-Government Collaboration* 2, no. 5 (2006), http://sangakukan.jp/journal/main/200605/0605-10/0605-10_e.pdf (or http://tinyurl.com/c9krc2) (accessed Oct. 29, 2008).
17. A.S. Rao, interview with Jeff Lindsay, Nov. 12, 2008.

CHAPTER

17

Innovation Fatigue in the Pulp and Paper Industries (Forest Bioproducts)

WHY "INNOVESTMENT" MATTERS

Exhibit 17.1   A paper mill using recycled paper (© Wolfgang Muecke)

In the fall of 2007, I (Jeff) was privileged to be one of about 400 people attending the induction ceremony for the Paper Industry International Hall of Fame. Many business leaders, scientists, and stalwarts of the pulp and paper industries were there in Appleton,

Wisconsin, where six people from three countries would be inducted into the Hall of Fame. After the introduction by Harry Spiegelberg, a retired executive from Kimberly-Clark Corp., the keynote speech was given by Eugene Van As, CEO of Sappi, a South African paper company with major investments in North America. For some, the speech put a painful damper on the excitement of the evening, but a few of us found it invigorating. Rather than praising the industry for its progress, Van As spoke more like a prophet of doom, calling the industry to rethink R&D and invest in innovation or face destruction. Many winced, but some heard a message of hope—if the industry would heed it.

Van As warned that declining investment in R&D and new technology was making the American industry non-competitive. With the market capitalization of the industry having steadily declined for the past 20 years, he warned that the pattern of spending less than depreciation on new equipment would continue to erode the industry unless there was a reversal in investment patterns. He observed that paper machines in Asia and Europe are larger and employ more recent technology than those in the U.S. Without a renewed willingness to build for the future instead of cost cutting for the next quarter, the U.S. industry may not regain its competitiveness. Now was the time to reverse these trends, Van As said, and to reinvigorate research to make the industry vibrant again. We agree with Van As, and believe it can be done.

One of the great declining industries in North America is the pulp and paper industry, or, more broadly, the forest products industry. With over $200 billion a year in sales and over 1 million employees, the U.S. forest products industry is one of the nation's largest sectors with a magnitude similar to the automotive industry. In 48 states, it is in the top 10 manufacturing employers.[1] In Canada, it is an $80 billion dollar a year industry and one of the largest employers.[2] (See Exhibit 17.2.)

Though North American paper manufacturers have been world leaders in efficiency and innovation, the innovation role is on the decline. With heavy cost cutting, R&D resources have been depleted and the competitive edge continues to become duller on average.

As one who began his career with paper-related research and education at the Institute of Paper Chemistry (now the Institute of Paper Science and Technology on the Georgia Tech campus),

Exhibit 17.2   Large rolls of paper being produced in a paper mill (© SemA—Fotolia.com)

I have witnessed the frustration of innovators in this industry over the past two decades. The lessons learned from the decline of this industry can teach us lessons for other mature or maturing industries as well.

A Proud History of Innovation

When I joined the Institute of Paper Chemistry in 1987 as an assistant professor, it seemed like the ideal academic establishment with abundant resources, direct linkages to industry, outstanding students and faculty, a strong sense of community, and a global reputation. Founded in 1929, professors and graduates of that private graduate school in Appleton, Wisconsin guided the rise of the pulp and paper industry in North America and much of the world. The Institute was the hub of a thriving community that provided many advances in areas such as paper physics, pulp processing, energy recovery systems, and environmental technology. Industry leaders regularly visited the Institute, and technology transfer from the Institute to industry was relatively direct and productive. There was an exciting and energizing atmosphere.

To many, the pulp and paper industry seems like an old smokestack industry ripe for outsourcing. However, it has been at the vanguard of many technologies now viewed as fashionable (see Exhibit 17.3). Current efforts to produce ethanol from cellulose and other biomass sources are yielding incremental improvements over the breakthroughs in biofuel work that began a century ago at the Forest Products Laboratory in Madison, Wisconsin. There has been relatively little progress in efficiency and yield over the "Madison Process" which was developed there in the 1940s.

Those familiar with papermaking also recognize that the energy recovery systems in kraft pulping represent advanced chemical recycling technology and biofuels technology. Energy recovered from the waste products of pulp making provides power and heat for the mill and may return electrical power to the grid as well.

Paper itself is an amazing nanocomposite, and paper researchers for decades have relied on intricate chemistry involving nanoparticles to craft paper properties. The bonds formed between paper fibers, for example, involve minute strands of cellulose chains called "microfibrils." Colloids and complex mixtures of particles, fibers,

- **Nanotechnology:** Colloidal chemistry and natural nanoparticles to control fiber interactions (retention aids), tailored filler particles to control properties. The paper industry may be the largest user of nanotechnology.

- **Green energy:** Over a century of practical bio-based energy production from the "black liquor" by-product of pulping; decades of experience in producing ethanol from cellulose; practical biorefineries for producing biodiesel and other biofuels.

- **Bioproducts:** Numerous products from the compounds in wood. The sugar xylitol, often derived from birch, is one of many examples.

- **Recycling:** Extensive infrastructure and technologies for recycling paper; extensive recycling of the chemicals used in pulping.

- **Microencapsulation:** An advanced technology used in carbonless and thermal papers with many applications elsewhere.

- **Process control and intelligent manufacturing:** The complex, integrated systems in paper mills employ some of the world's most advanced process control systems and advanced systems for managing raw materials, inventory, spare parts, and other aspects of the value chain.

Exhibit 17.3   Technological Contributions from the Pulp and Paper Industries

and polymers are at the heart of papermaking. Yet when "nanotechnology" became the rage in the 1990s, few recognized the contribution of papermaking to nanotechnology.

The use of microencapsulation (embedding chemicals in microscopic shells for subsequent release) has important origins in the paper industry. Appleton Papers, now known simply as Appleton, developed sophisticated microencapsulation techniques in the 1950s that led to the creation of carbonless paper, in which colorless reactants that form ink are separated with a microcapsule wall until the pressure of a writing instrument breaks the capsules and forms visible ink. Separating chemical components to allow for controlled release and reaction at a later time has become the basis of many product advances. In thermal papers widely used in cash registers, for example, microcapsules are also used to separate chemicals that are released when heat is applied, forming visible dyes. Recently Procter and Gamble turned to Appleton for microencapsulation technology for improved release of fragrances in Downy® fabric softener sheets. Microencapsulation is also used for time-released drug delivery, scratch and sniff materials, and self-rising pizza dough, where moisture and baking powder are kept separated through the use of fatty microcapsule walls that melt in the oven, allowing the components in the baking powder to react and generate the carbon dioxide gas that promotes rising of the dough.

The speed and efficiency of papermaking processes reflects the generations of creative engineering from many minds. Some mills produce paper webs roughly 5 meters wide at speeds over 100 km/hr. Hundreds of details in machine design, heat transfer, chemical processing, fluid mechanics, air handling, web handling, and other issues have been the subject of creative innovations for these gargantuan mills.

The raw materials of paper, of course, are bioproducts, a sustainable harvested crop that is replanted and carefully managed. In fact, the forests of the United States are more abundant than they were 20, 50, or 100 years ago. About 1.7 million trees are planted daily by the forest products industry, three times more than are harvested. The paper industry has had its environmental scandals, such as the dumping of waste products into rivers, but today has matured into a highly responsible industry seeking a viable partnership with the environment.

An often overlooked part of the forest products story is the significance of its products in many commercial sectors. In addition to the obvious products such as pizza boxes, paper towels, currency, juice cartons, books, newsprint, and copy paper, materials derived from wood and other cellulose sources are used in perfumes, cosmetics, food flavorings, shoe polish, roofing, and detergents. Companies in other sectors continue to turn to the paper industry to find solutions to related problems or to find novel materials to help in their innovation—such as the discovery that lightweight paper composites make great blades for wind turbines, resulting in exciting new product opportunities for Wausau Paper Company, for example. Other new product opportunities include applications of paper in edible form. *Edible paper?* Homaro Cantu, the master of innovation and chef at Moto restaurant in Chicago, is pursuing edible paper as a low-cost tool to deliver essential nutrients and even medicines to the poor in developing nations and to help fight hunger.[3,4] Papermaking technology for edible products actually has older roots extending at least back to the invention of Pringles® potato chips using several aspects of papermaking technology.

While others tap into the richness of technology in the pulp and paper industries to drive their innovation, this process has become less reciprocal as the pulp and paper industries have become less committed to innovation and lost or simply inhibited some of the talent that could make it happen.

The Need for Innovation—and "Innovestment"

Exciting areas of innovation remain, such as the development of integrated biorefineries where papermaking operations are combined with biorefineries to produce fuels from waste biomass. One example is the Flambeau River Biorefinery in Wisconsin, which uses birch wood in its papermaking operation, yielding xylitol as an important commercial byproduct of the sulfite pulping process. In addition, low grade biomass such as branches are being converted into fuel using a gasification process, with enough energy being generated to run the mill plus provide energy to the market. The pulp and paper industry has developed a variety of techniques for extracting fuels from byproducts of paper making and has shown remarkable leadership in the green energy area. However, this leadership has been relatively neglected and is in danger of being surrendered unless more effort is made to maintain its lead and to play a stronger and more visible role with others, according to

Ben Thorp, a former executive in the paper industry and president of the Flambeau River Biorefinery.[5]

In spite of the potential for innovation with the remarkable scope of product possibilities and technologies in the pulp and paper industry, it generally remains focused on paper as a commodity for books, boxes, printing, etc. Declining "innovestment"—driven by short-term financial metrics—has produced a declining industry, caught in a downward spiral of cost cutting. Global leadership is being lost. The rapidity of its decline, with lessons for prospective innovators, can be surveyed by looking at the place where my exposure to the industry began, a place once known to many as "The 'Tute."

The Microcosm at the 'Tute

Many of the most exciting innovations in the pulp and paper industry felt the touch of the Institute of Paper Chemistry throughout much of the twentieth century. Faculty members with decades of expertise and world renowned status in their fields walked the halls, while thought leaders from across the industry visited and advised the staff. Technology transfer was effective and relatively easy. Further, the student body of about 100 graduate students had a close-knit camaraderie that extended long past graduation and contributed to the sense of community among those in the forest products industry.

When I arrived in 1987, research at the Institute was well funded by the thriving forest products industry, with relatively little need for faculty members to devote their lives to finding external sources of funding. It seemed too good to be true. In fact, the late 1980s marked the beginning of a painful decline not only in the industry and its R&D community, but in the Institute itself.

The 1980s and early 1990s were an era of merger mania. The consolidation of the industry into a handful of major players inevitably resulted in efficiency measures to reduce costs and redundant efforts. Financial pressures not only reduced "redundant" R&D centers, but moved some companies to convert R&D into primarily business support. There trends also affected the Institute. Mergers reduced the number of supporting companies and also the total revenues received. Further, beginning in 1989 some industry leaders pressured the Institute to be "more relevant" and help solve more of their current problems in the mills. The Institute tried to comply, but the request was not well suited to the background of many faculty members.

During the frenzy of M&A activity, the Institute itself went through a radical change. In mid 1987, rumors circulated that a move for the Institute was being considered—an academic merger of some kind. These rumors were denied in a meeting of faculty and staff. Assured by the declaration, my wife and I moved ahead and purchased a home in Appleton, Wisconsin. Days after closing on our home, I opened the door around Christmastime to find a shocking headline on the front page of the *Post-Crescent* newspaper: "IPC to Move." A board member had leaked the story: the Institute was planning to move out of the "isolated" community of Appleton to form an alliance with a major research university still to be determined. Had we known that a move was being considered, we could have saved many thousands by not having to sell our home (at a loss) shortly after buying it. But that was a small price to pay, compared to the harm done to the Institute. Faculty members and students were outraged. Information had been withheld in a desire to help the Institute for the short term, but at the cost of valuable intangibles such as trust.

A leader in a local paper company, an expert in organizational behavior, explained that the move of the Institute looked like a textbook example of how not to handle a major organizational change. When change is needed, openness and communication are vital. Respect for people's feelings and needs must be shown, even when the reality may be grim. By doing all possible to be open and respectful, goodwill and cooperation can be maintained, even in the face of difficult circumstances. But when trust is lost and other wrong messages are sent, dramatic losses may follow. In this case, about 50 percent of the faculty and staff—including many of the most respected—remained in Appleton or went elsewhere when the Institute moved to Georgia Tech, where a luxurious $43 million building was not enough to maintain the image that the 'Tute once had.

Student morale was hurt, and uncertainty about the new Institute made recruiting of top students more difficult and costly.

There were increasing financial pressures also as mergers in the industry cut the number of member companies supporting us. Overhead rates were higher than ever, compounding the difficulty of seeking additional money for research. Further, there were dramatic changes underway in the leadership and attitudes of the paper industry. Whereas the Institute was once a gathering place for CEOs from across the industry to periodically discuss emerging technology and contemplate the future, new corporate leaders increasingly focused on shorter term results and left responsibility for technology and innovation to managers whom they sent to the Institute in their place.

In spite of this discouraging backdrop, Institute leaders countered with successful efforts in several areas. Woody Rice, with years of executive-level experience working with the paper industry, was enlisted as Vice President of Development and Government Affairs to help advance the new Institute. He would later serve as President. Woody recognized that the paper industry was increasingly becoming global, and that Asia would need to be part of the Institute's ecosystem. Zealous efforts were made to build international ties and to bring in support from Asian companies. Woody was also behind many efforts to help faculty members and students succeed under the new circumstances. These efforts included helping researchers recognize that invention and discovery alone are not enough, but needed the extra steps of commercialization and adoption to make any difference. Woody taught the importance of marketing, whether it's an individual's work or the role of the Institute as whole. The widely misunderstood and underappreciated pulp and paper industry needs more of this kind of thinking.

While many other universities were becoming increasingly difficult for companies to work with due to demands regarding IP rights from collaborative work (see Chapter 16), Woody was a passionate champion for improved university-industry relations and found ways to respect corporate needs while also benefiting the Institute. For example, special procedures were developed to better preserve confidentiality and clarify IP issues for some sensitive research projects for corporations. Further, with his understanding of industrial needs and perspectives and the constant efforts of his team to reach out to the industry, he was able to bring in several new member companies such as Kimberly-Clark Corp. and others with highly proprietary R&D programs. These efforts did much to sustain the Institute in difficult times.

However, in spite of some success, the burden of the move and the declining support of industry ultimately would require significant restructuring and a complete merger with Georgia Tech. Long before that point was reached, cost-cutting pressures resulted in requirements for faculty to bring in very high levels of external funding. To reach these goals, some of us felt that we had to pursue every opportunity that had money attached, whether it made sense or not. When research no longer seems meaningful, innovation fatigue is nigh. It was time to move on. I loved the Institute and wanted it and my peers to succeed, but increasingly had doubts about its future.

Joining Kimberly-Clark in 1994 was another dream come true. The spirit of cooperation among team members in the Family Care Division (its name at the time) was inspiring. There was excitement in the air as dozens of people collaborated to bring a new class of tissue technology online. I was also impressed at the level of proprietary knowledge in technical areas of interest to me. Much of this contributed to the success of the "uncreped through-air dried" (UCTAD) system that I was supporting—a bold new way of making soft, flexible tissue without the complex and highly constraining techniques used for conventional tissue. This was an exciting time and place for innovation.

After IPST fully merged with Georgia Tech, it lost some of its flavor and unique status in the industry, but still plays a valuable role. The industry itself continued its decline. In spite of the huge potential in resources and capabilities for leadership in areas such as biofuels, the industry did not recognize and invest in its potential. As Ben Thorp warned in evaluating the biofuels potential of the industry, "Continuation of business as usual will surely mean loss of leadership and faster decline."[6]

Other Fatigue Factors for the Industry

The American Forest and Paper Association (AF&PA) has identified a variety of factors that are threatening the competitiveness of the industry:[7]

- Availability of affordable, high quality fiber
- Cost of environmental regulation
- Tax rates
- International trade practices
- Labor costs, especially healthcare costs
- Energy costs
- Investment in technology

In its discussion of regulatory and tax burdens, AF&PA observed that the "pulp and paper industry, one of the most capital intensive sectors in the U.S., spends on average 15 percent of its total capital investment on environmental protection." This burden is not faced by foreign competitors: "For example, capital expenditures per ton for environmental protection are only about 60 percent as high in Brazil and 40 percent as high in China as expenditures in the U.S." The extensive reporting requirements, frequent inspections, and inflexible deadlines (often bringing fines and penalties) are cited as additional burdens not equally shared by competitors outside of North America and Western Europe.

Regarding taxation, AF&PA has this blunt observation:

> The U.S. tax system discourages investment by the domestic forest products industry, while competing countries use their tax codes to foster the industry's growth. In fact, our tax system poses greater obstacles to corporate timber production and paper manufacturing than that of any major competing country except Canada.
>
> For non-corporate investment in forestland, estate tax laws force many inheritors of family-owned tree farms to either sell these properties for commercial development or to prematurely cut their trees to pay the tax bill.

A Few Recommendations

Calling upon the industry to spend more on R&D is obviously only part of the solution. Fatigue factors from regulation and tax law weigh heavily upon the industry, as do a variety of strategy and organizational fatigue factors, along with the normal fatigue factors encountered at the personal level. An aggressive, multi-faceted effort is needed for this industry to regain global leadership. We see glimmers of hope in some areas such as renewable energy, but these are exceptions to the rule so far.

Many observers see the need to rebuild R&D in the pulp and paper industries, but that does not necessarily mean a return to the typical R&D centers before the trimming in the late 1980s and the 1990s. Many of these groups were disconnected from the needs of the companies they served, or else were focused solely on business support and not the future of the company. Waynne Despres, a former papermaker now leading WHBD Associates in Ottawa, shares that skeptical view of past R&D efforts, and instead calls for setting up two small, centralized groups within each company, one for manufacturing support and the other for R&D.[8] The support group would have several seasoned engineers who can solve mill operating problems and train mill technical staff. That team could also work with a capital planning/project management group and help them guide and manage larger projects. The R&D group would primarily manage outsourced research projects that could be conducted by various organizations like Paprican, or conducted with supplier companies like Metso Paper. We find Despres's proposal to be one reasonable path companies should consider, although we recommend the following for the R&D or innovation team:

- Team members should be skilled in open innovation and develop the connections and awareness to find capable partners and capable technologies.
- The team should be staffed with capable innovators who can add value to outside innovations.
- The team needs to be familiar with the full scope of the business and business plans, and should meet regularly with senior management to maintain their awareness of corporate needs and vision.
- The team should include technical people with proven track records of innovation as well as experienced marketers who can assist in connecting innovation efforts to market opportunities, and translate market insights to corporate needs.
- The team needs to be connected through multiple channels to the business units to interact with others and encourage their contributions, actively working to eliminate NIH behaviors. Seeking, encouraging, and pursuing internal innovations from throughout the company should be an objective, as well as finding external innovations.
- The team needs to be savvy in intellectual asset strategy and work closely with Legal to ensure that intellectual asset opportunities and threats are proactively addressed.

Ultimately, there is a need for leadership to listen to new voices. Not only the voice of stockholders and analysts demanding better numbers next quarter and unreasonably high or rapid return on invested capital, but also the voice of the innovator, helping to create a shared vision of the capabilities of the technologies and assets before them, a vision of new business growth and, in some cases, new business models. Hearing this voice as it once was heard may be difficult, as we learned in an interview with Dr. Doug Dugal,[9] a former Director of the Institute and respected thought leader in today's pulp and paper industry. During the height of the paper industry, he explained, many of its leaders were graduates of the Institute or held other technical degrees and could speak the language of the technical community and listen to its input. Adding our voice to Dr. Dugal's, we would encourage leaders today to not only learn to listen to the technical community, but, as Clayton Christensen has urged, to recognize that their leadership affects the entire body of employees and their communities. There may be short-term pain as needed "innovestments" for the future are made.

Dr. Dugal told us that the revival of the North American industry is possible, but the task demands leaders who are "gutsy people" who can listen to voices other than those coming from the Street demanding unreasonably high short-term returns on the heavy capital investments required in the paper industry. "Gutsy people" are needed to set the vision, guide long term growth, and pursue meaningful innovation.[10]

We would encourage the industry to further strengthen itself through open innovation, both in finding new industrial applications of its technologies through cross-industry collaboration, as well as finding external technologies that can enhance growth opportunities for paper-related products and businesses. One exciting area where that is beginning to occur is the production of biofuels from forest products. For example, Chevron and Weyerhaeuser Corporation recently combined forces in a joint venture for large-scale production of liquid transportation fuels from forest-derived resources. Others are developing integrated biorefineries to convert byproducts from pulp and paper production into fuels. Such efforts build upon a long history of power generation from pulp byproducts and of producing value-added materials from the wastes of the pulping process, but the full potential is just beginning to be tapped after years of painful delay.

Other recommendations, including guidance to government, are covered in the general recommendations we make in the next section of this book.

Learnings

- Mature industries can be at risk of decline if they fail to reinvest in innovation and ensure that a vision and strategy for the future is in place.
- Driving innovation in light of the challenges posed by economic stress and various external fatigue factors requires courage and fortitude, but cannot be neglected.
- Innovation for mature industries may best be stimulated by open innovation to find new partners, opportunities in new markets, and new business models that allow established capabilities and technologies to be used in new domains.

Notes

1. "Economic Impact," American Forest & Paper Association, 2008, available online at www.afandpa.org/Content/NavigationMenu/About_AFandPA/State_Economic_Brochures1/Economic_Impact.htm (or http://tinyurl.com/paperind) (accessed Nov. 23, 2008).
2. Forest Products Association of Canada, "Investing in our Future," www.fpac.ca/en/industry/innovation_economy/investing.php (accessed Oct. 6, 2008).
3. Jennifer Reingold, "Weird Science," *Fast Company*, issue 105, May 2006, www.fastcompany.com/magazine/105/open_food-cantu.html (or http://www.fastcompany.com/node/56689/print) (accessed July 13, 2008).
4. Pete Wells, "New Era of the Recipe Burglar," *Food and Wine*, Nov. 2006, www.foodandwine.com/articles/new-era-of-the-recipe-burglar (accessed July 13, 2008).
5. Ben Thorp, "Paper Industry Must Protect Its Lead Status in Cellulosic Innovation," *Pulp and Paper Magazine*, May 2007, www.risiinfo.com/magazines/May/2007/PP/pulpandpaper/magazine/7778.html (or http://tinyurl.com/bthorp) (accessed March 29, 2008).
6. Ibid.
7. American Forest and Paper Association, "U.S. Forest Products Industry—Competitive Challenges in a Global Marketplace," www.growthevote.org/page.asp?g=AFPA&content=White_Paper_re_Competitiveness_Summary & parent=AFPA (or http://tinyurl.com/growvote), June 5, 2005 (accessed July 14, 2008).
8. Perry J. Greenbaum, "Research & Development: Harvesting Technological Progress," *Pulp and Paper Canada*, Oct. 2003, available online at http://tinyurl.com/greenbaum (accessed March 7, 2009).
9. Doug Dugal, interview with Jeff Lindsay, Oct. 16, 2008.
10. Ibid.

PART

V

FURTHER GUIDANCE

CHAPTER

18

Guidance for the Lone and Corporate Inventor

Several lessons have come from the prior discussion of fatigue factors, such as the importance of documenting inventions and confidential disclosures, and of taking steps to create valuable intellectual assets to protect the invention. We've reviewed the importance of having reasonable expectations and not being, well, delusional in one's approach. We've discussed the importance of understanding the perspectives of others, especially the lens of risk that potential partners and buyers will use to view outside technology. We've emphasized the need to be persistent, while also getting good advice and knowing when it's time to regroup and refine (or sometimes abandon) the concept. We've discussed ways that innovators can be treated like immigrants and excluded by others when it would be wiser to include them and more fully use their talents—problems which innovators overcome by building the right ties and developing new skills. Here we review several additional principles to give innovators a passport for success. We begin with an overarching concept we use to help inventors seeking to bring their product to the market through the power of a major partner. Then we discuss several general principles that can be of value to lone inventors and those in corporations seeking to chart their paths in the sometimes foreign lands of business.

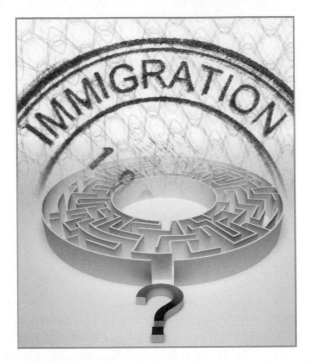

Exhibit 18.1 **How do "immigrant" innovators gain passports for success?**

Completing the Circuit of Innovation

One of the models **Innovation**edge uses to help innovators understand how to license their technology and bring it to market is the concept we call "Completing the Circuit of Innovation™." The Circuit of Innovation™ is based on an analogy to an electrical circuit. (See Exhibit 18.2.)

Like an electrical circuit involving a microprocessor (the genius of the inventors), the pathways that connect the intelligence of inventors and innovators in general to the power of the market involves multiple components that must be in place for the energy to flow constructively in the circuit. If a component is missing the circuit will fail and useful work will not be done. At the simplest level, the Circuit of Innovation™ uses a market plan and a holistic intellectual asset strategy (360° IA™) to join inventors with prospective partners in the marketplace.

The market plan involves identification of the market segments and prospective partners that should be pursued and in what order.

Exhibit 18.2   The Circuit of Innovation™ model

The story to be told must relate the "reason to believe" and help the audience understand how the invention or new offering solves a problem or makes life better. The market plan, as developed in work with clients at **Innovation**edge, is typically based on recognizing the innovation as part of a pipeline of opportunities rather than a single offering.

While crafting the market plan, a holistic approach to intellectual assets, or 360° IA™, is also pursued. This involves more than conventional product and process patents. In addition to creative patent approaches that some call "business method patents," many non-patent intellectual assets are considered as well, including digital intellectual assets such as domain names; Web-based audio, video and static channels; defensive publications; supplier agreements; and other assets. The goal is to create a compelling IA story that synchs with the marketing story. Likewise, knowledge of the marketing strategy should inform IA strategy.

Defensive publications are an important and frequently overlooked low-cost IA tool that can strengthen the IA story. Though they don't give ownership of technology as patents can, they can deliver many benefits such as adding value to a core patent estate by creating prior art to limit future competitive patents in the space. We have seen companies and inventors who create a new product category later face serious challenges in introducing improved products due to numerous competitive patents for minor improvements of the technology. In some cases, the pioneers had already thought of the improvements and had considered patenting them (or describing them in a related patent) but chose not to, feeling they were "too obvious" or not worth the cost. However, when a competitive patent captures some new benefit, however minor, that the market wants, an improvement patent can become a serious roadblock. One solution is to regularly update an IA estate by crafting short strategic documents describing potential improvements (new features, uses, materials, alternate designs, combinations with competitive technologies, etc.) in order to create useful prior art. Caution is needed to avoid disclosing something that should be patented. For corporations, broad internal communication and approvals should be in place before publications are released. Venues such as IP.com can provide rapid, inexpensive, time-stamped publication of documents in a forum increasingly searched by the PTO. There is much more that can be said about strategies for crafting publications, guidance on incentives, venues to consider, unusual objectives to pursue, and other tactics—see *InnovationFatigue.com* and *Innovationedge.com* for more.

When the Circuit of Innovation™ components are in place, it's possible to execute the strategy by connecting to the right partners to get the invention plugged into the market. It's an exciting process with many pitfalls, and one of the areas where inventors can be rejected, worn down, or inadequately rewarded if they don't get the right assistance. Few have the skills, knowledge, and connections to make it happen on their own. Getting the right help, making the right connections, and pursuing the right strategies can give one the edge.

There are numerous "circuit breakers" that can interrupt the flow of creative energy in the circuit. For example, the circuit can fail if the marketing plan doesn't work, if the intellectual assets are weak, if the invention is not a good fit for the market, if targeted partners are uncooperative, or if deals are structured poorly. Many of the fatigue factors discussed in this book can also act as circuit breakers in this model. In spite of these challenges, with proper diligence, proper assistance, and a bit of luck, success is possible for many.

The Circuit of Innovation™ model applies not only to small entrepreneurs and inventors, but can also guide corporate new product development efforts. The circuit is related to the "Horn of Innovation™" concepts from Chapter 2, where we discuss the importance of involving innovators in a feedback loop to allow for constant adjustments to stay in tune with the market and other factors. In the circuit model, the creative energy of innovators flows throughout the circuit, not just to one component such as the IA strategy. Specialists may handle tasks such as drafting patents, preparing marketing materials, and delivering the pitch to partners, but the energy and vision of innovators helps inform and guide these efforts to various degrees. They also must be aware of the feedback from the market to continuously refine and guide their efforts.

Expanding the Scope of Intellectual Assets: Trademarks and More

A broad approach to intellectual assets is more important than ever. Unusual approaches such as "business method patents" can be considered. Low-cost publications can play a role in reducing the threat of competitive patents by creating prior art. Digital intellectual assets such as domain names are often neglected until too late. Trademarks can be another valuable avenue to explore.

David Orozco of Northwestern University has explored how various forms of IP combine to create value for the owners and how they relate to the consumer experience.[1] Patents protect function, copyrights can protect commercial expression (ads, for example) of that function, design patents protect aesthetic aspects of the product and its packaging, and at the highest level, trademarks protect the brands that are based on the consumer perception of the product.

The power of trademarks in protecting a company is illustrated in a recent case involving Adidas, owner of trademark for a tennis shoe with three stripes on the side. In May 2008, an Oregon jury ruled that Payless Shoes should pay *$308 million* to Adidas for infringing that trademark. Payless may have hoped to evade the three-strip trademark of German-owned Adidas by using four stripes, but Adidas successfully argued that their stripes create a distinctive mark that is a sign of origin, and that both two-stripe and four-stripe shoes may cause confusion in the minds of consumers. Three simple parallel stripes have become a distinctive part of the Adidas brand.[2] This coverage may last as long as the brand does, unlike the limited coverage afforded by patents. Adidas, of course, relies on both utility and design patents as part of its IA strategy.

In recent years, U.S. trademark rights have been expanded to cover not just traditional logos and names, but to also cover colors, scents, characteristic sounds, and three-dimensional shapes. Examples include:

- Yamaha's distinct water spout from its WaveRunner® personal water craft. As U.S. Trademark 74321288 states, "The mark is comprised of a three-dimensional spray of water issuing from the rear of a jet propelled watercraft and is generated during the operation of the watercraft."
- Tiffany's famous robin-egg blue gift box (U.S. Trademark 75360201).
- Intel's five musical notes (U.S. Trademark 78721830).

Though harder to obtain than design patents, trademarks can have an unlimited life, in sharp contrast to the 14-year-life design patents have from the date of filing, or the 20-year life of regular utility patents. Under U.S. law, trademarks can be used to sue both manufacturers and distributors of infringing products. While patents appear increasingly under attack, trademarks seem more respected and more likely to maintain value, if the owner is diligent in protecting trademark rights.

The combination of patents and trademarks for competitive advantage is illustrated by Apple's approach to protecting its iPod® MP3 players.[3] In addition to traditional trademarks for the iPod® name and the two-dimensional appearance of its navigation pad, Apple has pursued non-traditional trademarks as well, including one for the three-dimensional shape of the iPod® (U.S. Trademark 78925932). Anticipating the rise of accessories, Apple has registered a "Made for iPod"® trademark showing the text and a simple iPod® icon.

We recommend that innovators look for creative combinations of both trademarks and patents, as well as other forms of intellectual assets.

The Need for Multidisciplinary Skills: Da Vinci in the Laboratory

We've discussed a variety of attributes that innovators need to overcome fatigue factors. In addition, they also need fundamental skills— more skills than ever. Those who pursue "the slight edge" concept by continually adding to their education, skills, experiences, and networks will be poised to innovate at a far more meaningful level. Multidisciplinary innovators are needed more than ever. It's time not for more Edisons or Einsteins in the boardroom or laboratory, but for Da Vincis.

As the world becomes increasingly "flat," work requiring specific knowledge and skills can be outsourced across the world. Doesn't that mean that deep specialization should be the best path of the innovator, allowing others to fill in missing skills? Can an entrepreneur succeed by simply bringing all the pieces together and letting others do the hard work of developing and applying knowledge-based skills? Perhaps, but innovations based on deep expertise often require breadth and multidisciplinary skills for the value to be recognized and exploited. Multidisciplinary inventors and entrepreneurs are needed to know where to drill into the readily available depths of knowledge and skill. They are needed to catalyze synergies across technical boundaries and recognize new relationships that traditional specialists might miss. They need to learn rapidly, to see patterns and opportunities, to know where new connections should be forged, and have the confidence and courage to persist and deliver— such attributes may be far more important that specialized technical knowledge.

This is not to discard Adam Smith and his rationale for economic growth through specialization (division of labor) and trade. The modern "Da Vincis" we speak of are a new breed of specialists in their own right. Not necessarily in narrow branches of genetics, nanotechnology, or telecommunications, but specialists in the art of innovation, in knowledge harvesting, and in creating cross-disciplinary ecosystems, coupled with deep expertise in several traditional categories. Their discipline requires knowledge in many traditional disciplines. No one of these specialists has all the insights and capabilities needed for success: wealth creation comes when they trade with other specialists, including other Da Vincis, magnifying the value of their own specialty.

If Da Vinci were an entrepreneur today, his combination of scientific prowess, artistic talent, engineering acumen, and strong networking might bring a flood of innovation into the marketplace. The breadth of knowledge and experience of a modern Da Vinci can guide teams of inventors and technical experts with a vision of what can be done. For the innovations we need most, we need to encourage Da Vincis and bring them into our boardrooms. This is their era.

Da Vinci was not simply a dabbler who occasionally read articles on many topics. He paid the price to develop impressive skills in painting, architecture, the elements of mechanics, and human anatomy, and to develop works and inventions based on those skills. Sweat equity—paying the price, putting in the time—is needed more than ever. The lazy are less likely to be lucky when it comes to innovation.

An example of the benefits of a diverse skill set in a single person can be found in Nathan Myrhvold, former Chief Technical Officer of Microsoft and current CEO of Intellectual Ventures, a firm that acquires and develops portfolios on intellectual property in areas ranging from theoretical physics to computer security. Nathan is a polymath, with competence—not just fleeting familiarity—in fields such as computer science, physics, and photography. He is an inventor, an entrepreneur, and a visionary who can guide other inventors in creating new inventions in targeted areas.

Another example is Nikolai Tesla, inventor of AC power systems that now light up the world and also the genius behind wireless transmission of energy so critical to modern radio and television. Margaret Cheney and Robert Uth in *Tesla, Master of Lighting*[4] describe him as a Renaissance man who invented brilliantly across a half-dozen fields of science. He even wrote poetry, was an environmentalist, advocated health and nutrition, and managed his own press relations with sophistication.

"Da Vincis" might include the passionate, multidisciplinary scientists, the "innovation finders," that Jean-Pierre Garnier sought in GlaxoSmithKline.[5] Such talent is rare—Garnier estimates that only 1 percent of scientists fit the mold—but increasingly needed. A challenge for Da Vincis is that they don't remain comfortable in any given narrow task. Breadth and vision is their passion—but this can be annoying to some managers. Learning to recognize and benefit from these individuals takes deliberate effort and sometimes systemic change. Without recognition and support, a Da Vinci will become an immigrant trapped and frustrated in a strange land, rather than the citizen of the world they are meant to be.

We would also suggest that the vast range of inventions from Philo Farnsworth (see Chapter 3) might qualify him as a multidisciplinary and visionary innovator. Had he developed the connections and received the sponsorship Leonardo had, perhaps his contributions might have been more acclaimed and more successful.

Endurance and Patience: Still Vital for Innovators

At the personal level, successful innovators often conquer fatigue factors by sheer endurance. As we've said before, it's essential for innovators to persist and endure, for new products or new business models won't succeed right away. As with a hornist learning to play the horn well, years of effort are often required to develop the right skills, overcome technical challenges, or drive social acceptance.

Endurance was vital for Norman Kraft, VP of Technology in the Kraft Foods Company. He had a great idea in 1930 for making cheese slices. Not sliced cheese, but cheese slices. Taking a block of cheese and slicing it would require extensive labor. Instead, Norman envisioned a process to form cheese into slices. Hot processed cheese would be cooled using a chilled roll and other equipment to create a ribbon of cheese that would be cut and stacked. The product, Kraft® Deluxe Pasteurized Process Cheese Slices, went commercial in 1945—15 years after the initial conception of the invention. It was worth the wait, for it quickly became the most profitable product in the 50-year history of the company at that time.[6] Numerous voices had said it could not be done, but Norman persisted. "During that time we had to work hard to keep the idea alive, in spite of people saying it won't work." Today, cheese slices based on his invention remain a significant part of the cheese market and make life more convenient for many—but 15 years seems painfully slow, and surely the invention could have been accelerated.

Many inventions have much faster paths to market, but few do so without significant trials that inventors must face and conquer. Rarely is the journey so dramatic and painful as that of, for example, Ignaz Semmelweis, a Hungarian immigrant. (See Exhibit 18.3.) In 1847 he discovered that contact with cadavers by medical students at an Austrian maternity clinic made the women in childbirth they subsequently treated much more likely to die from infection.[7] Decades before germ theory would be developed, he introduced handwashing practices with hypochlorite solutions to eliminate "cadaverous particles," reducing patient mortality from 10 percent to about 1 percent. However, this innovation was at odds with the established disease theory of his day which emphasized "vapors" as a primary disease vector. In his role as an assistant to a medical professor, he was

Exhibit 18.3   Ignaz Semmelweis, from an 1860 copper plate engraving by Jenö Doby

unable to drive the social aspect of innovation. He was too much the immigrant, literally, but more importantly, metaphorically, lacking the connections and support to influence the elite citizens of the medical community. Weakness in his communications contributed to the resistance.

In spite of his success in solving one of the most severe problems in medicine, he was largely ignored, dismissed from the clinic, and even harassed. Outraged, he returned to Hungary and continued his battles, denouncing the medical establishment and calling them murderers, a technique that rarely overcomes barriers. Those close to him thought he was going crazy (inappropriate personal behaviors compounded the problem, and possibly syphilis). They had him committed to a mental institution where he died two weeks later in 1865.

Semmelweis persisted to the end of his life, but persistence is often not enough. He failed to develop the network needed for his concepts to gain acceptance. He failed to garner adequate support of influencers, failed to communicate his message effectively, and failed to understand the reasons behind the resistance he faced. In most cases, those who appear to be barriers aren't actually murderers and criminals, and understanding the lens they use to view the innovation can help bridge chasms of misunderstanding. With improved understanding and more constructive efforts on Semmelweiss's part, possibly coupled with mentoring and other assistance—the encouragement that innovators so often need from outside—he may have found much greater success in his lifetime.

We hope the principles in this book may help future immigrants of all kinds to avoid the sometimes disastrous pitfalls that can befall innovators. Our hope is that this book may not only help inventors and entrepreneurs directly, but also guide those around them and those who influence them to better provide the encouragement and support needed for innovation to flourish.

Recommendations to Innovators

- Learn to use the Circuit of Innovation™.
- Don't rely on traditional patents alone, but consider a broad array of intellectual assets including defensive publications, business method patents, trademarks, digital IA such as domain names, and so forth.
- Develop and apply multidisciplinary skills.
- Be patient and persistent! The journey to success can be long and challenging.

Notes

1. David Orozco, "The Meaning of Intellectual Property," working paper, Kellogg School of Management, Northwestern University, Feb. 10, 2006, www.ipthought. com/articles/The_Meaning_of_IP.pdf (accessed May 12, 2008).
2. Slaven Marinovich, "Much Ado About Adidas Stripes," *BusinessWeek,* April 28, 2006, www.businessweek.com/innovate/content/apr2006/id20060428_729369 .htm (or http://tinyurl.com/yobwql) (accessed May 12, 2008).
3. David Orozco and James Conley, "The Shape of Things to Come," *Wall Street Journal,* May 12, 2008, R6, R12.

4. Margaret Cheney and Robert Uth, *Tesla, Master of Lightning* (New York: Barnes and Noble, 1999), vi.
5. Jean-Pierre Garnier, "Rebuilding the R&D Engine in Big Pharma," *Harvard Business Review* 86, no. 5 (May 2008): 68–76.
6. This account is taken from a poster in the Kraft R&D Center, Glenview, IL, viewed April 2008.
7. Wikipedia contributors, "Ignaz Semmelweis," *Wikipedia,* http://en.wikipedia .org/wiki/Ignaz_Semmelweis (accessed Oct. 14, 2008).

CHAPTER 19

Energizing Theory

DISRUPTIVE INNOVATION AND DISRUPTIVE IA

While "disruptive innovation" has become a mere buzzword in the mouths of some people, the concept has great value when properly understood. This knowledge can be an energizing factor for inventors and corporations alike. With it, the prospective innovator can recognize opportunities and position innovation in ways that add a "disruptive" advantage. The business leader can use the theory of disruptive innovation to proactively avert external threats while nurturing opportunities for future growth. We also point out how a low-cost intellectual assets (IA) strategy can help solve one of the conundrums of disruptive innovation, the tendency for valuable disruptive innovations to be rejected by successful corporations. We believe our recommended "*disruptive intellectual asset strategy*" fills an important gap in the literature on disruptive innovation, more completely discussed in a 2009 article in the *Journal of Product Innovation Management.*[1]

We will see that disruptive innovation requires looking beyond technology and new products *per se* to understand the barriers that are leaving the often unrecognized or unexpressed needs of non-users and low-end users unfulfilled. We must consider innovation in terms of business models, services, and customer experiences to provide new levels of convenience, access, and cost effectiveness. By pursuing broader forms of innovation and seeking disruptive opportunities, game-changing innovation can be introduced in the marketplace with a lasting, asymmetric advantage that motivates incumbents to flee rather than fight, giving the market entrant a precious foothold from which to grow with further "sustaining" innovation.

Whether an innovation is disruptive or not is not a function of the technology or magnitude of the innovation, but the business model in which it is implemented. Finding the disruptive business model often requires good instincts and market insight about gaps and unmet wants and needs.

Introduction to Disruptive Innovation

When Kleenex® facial tissue was introduced in 1924, makers of handkerchiefs had little to worry about. The innovative soft paper product was only being marketed to women as a tool for cold cream removal, a niche product at best. In the following years, Kimberly-Clark would learn about new benefits of this product directly from the marketplace. Passionate consumers wrote the company about the benefits of Kleenex® facial tissue in dealing with the common cold. With this unexpected feedback from the marketplace, marketers repositioned the product in the early 1930s as "the handkerchiefs you can throw away." A niche product would soon grow into one of the world's most famous brands, and the handkerchief industry would face a competitor out of nowhere with a competitive advantage that couldn't be overcome: the upstart enjoyed an "asymmetric" advantage in terms of its skills, assets, technology, and supply channels—in other words, it would be far too expensive and difficult for a handkerchief manufacturer to ever consider creating tissue manufacturing assets and expertise from scratch, and the benefits offered by the paper product were ones that could not be affordably built into their cloth-based products.

As Gustafson and Chester explain in their history of the handkerchief,[2] the emergence of Kleenex® facial tissue did not deal a sudden death blow to the industry, but resulted in steady erosion over several decades. By the 1960s, the handkerchief was no longer an essential part of a man's wardrobe, while the vast majority of households purchased facial tissue.

Kimberly-Clark had nothing to fear from the textile industry, but recognized that other paper companies or consumer product companies might want to encroach into their highly profitable field. Intellectual property would then be an important element of maintaining their competitive advantage. K-C filed numerous patents, trade secrets, and trademarks and continues pursuing patents in the facial tissue area to this day. Recent examples of patent-protected innovations include anti-viral tissues that help prevent the spread of germs, tissues that release menthol or fragrances from microcapsules when they are used, tissues with lotion that doesn't make a mess, and tissue in boxes with 3-D optical effects from clever flat plastic lenses.

Other products launched or made famous by this company have also disrupted previous long-standing icons of consumer life. Consider the impact of disposable diapers on cloth diapers or the impact of Huggies® Pull-Ups® training pants on cloth training pants, or the impact of disposable wipes on cloth towels. The newcomer was "worse" in terms of some previous metrics—washability, for example—but created new benefits of convenience that drove consumers to adopt the new concept.

The Theory of Disruption or the "Christensen Effect"

Professor Clayton Christensen of Harvard's Business School has sought to explain common aspects of business success and failure in terms of "disruption innovation." His popular theories are elaborated in three books, *The Innovator's Dilemma* (1997),[3] *The Innovator's Solution* (2003),[4] and *Seeing What's Next* (2004).[5] Christensen begins by analyzing the failure of many once-successful businesses that missed important innovation opportunities, and shows how businesses can greatly increase the chances of success in innovation.

In Christensen's model, disruptive innovations are generally those that allow a new product or service to get a foothold in a market by appealing to nonusers or low-end users of a previous product or service. According to Christensen, "Disruptive innovations typically enable a larger population of less skilled people to do things previously performed by specialists in less convenient, centralized settings."[6] Disruptive innovations are often "worse" in terms of the established metrics and customer expectations in the existing market, but offer new benefits such as reduced cost, increased convenience or ease of use, or other features that may appeal to current non-users.

To be disruptive, the innovation is generally introduced in a way that motivates the incumbents in the area to avoid direct competition. Rather than fighting a head-on battle with the market entrant, the incumbents are motivated to focus efforts on mainstream or high-end customers. Because disruptive innovations are typically ignored by the incumbents, they give the newcomer a chance to get a foothold in the market, from which further sustaining innovations can be pursued. The temptation to ignore disruptive innovation can be powerful because the loss of low-end, low-margin consumers may actually improve revenues in the short run and allow a company to focus more on the high end where increased profit margins can be found. Eventually, as the disruptive innovation improves and attracts more customers, it can become a source of genuine pain to the incumbents, but by the time they feel the pain and are motivated to respond directly, it can be far too late (see Exhibit 19.1).

The Path of Disruption

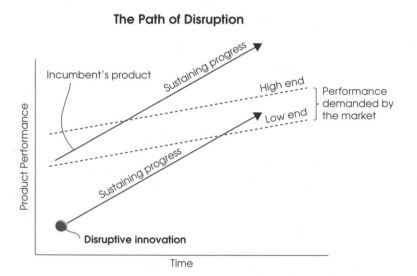

Exhibit 19.1   The path of disruption shown on a plot of performance versus time. A "worse" innovation, ignored by the incumbents but appealing to new customers or low-end customers, can undergo sustaining innovation until it becomes a threat to the mainstream customers of the incumbent. The incumbent is motivated to focus on higher end customers, surrendering the lower-margin end, overshooting the actual needs of the market and feeling little financial pain until it is too late. (Adapted from the works of Clayton Christensen and used with permission.)

Sustaining innovation is what most businesses pursue most of the time: improvements in products and services to meet the needs of existing customers in existing markets. Unfortunately, this logical process of constantly improving performance for existing markets and consumers can result in a product that overshoots the level of performance demanded by many customers, or can result in missed opportunities to reach non-consumers who want other benefits. Managers trained to look for improvements for mainstream customers based on established metrics may miss the opportunities to address the needs of low-end users or nonusers.

Understanding disruption can provide a powerful benefit when it comes to new product development. Christensen cites statistics indicating that competing with an established competitor in an existing marketplace without the benefit of disruptive technology usually dooms the effort: only about 6 percent of non-disruptive new businesses succeed. When the entrant has the advantage of disruptive innovation, the likelihood of success increases to about 37 percent.[7]

As an example, Christensen cites the rise of the transistor radio represented a disruptive technology that disrupted vacuum tubes. Radios with transistors initially were much worse than tubes in terms of sound quality, but the transistor radio offered a new benefit that could not be matched by tube radios: portability. Teenagers now could have music with them wherever they went, creating a large market for Sony's disruptive transistor radio. Meanwhile, Motorola invested millions into trying to implement the transistor into established products via established value chains, namely, high-end console radios sold through furniture and appliance stores. It would take years before the transistor radio would be good enough for the customers in that market. Meanwhile, Sony used the rapidly growing business of portable transistor radios to develop a new value chain for transistor electronics, developing resources and skills that would give them a massive advantage. By the time Motorola felt the pain from Sony's growth, it was too late—they were too far behind, and lacked the supply chain and value network to implement transistor electronics. For Sony, the transistor radio succeeded not because the transistor radio was inherently disruptive, but because Sony developed and pursued the right business model that made the innovation disruptive.

Other examples of disruptive innovation before our eyes include online brokerages, remote health care services, mail-order delivery of DVDs, and Nintendo's Wii® gaming platform.[8] In the last example, the Wii® system does not provide more advanced technology or higher-resolution graphics, but uses lower-end technology with a disruptive new business model that makes the gaming experience more accessible to customers.

Facing the Barriers

It's always easy to blame short-sighted business leaders when disruptive innovations are passed over or killed internally. Indeed, myopia is a common problem well meriting condemnation, such as Ted Leavitt's classic treatment of "marketing myopia" in 1960.[9] However, myopia or stupidity is not the reason why disruptive innovations are so often killed. Rather, Christensen explains that it stems from managers making *sound* decisions to achieve exactly what they have been trained and asked to do, and that is to focus on their customers—existing customers—to deliver the performance they are asking for. This process may cause disruptive innovations to be rejected as poor fits or poor solutions.

To overcome the barriers to disruptive innovation in a company, Christensen recommends special units with different systems, cultures, and expectations to break free of the systems that reward managers for filtering out disruptions. New values and processes may be needed, and the personal support of visionary executives may be needed. Units aimed at disruption may need to be separate from the rest of the corporation, in some cases. The staff may need different skills than those at the core of the business, where sustaining innovations are usually desired.[10]

Reorganizing to drive disruptive innovation is a difficult proposition for a large company. Smaller companies are much more likely to have the flexibility and cost structures that can pursue emerging growth markets without every decision being backed by extensive analysis.[11] But large or small, we suggest that a corporation can also turn to creative, proactive intellectual asset strategy to level the playing field when it comes to disruption.

A Proposed Solution: Disruptive Intellectual Asset Strategy

While organizational change to support disruption is often difficult and costly to bring about, intellectual property and other forms of intellectual assets may be a tool that can allow small groups within a company to aggressively defend it from external disruption and prepare for future commercial exploitation of disruptive innovations. The innovations may be killed for a period of time by normal screening processes, but when such innovations become recognized as important in the marketplace, the corporation with "disruptive intellectual assets" may be able to resist the assault of a disruptive entrant and later pursue the new opportunity on their own. A corporation with "disruptive intellectual assets" may be able to profit from an opportunity that otherwise would have been a disruptive weapon against it.

Proactive intellectual assets, especially patents and defensive publications, can be part of a two-pronged approach to deal with disruptive innovation at early stages. Initial "defensive" efforts from a small team can nevertheless result in business opportunities years later when the company is willing to pursue the related innovations commercially.

A team dedicated to seeking intellectual assets in disruptive areas need not develop technical breakthroughs, but by searching for disruptive threats and opportunities, it may identify disruptive applications for emerging technologies, find disruptive business models for existing technologies, or recognize and avert threats from distant quarters. With such vision, low-cost intellectual assets can often be generated to lay some kind of foundation. Targeted innovation sessions (not mere brainstorming) or small-scale projects informed with the right theory and vision can deliver significant IA territory. "Da Vinci in the Boardroom" becomes a relevant section of this book for such efforts, for multidisciplinary inventors and teams will be needed, and open innovation can be a critical component for the early defensive efforts related to disruptive innovation. Given the importance of the business model to disruptive innovation, the team should be familiar with business method patents[12] and the opportunities that they may provide. Business model ideation must be part of any effort to generate "disruptive IA."

The key to "disruptive intellectual asset strategy" is recognizing that many companies are more concerned about averting risk than pursuing distant opportunities. An emphasis on averting risk can sometimes mobilize needed resources for proactive efforts long before resources could be mobilized to pursue the commercial opportunity. Behind the risk aversion is the patient desire to also open doors for future growth.

Insights from Kimberly-Clark's Efforts

In past experience at Kimberly-Clark Corporation, deliberate eff-orts were taken in the past decade to advance open innovation and strengthen the pursuit of disruptive innovations, particularly through the use of low-cost intellectual asset strategies using founda-tional patents coupled with aggressive defensive publications. This included pursuit of IA across the supply chain, including IA gene-ration around business methods such as marketing techniques, consumer research tools, RFID applications, Enterprise software systems, supply chain management, and intelligent manufacturing. In several cases, we found that early patents dealing with disruptive threats from a defensive standpoint proved to have value years later.

Our experience taught us that some of the normal barriers to disruptive innovation identified by Christensen could be overcome with an aggressive IA strategy led by small teams with the flexibility to pursue "defensive" projects with additional potential benefits, such as laying a foundation for future disruptive innovation.

At Kimberly-Clark, in the late 1990s, we formed a group called the Cross-Sector Business Method group (CSBM) with the mission of pursuing "business method patents." This loosely knit cross-functional group met regularly to consider IA strategy and make filing and pub-lication recommendations. The group also reached out to other groups across the corporation who did not normally get involved with patents to help identify when there might be an innovation that could be protected. These efforts resulted in many new inventors par-ticipating in patent filings in diverse areas beyond the currently mar-keted consumer products of the company.

CSBM's early pursuit of patents in the RFID area were initially low-cost projects primarily for defensive purposes. Years later, when Kimberly-Clark was investing heavily in RFID technology and was becoming recognized as a leader in solving the problems of imple-menting the technology in the supply chain, the early patents became useful components in a growing patent estate, one that enhanced our interactions with some partners and opened up a variety of options for potential competitive advantage.

Again, low-cost early IA efforts in potentially disruptive areas can be justified primarily by their defensive value, but may be useful

Bonus Tip for Patent Strategy: Overcoming Obviousness with Disruptive Innovation Theory?

We have previously discussed the recently raised bar for patent seekers relative to the complex standard of "nonobviousness" to qualify for a U.S. patent. We suggest that in some cases, the theory of disruption might be useful in arguing that an invention is nonobvious. Some inventions make an existing product "worse" in some way, defying the demands of high-end, mainstream customers while appealing to low-end customers or non-users, often ignoring some conventional wisdom while providing new benefits such as convenience, ease of use, etc. If you can show that your invention defies the normal trajectory of sustaining innovation, then you may have a stronger case for nonobviousness. In these cases, why not consider adding a discussion of disruptive versus sustaining innovation in your background section? Why not show how the attributes of your invention in terms of generally accepted metrics makes your invention worse, undesirable, and certainly nonobvious in light of prevailing wisdom and market forces?

In this approach, the patent text (the "specification") may describe how the inventors found, perhaps through serendipity or other processes, a previously overlooked user need or an unexpected opportunity to meet the needs of former nonusers. The text could refer to the widely accepted theoretical framework of Clayton Christensen and others to show why the invention was not only unlikely to be pursued by those of ordinary skill in the art, but even likely to have been stamped out by experts such as experienced product developers and managers at the earliest stages had those of ordinary skill in the art attempted to pursue a similar path. If established market filters and metrics would brand a useful invention as hopelessly "worse," the case for nonobviousness may be strengthened.

Can business theory help in patent prosecution? We think so and feel this approach, when appropriate, is worth considering to help others understand why an invention is nonobvious. Whether disruptive theory is used or not, the art of framing and telling the story of the invention may be increasingly valuable in overcoming obviousness challenges to patents. We advise, however, that this suggestion is somewhat speculative at the moment and needs more time to be actually tested and refined. Please discuss these suggestions carefully with your patent attorney or agent first.

years later when new business opportunities in that area are being sought. In pursuing this approach, it is often much easier to convince a small portion of a company to pursue defensive IA in light of a disruptive threat than it is to convince the corporation to develop a potentially disruptive innovation.

While there are other views critical of Christensen's theories,[13] we have found them to be consistent with some of our experiences and helpful in guiding strategy. We hope that the theory of disruptive innovation and the concept of "disruptive intellectual assets" will guide many inventors and companies in more effectively dealing with the threats and opportunities of disruption.

A Few Recommendations

- Apply the theory of disruptive innovation to strengthen your business model and gain competitive advantage.
- Be aware of the disruptive potential of emerging technologies, market trends, and competitive actions.
- Use low-cost "disruptive intellectual assets" to lay a foundation for future disruptive innovation and to mitigate disruptive threats.

Notes

1. Jeff Lindsay and Mike Hopkins, "From Experience: Disruptive Innovation and the Need for Disruptive Intellectual Asset Strategy," *Journal of Product Innovation Management*, in press, 2009.
2. Helen Gustafson and Jonathan Chester, *Hanky Panky: An Intimate History of the Handkerchief* (Berkeley, CA: Ten Speed Press, 2002), 9.
3. Clayton M. Christensen, *The Innovator's Dilemma* (Boston: Harvard Business School Press, 1997).
4. Clayton M. Christensen and Michael E. Raynor, *The Innovator's Solution* (Boston: Harvard Business School Press, 2003).
5. Clayton M. Christensen, Scott D. Anthony, and Erik A. Roth, *Seeing What's Next* (Boston: Harvard Business School Press, 2004).
6. Clayton M. Christensen, "Innovation in the Connected Economy," *Perspectives on Business Innovation, Cap Gemini Ernst & Young Center for Business Innovation*, Issue 5 (2000): 6–12, www.leader-values.com/content/detail.asp?ContentDetailID=37 (accessed Dec. 21, 2006).
7. Christensen, *Innovator's Dilemma.*
8. Michael Urlocker, "Spend Three Minutes to Become More Competitive than Sony," *Urlocker On Disruption Blog*, www.ondisruption.com/my_weblog/2007/02/give_me_three_m.html (accessed March 13, 2007).

9. Ted Leavitt, "Marketing Myopia," *Harvard Business Review*, 38 (July–August 1960): 24-47.

10. Christensen and Raynor, *Innovator's Solution*, 178–183.

11. Clayton M. Christensen and Michal Overdorf, "Meeting the Challenge of Disruptive Change," *Harvard Business Review on Innovation* (Boston: Harvard Business School Publishing, 2001), 103–129.

12. The term "business method patents" is a loosely defined term that has become widely used since the Federal Circuit ruled in 1998 and 1999 that methods of doing business are not unpatentable *per se*. The term comprises many systems and processes involving transactions of information, especially computer-assisted methods such as e-commerce techniques, but can also refer to more general systems. See, for example, Gregory A. Stobbs, *Business Method Patents* (New York: Aspen Law and Business, 2002).

13. Kitty Wan-Ting Chiu, "Commercialization of Disruptive Technologies: Revisiting the Value Network Theory and the Failures of Leading Incumbents in the Hard Disk Drive Industry," draft of a paper from the Department of Strategic and International Management, London Business School, June 21, 2007, www.value-networks.com/howToGuides/VN%20Theory.pdf (accessed June 27, 2008).

CHAPTER

20

Further Guidance for Management

Much of the guidance we offer to management has already been introduced in previous chapters. Here we offer some additional thoughts that may strengthen efforts to build an ecosystem of innovation that can overcome some critical fatigue factors.

Each corporation has an "Innovation Spectrum™" as shown in Exhibit 20.1 in which elements ranging from the "tangible" (e.g., contractual, formalized, or physical) to the intangible affect the ability to innovate. These can also be grouped in four categories: (1) Strategy and Vision, (2) Culture and Motivation, (3) Organization (People and Processes), and (4) External Customers, Markets, and Systems. We show this to hint at some of the additional elements that can be considered to strengthen corporate innovation. A detailed discussion of the Innovation Spectrum™ is beyond the scope of this book, but we will consider a few energizing factors related to culture, organization, and relationships with external entities.

Creating a Culture that Inspires Inventors and Innovators

While many books have been written on how corporations can strengthen innovation, here we offer a few thoughts based on our awareness of innovation fatigue factors and their impact on individuals

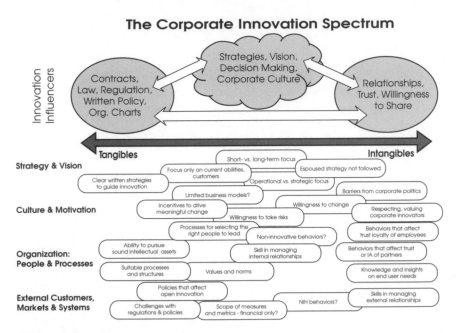

Exhibit 20.1   The Corporate Innovation Spectrum™

in corporations, large and small. Large companies, though, deserve particular attention here for their cultures can easily gravitate toward innovation fatigue, with challenges that are often missed by consultants advising top executives. The consultants, after all tend to gain information from the same sources management uses and are highly motivated to tell management things they want to hear. Without the benefit of new perspectives, innovation fatigue can remain a chronic undiagnosed problem even when top leaders feel they are on the cutting edge of innovation.

The success that drives some companies to become giants can also bring resilient institutional barriers to innovation. Large companies naturally tend to implement complex processes and grow bureaucracies where individual needs are easily overlooked. The tangible aspects may look healthy—solid physical resources, detailed formalized processes, good funding—but the intangibles such as relationships of trust and the willingness to share may be weak. Failure to see the employees as individuals, especially in the innovation organs of the company, can lead to atrophy and innovation fatigue as crucial intangibles erode (see Chapter 7, for example).

The Horn of Innovation™ model (Chapter 2) also applies. Seeing innovation as all about process and not about the artistry of innovators is like preparing for a brass quintet performance by focusing on obtaining top-notch brass without concern for who will provide the "buzz" that generates the music. If talented musicians aren't interested in playing, even the world's best brass will leave the audience disappointed.

Jean-Pierre Garnier, CEO of GlaxoSmithKline, recognized related problems in the pharmaceutical industry, observing that scientists were buried in large corporate pyramids where decision-making processes slowed, communication was hindered, and scientists promoted into management lost their scientific edge. In the late 1990s, he began an experiment by breaking R&D into multiple focused centers where research scientists were given more freedom and recognition. Only two or three layers of management exist between scientists working on the bench and the CEOs of each center. Passionate, gifted scientists were chosen as "product finders" who must be protected, encouraged, and supported. One of his goals is "inspiring and nurturing leaders who are also accomplished scientists" as well as to inspire motivated, driven scientists on the bench to succeed. He recognizes that scientists care a great deal about external recognition and has enabled this, but also has implemented financial incentives to reward those who assist in important advances. These are part of a comprehensive effort to rebuild GSK's R&D engines, creating a cultural shift that will return high productivity to R&D.[1]

Changing a culture can be painful. The first step must be to recognize when there is a problem. When top leaders are removed from the innovation centers of the corporation, unaware of what the product developers, scientists, engineers, or marketing teams behind innovation are experiencing, they may rely solely on glowing reports from other leaders who are removed from the reality of innovation fatigue, when it exists. Some incumbent leaders have had the awareness—or the listening ear—to recognize that innovation problems have crept into the corporation, and some have been visionary enough to implement a successful culture shift. Too frequently, though, the cultural barriers to innovation are buttressed by the priorities and behaviors of management, and require some dramatic stimulus for change to occur. This can occur with a change in top management, a business crisis faced by the company, or competitive surprises analogous to the Soviet Union's successful launch of Sputnik which shocked the United States into action. Many corporations will face their own "Sputnik moment," but many will respond with cost cutting or other non-strategic changes rather than rising to the occasion and heading to the moon with renewed, targeted innovation.

Many subtleties in an organization can contribute to a culture of innovation. One of these, for example, is managing rejection. Inventors know that most of their ideas will fail, but there is a human side to innovation failure which needs to be considered. Many times R&D personnel feel that they throw their work over a wall and wait in vain to hear anything from the other side. When invention disclosures are rejected without communication to the inventors, as often happens, inventors feel isolated and discouraged. Further, a valuable teaching opportunity is lost.

In our past efforts at Kimberly-Clark Corp. to strengthen intellectual asset systems, we encouraged intellectual asset review boards to communicate openly with inventors regarding decisions. We encouraged groups to invite inventors into review board meetings to interact with the decision makers and better learn what screening criteria were used. We also required the boards to have written strategy statements explaining what kind of invention disclosures were being sought to fulfill current strategies. Clear communication helped inventors understand the process, refine their approach, and align their efforts more closely with corporate needs. We feel that was an important step in reducing barriers and fatigue factors. It's one of many steps that can contribute to a culture of innovation, and that helps channel and adjust the "buzz" of innovators to deliver output in tune with corporate needs and the marketplace.

Case Study: Multidisciplinary Innovators in the Oil and Gas Industry and the Rise of Inficomm

While innovators with multiple skills will be increasingly valued in our forecast of the future, companies can use existing resources to gain some Da Vinci-like benefits by actively promoting open innovation to bring different skills into their innovation engines. The oil and gas industry provides an instructive case in point.

According to the International Energy Agency, the global energy demand will increase by 50 percent by year 2030. To keep up with such a demand growth, technological innovations are required at a rapid pace. However, one serious problem arises: who will do the work?

With relatively low energy prices during the period from about 1980 to 2000, the oil industry witnessed two decades of minimum investment in new oil and gas projects. This was terribly shortsighted in light of the industrialization of China and India which has driven global energy demand. Also during this time, the industry went through numerous mergers and acquisitions with half a million jobs lost for "efficiency." In the past few years, as energy prices rose dramatically, the oil and gas industry faced increasing needs to expand exploration and production with a drastically reduced workforce. In U.S. universities, enrollment in relevant fields eroded for years. For example, over 12,000 students were enrolled in petroleum engineering in 1984 but there were only 2,000 in 1997.

Now the industry is faced with a massive manpower challenge to cope with growth fueled by global energy demand. Some chemical engineering departments have struggled to maintain faculty members who are being lured into lucrative R&D positions in energy companies. Companies that recruit chemical engineers are finding surprisingly high competition for top students due to a surging demand in the oil and gas sector. Unfortunately, the small supply on the market of those with traditional energy-related training cannot meet the demand for highly talented individuals to support growth and innovation. The need for *innovation via technology development* to meet the existing and future challenges in energy requires additional manpower not readily available through traditional channels.

To find the innovators of the future, the oil and gas industry has been forced—perhaps fortuitously—to find innovation talent in new fields. One could argue that the expansion to numerous other fields was logical on its own and would have happened even if there had been a glut of qualified manpower in traditional fields, but we think necessity helped foster at least a little of the inventive hiring we have seen. By design or necessity, the oil and gas industry is beginning to reap the benefits of aggressive multidisciplinary innovation. Experts are now crossing borders and bringing new technologies, skills, and perspectives to an industry that is becoming far more high-tech and innovative than the public recognizes.

An instructive example is the development of a sophisticated data system for oil drilling that arose through collaboration between Chevron Corporation and Los Alamos National Laboratory.

The Future Oil Field and Need for Data

As reservoir management becomes increasingly complex, the need for real time data is also increasing. Companies across the industry recognize this and have launched efforts to create a data-rich and highly networked oil field. A major obstacle in this area is the ability to obtain accurate and continuous data from downhole (from the lengthy bore drilled into the earth) during production. Oil wells are difficult environments for communication equipment, and existing technologies are challenged by several factors such as bandwidth, battery life, reliability, and the need to cease production to take measurements among others. In spite of considerable efforts and many innovative products, getting real time data from downhole is still a significant struggle for well operators.

Solutions from an Unexpected Place

One day, a Chevron engineer turned to his former associates at Los Alamos National Laboratory (LANL) with the hope that outsiders might offer a solution to the problem. Engineers from Chevron and open-minded scientists from LANL started working together in order to find the common ground. LANL had worked on and developed a technology called Inficomm (short for Infinite Communication) to address the complex communication needs of the battlefield.

Inficomm is based on the concept of "modulated reflectance" where wireless communication is carried out with electrical power needed only at one end of the communication chain. At the other end, transmitter or receivers can be entirely passive, drawing their energy from the electro-magnetic broadcast of a single source. The approach is essentially a high-tech version of a mirror sending Morse code via reflected sunlight. By diligently delving into the science of electro-magnetic propagation, the team realized that underlying principle of Inficomm would indeed apply to the downhole environment. This is where science and engineering started converging.

Following a two year collaborative development effort, Inficomm has demonstrated the ability to transmit complex data and has gone through multiple field tests. The sensors are battery free, wireless, and have demonstrated operating lifetimes exceeding industry standard systems by orders of magnitude. Much intellectual property has been created and efforts are underway to fully commercialize

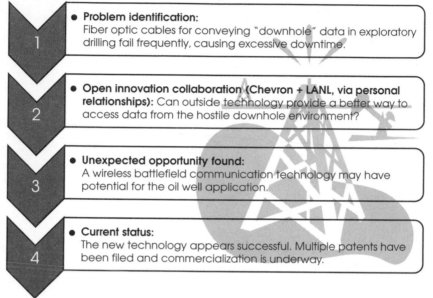

Drilling for OI Success
An Example from Chevron

1 ● **Problem identification:**
Fiber optic cables for conveying "downhole" data in exploratory drilling fail frequently, causing excessive downtime.

2 ● **Open innovation collaboration (Chevron + LANL, via personal relationships):** Can outside technology provide a better way to access data from the hostile downhole environment?

3 ● **Unexpected opportunity found:**
A wireless battlefield communication technology may have potential for the oil well application.

4 ● **Current status:**
The new technology appears successful. Multiple patents have been filed and commercialization is underway.

Exhibit 20.2   Chevron successfully applied multidisciplinary open innovation to solve a costly problem

the system. This successful example of multidisciplinary OI is summarized in Exhibit 20.2.

Open Innovation as an Energizing Factor: Completing the OI Circuit

Open innovation (OI), the system of opening your innovation pipeline to consider external inventions and technologies, has been the key to success for many companies and for entire industries. However, OI can contribute to innovation fatigue when it is implemented poorly. OI done right can be one of the greatest energizing factors of all, adding energy to a company's inventors and to the entire corporation. For this energy to flow, the circuit of open innovation must also be properly completed.

At the CoDev 2008 conference on open innovation,[2] chaired by Cheryl Perkins, we met Dr. Scott Rickert, CEO of NanoFilm (Valley View, Ohio) and one of the keynote speakers. In an interview with

Jeff, Dr. Rickert described what was happening at this conference as "the hope of America." We found his words to capture the vision of what OI can do not just for a company, but for a nation:

> What other country would you see this kind of conference taking place? What you see happening here is our secret weapon that can keep America strong in the marketplace of the world. We know how to partner, we want to partner, we love to partner. And it's the key skill that will help this nation become greater.

To be sure, open innovation is now catching on in a variety of nations, and in the future Dr. Rickert and we anticipate open innovation conferences around the world. But the theories, skills, and mindset that can turn open innovation into a powerhouse of economic success have strong roots in North America. Those roots are especially deep in the pharmaceutical industry.

In the late 1990s and early 2000s, Schwarz Pharma's dramatic rise to success illustrates the pioneering implementation of OI as a matter of deliberate and aggressive strategy by a visionary company. Long before the term "open innovation" was circulating in business schools and the press, Schwarz Pharma embraced a model of open innovation that they referred to as "search and development."[3] Schwarz recognized that the growing costs of regulatory approval for new drugs coupled with the increasingly small odds that any compound could become a useful drug would limit the ability of the small company to succeed in the marketplace. They didn't have thousands of scientists to explore compounds, but there were thousands of scientists at biotechs and start-ups developing and screening compounds. To succeed, they would become a niche branded company, focusing on neurology and urology, where there were unmet needs in the marketplace with abundant but fragmented R&D efforts that could be exploited. Schwarz believed its model was best suited for mid-sized companies like it with less than 5,000 employees. Klaus Veitinger, President and CEO of Schwarz Pharma, Inc., a wholly owned affiliate of Schwarz Pharma, wrote that such companies should no longer be constrained by internal discovery, but should expand to a worldwide scope in finding outside discoveries. It was a model built largely on open innovation, coupled with internal added-value as Schwarz brought its corporate resources to bear in developing and marketing the drugs that others invented.

Schwarz employees weren't about to be laid off because the company was looking outside. Instead, they were about to become far more productive, involved, and rewarded by turning externally mined rough stones into polished gems. Knowing what was wanted and why, Schwarz employees were able to screen opportunities, develop the right relationships, and forge valuable partnerships that led to a series of successful drugs.

With good IP, a sound OI strategy, and proper execution, Schwarz completed the circuit of innovation and unlocked vast profits in the marketplace. Schwarz's market cap went from $500 million to $5 billion in a few years, when it was acquired by UCB Group in Brussels.[4] Their success was not built on one chance discovery of a blockbuster drug, but followed directly from a strategy "which holds that a mid-sized company should never be constrained by internal discovery" and which takes advantage of "the fragmentation of drug discovery," reducing research risk by tapping into the flow of new ideas harvested through global search and development.

The evolution of open innovation, unfortunately, has come at a time when many companies are downplaying the role of internal expertise. Some companies approach open innovation as a way to cut jobs in R&D. However, for OI to be most effective, internal expertise is added to external technology to create further innovation. Closed—as in shut-down—internal R&D does not facilitate OI, and may deprive it of its potential. The companies doing the best OI also have some of the best internal innovators, and are quick to bring them on board when outside technologies are being considered. Value-added OI with contributions from engaged, empowered, and energized internal innovators involved must be the model for future success.

Open Innovation Fatigue Revisited: The Persistence of Closed Innovation

Just as "innovation" can become an overused mantra without substance, "open innovation" can suffer the same fate. It's increasingly popular to speak of open innovation, but many of the same "not invented here" fatigue factors and other barriers remain firmly in place in some companies. For open innovation to succeed, it must fit within a culture that actually values innovation. Innovators within as well as outside the corporation can work together to create synergy, rather than simply importing as-is technology—something competitors can do just as well.

Close associates of one major Fortune 500 company told us this:

> Our leaders often told us how we were celebrating Open Innovation. This seemed to be a code word for decreasing the reliance on our technical community, for decreasing R&D headcount, for outsourcing R&D, and for spending more money on marketing rather than innovating.

Unfortunately, this is not unusual. Failure of management to understand the potential of their own employees results in misguided outsourcing efforts, not recognizing that lower-cost groups with similar technical skills may not have the company loyalty, passion to innovate, the market experience, and the skills necessary to deliver the innovation that could best exploit corporate competencies and provide a competitive edge. It is too easy to see one's employees solely in terms of costs on a balance sheet, not recognizing their value. Part of the difficulty is failure to consider the numerous transactions of intangibles that employees may provide.

The intangibles of a corporation—its know-how, knowledge, relationships with partners and customers, loyalty, reputation, etc.—can provide far more value than the tangible assets, as Baruch Lev,[5] Verna Allee,[6] and others have shown. However, intangibles are poorly tracked and evaluated using traditional accounting techniques and organization charts or maps, and thus may be undervalued (though the contributions of brand recognition and other intangibles may be greatly overvalued in some cases). Recognizing the network of relationships and exchanges of intangibles created by the technical community and other groups within a corporation is essential in understanding and fostering value creation. The internal and external ecosystems around a company's innovator community, for example, should be understood to more fully nurture a culture of innovation and collaboration. In our work with organizations, we have found great value in applying Value Network Analysis and related tools toward this end.[7]

We recommend training employees, including management, to understand the benefits of outside connectivity, especially in the technical community. Provide rewards, visibility, and perks to motivate open innovation thinking. Encourage senior R&D staff to give presentations at universities, be guest lecturers, participate in forums and conferences, and look for synergistic relationships. Encourage them to read one of our favorite books on these topics, *Never Eat Alone* by Keith Ferrazzi.[8]

OI is not about simply sending out scouts. The real opportunities in open innovation are when creative minds—scouts, researchers, managers—look for what can be created by coupling internal capabilities with external resources. External technology plus internal inventiveness provides the most dramatic benefits from open innovation efforts.

Traditional closed internal innovation often runs parallel but unconnected to OI efforts. For OI to be most valuable, there must be value added through synergy and innovation from within. Internal innovators must be kept in the loop and allowed to add value to external innovation for there to be true competitive advantage to OI. Otherwise, the external innovation can be exploited by competitors just as well.

Corporate Energizer: Communities of Practice to Support Innovation

One of the smartest approaches a corporation can take to re-energize their innovation community is to create one or more communities of practice in areas of interest such as intellectual assets or new product development. At Kimberly-Clark, an important step forward in the late 1990s was the formation of the Intellectual Property Chapter. As a community of practice, it serves as a forum for anyone interested in intellectual asset issues. The legal team, managers, R&D staff, new product developers and other prospective innovators came together for training, discussion, and problem solving. It led to the institution of patent facilitators within K-C with formal career tracks and strengthened roles in the corporation, and led to a variety of recommendations for policy changes and other initiatives to strengthen innovation at K-C. Over a decade later, we understand it still plays a valued role.

Another example of successful communities of practice comes from the oil and gas industry. Royal Dutch Shell has linked 13 communities of practice with involvement of more than 10,000 users. Shell's Exploration and Production business estimates that it realizes at least $200M benefits annually due to community-driven knowledge-sharing initiatives.[9]

University Considerations

Some of our guidance to corporate managers may also apply to university administrators. Recalling the "Horn of Innovation™" model of Chapter 2, university innovators need to be included in the feedback loop and be actively involved in the process of commercialization. Robert Litan, Lesa Mitchell, and E.J. Reedy of the Kauffman Foundation make a related point in their working paper, "Commercializing University Innovations: A Better Way."[10] They argue that professors, via their expertise and networks, will often be more capable of recognizing the commercial opportunities of their technology than Technology Transfer Office (TTO) employees, and thus must be more fully included in the process of licensing and commercialization. They propose a variety of models that may be considered, including one of giving university inventors "free agency" status to pursue commercialization through the TTO or via other routes.

We favor models that keep inventors included and part of the iterative feedback loop of commercialization, preferably with aligned incentives between inventors, administrators, outside partners, and others. For aligned incentives, for example, innovation-related metrics may well be considered in criteria for tenure.

Student inventors are sometimes overlooked in crafting policies pertaining to intellectual property and innovation at universities. Much of the innovation from universities is driven by the creativity of students in collaboration with professors, but in some cases student contributions have been ignored and credit misallocated. Ensuring that the contributions of students, staff, and faculty are all fairly recognized and rewarded should be a leading concern of those seeking to guide university culture and policies.

Other university-related recommendations for policymakers are provided in Chapter 24.

Notes

1. Jean-Pierre Garnier, "Rebuilding the R&D Engine in Big Pharma," *Harvard Business Review* 86, no. 5 (May 2008): 68–76.
2. Organized by the Management Roundtable, Chicago, Illinois. The CoDev 2008 conference was held in Scottsdale, Arizona, Jan. 21–23, 2008.

3. Klaus Veitinger, "Midsized Players—A Model for the 21st Century," *Pharmaceutical Executive*, Oct. 1998, 86–94.
4. Schwarz Pharma AG is currently owned by UCB Group in Brussels.
5. Baruch Lev, *Intangibles: Management, Measurement, and Reporting* (Washington, D.C.: Brookings Institute Press, 2001).
6. Verna Allee, *The Future of Knowledge* (Philadelphia: Butterworth-Heinemann, 2003).
7. Jeff Lindsay, "The Cosmic Org Chart Is Broken: Dark Energy, Dark Matter, and the Analogy to Intangibles in Business Ecosystems," *Sharp Innovation Blog (SharpIP.com)*, March 7, 2009, http://sharpip.blogspot.com/2009/03/cosmic-org-chart-is-broken-dark-energy.html (or http://tinyurl.com/sharpip).
8. Keith Ferrazzi, *Never Eat Alone* (New York: Doubleday, 2005).
9. R. McDermott, "Nurturing Three-Dimensional Communities of Practice: How to get the most out of human networks," *Knowledge Management Review* (Fall 1999) and S. Haimila, "Shell Creates Communities of Practice," *KMWorld Magazine* (Feb. 19, 2001).
10. Robert Litan, Lesa Mitchell, and E.J. Reedy, "Commercializing University Innovations: A Better Way," working paper, National Bureau of Economic Research, April 2007, http://sites.kauffman.org/pdf/NBER_0407.pdf (accessed Nov. 22, 2008).

CHAPTER

21

Da Vinci in the Boardroom?

Exhibit 21.1   Da Vinci's "Vitruvian Man" symbolizes the well-rounded, well-connected, visionary innovator whose voice can help guide strategy and policy at high levels

Adding Value to Open Innovation, or, New Lessons from the Renaissance

We have previously discussed the need for innovators to follow Da Vinci's example of developing multidisciplinary skills and healthy ecosystems of connections to others. Now we address corporations in a call for "Da Vinci in the boardroom." Da Vinci? Is that practical? Yes, we think so, but perhaps not for the Da Vinci taught in grade school.

Our call does not contemplate clones of the most singular genius of all time, but multidisciplinary masters of innovation, and more specifically, masters of what we call Added Value Open Innovation (AVOI). We'll add a little spice by drawing upon modern controversy over the works of Da Vinci and the rise of the Renaissance—not from *The Da Vinci Code*, but from the work of an amateur historian, Gavin Menzies, author of *1434: The Year a Magnificent Chinese Fleet Sailed to Italy and Ignited the Renaissance*.[1] Menzies argues (some say "speculates") that massive Chinese fleets of large ships sailed and mapped the world long before Columbus, Magellan, and other European explorers set sail. He argues that a visit of the Chinese fleet to Italy in 1434 brought a massive infusion of knowledge about the globe into elite European circles that inspired and even enabled "discovery" and exploration of other lands. The claims regarding Chinese fleets are not accepted by many historians. However, Menzies has found interesting evidence about possible sources for some of the brilliant works of Da Vinci and his predecessors.

Whether it came to Europe via a massive Chinese fleet in 1434, from Arab sailors or travelers on land, the Renaissance may have been helped along by the world's first mass-produced book—not the Gutenberg Bible, but the *Nong Shu*, printed in 1313 by Chinese author Wang Zhen. Wang Zhen is the apparent inventor of the world's first wooden moveable type printing press[2] (moveable type printing *per se* had its origins, of course, in earthenware moveable type from Chinese inventor Bi Shen three centuries earlier). The *Nong Shu* is replete with drawings and descriptions of practical mechanical devices, agricultural tools and methods, architecture, and scenes from everyday life.

Scholars had previously recognized that Da Vinci drew upon (literally and figuratively) the works of Francesco di Giorgio Martini (1439–1502). Di Giorgio described a parachute similar to Da Vinci's, as well as numerous mechanical devices, pumps and hydraulics systems, mills, cranes, and a large number of the other topics treated by Da Vinci. Di Giorgio prepared hundreds of drawings that bear remarkable resemblance to many of the drawings in the *Nong Shu*, according to Menzies. Da Vinci created more masterful three-dimensional drawings and many brilliant improvements, but his role as sole originator may need revision. Toothed wheels and gears, pulleys, ratchets, camshafts, and numerous other devices Da Vinci described could have Chinese origins, either in the *Nong*

Shu or elsewhere. The impressive paddle boat, for example, dates to 418 A.D., over a thousand years before Da Vinci's. The same may hold for the dismountable cannon and other gunpowder weapons, mortars, suspension bridges, and many Da Vinci themes.

Of course, independent invention often occurs without one inventor borrowing from another, but Menzies points to the published work of Di Giorgo that Da Vinci possessed, filled with notes and drawings from Da Vinci in the margins. Menzies finds nearly slavish copying of elements of the *Nong Shu* in the less inventive work of Di Giorgio.

If Menzies is correct, then the mysteriously high concentration of talent in Tuscany at the beginning of the Renaissance is not so much because "God waved a magic wand" over that blessed area, but because an infusion of advanced knowledge from China allowed brilliant men in an innovative culture to make use of and improve technologies acquired from outside sources. In other words, the Renaissance was driven by Added Value Open Innovation (AVOI). Some critics of Menzies' point to the rich wealth of knowledge and maritime expertise of the Arabs (who also had contact with China) as a more likely means for infusing foreign knowledge into Italy to help drive the Renaissance. In either case, we suggest the Renaissance may have been driven more by open innovation rather than a few rare geniuses on their own—nurtured by a decisively pro-innovation culture.

The innovative culture of Italy was largely enabled by the wealth of the Medicis, the powerful bankers and merchants of Florence who generously supported the advancement of knowledge.

A handful of brilliant minds given access to outside riches of knowledge and abundant encouragement from industrial and financial giants was a recipe for one of the world's most important eras of innovation. It's a recipe for success that we believe can be created again, though perhaps to a much smaller degree—thus our call for Da Vinci in the boardroom.

Da Vinci and Open Innovation

Menzies argues that Da Vinci was more a multidisciplinary improver and adapter than a master originator, though still a genius and master of innovation. Some Da Vinci fans may be discouraged by this tentative new perspective, but there is a hopeful aspect to it.

A nation or organization can have an outpouring of innovation not by finding an almost supernatural genius, but by a more practical "Da Vinci" process:

1. Create a culture of innovation within the organization, in which talented, multidisciplinary innovators are recruited, nurtured, and encouraged.
2. Pursue open innovation, gaining access to the rich sources of invention from outside.
3. Encourage internal innovators to add value to open innovation's fruits.
4. Bring the results to the market and let the world (and the organization—including the internal innovators) reap the benefits.

This approach does not require finding the world's leading genius, but bringing together multiple innovators to create a composite Da Vinci capable of building on wide-ranging external technologies and various business models to craft fruitful added-value innovations. This process can lead to a more efficient and targeted pursuit of the next great inventions that are "in the air," ripe for harvesting, similar to what Malcolm Gladwell observes in his analysis of Intellectual Ventures' inventing efforts.[3]

Others have discussed IP strategy in books with titles like *Edison in the Boardroom* and *Einstein in the Boardroom*. Based on our understanding of emerging needs in business, and recognizing the increasing importance of multidisciplinary skills, we call for "Da Vinci in the Boardroom." This is also a call for increased recognition of the value that internal innovators can deliver, knowing that many will be at their best when stimulated by external bounties of intellectual assets that they can adapt to meet business needs.

Notes

1. Gavin Menzies, *1434: The Year a Magnificent Chinese Fleet Sailed to Italy and Ignited the Renaissance* (New York: HarperCollins, 2008).
2. Wikipedia contributors, "Wang Zhen," *Wikipedia*, http://en.wikipedia.org/wiki/Wang_Zhen_(official) (accessed Oct. 28, 2008).
3. Malcolm Gladwell, "In the Air: Who Says Big Ideas Are Rare?," *The New Yorker*, May 12, 2008, 50–60.

CHAPTER 22

The Impact of Financials on Innovation

Aparamount factor affecting innovation is the financials of an organization. The very existence of a company and the job of every employee is determined, at least in part, by that all-important collection of reports, graphs, and numbers.

We will examine how the business world has traditionally measured an organization's financial performance and discuss some of the newer methods which are being developed to calculate corporate value and growth including intangible assets. We'll also discover

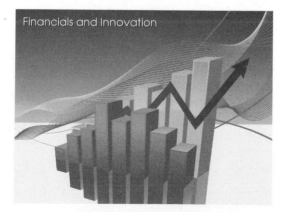

Financials and Innovation

Exhibit 22.1   Financials: what impact do they have on innovation?

some of the most common ways these financials can impact the development of innovation—not always in a negative way. Finally, we'll share some ideas for making positive changes.

How to Measure Financials and Their Impact

Traditional Financial Metrics

There always has been and always will be a need for some standardization in any reporting dealing with money. Accounting standards allow those who use industry financials to more easily utilize the results and more accurately compare apples to apples. Today's standards are usually referred to as "Generally Accepted Accounting Principles" (GAAP), developed and updated by an authoritative organization.

Here's a quick history lesson. The Securities Act of 1933 and The Security Exchange Act of 1934 required publicly-traded companies to file certain reports with the Securities and Exchange Commission (SEC). This U.S. regulatory agency has the authority to create and enforce accounting standards, but has always encouraged the private sector to develop its own guidelines. Since 1939, several national industry groups have been formed to deal with specific issues and began to formulate the GAAP. In 1973, the Financial Accounting Standards Board (FASB) was established as part of an independent organization designed to issue statements of standards and define the Generally Accepted Accounting Principles. The SEC has given authoritative support to the FASB standards. One historic revision to corporate financial metrics came about when Congress passed the Sarbanes-Oxley Act in 2002. Based on all the issues raised by several major accounting scandals (Enron, WorldCom, etc.), this law required many expensive, complicated measurement changes for the largest public companies and threatened serious penalties for failure to comply as of 2004.

Beyond the private sector, the Government Accounting Standards Board (GASB) was formed in 1984 to set standards for local and state financial reports. In addition, the International Accounting Standards Board (IASB) became the newest group encouraging worldwide cooperation in developing consistent international accounting principles in 2001. Both the GASB and the IASB follow the same model as the FASB.

Financials traditionally have offered an accountant's-eye-view of an organization's economic performance. Whether issued monthly, quarterly, or annually, the measurements used to analyze results usually begin with the basic income reports, balance sheets, and profit-loss comparisons. Depending on the size and complexity of the organization, some dig deeper to examine return on investment (ROI), capital expenditure, market penetration, market capitalization, total shareholder return, economic value added, the price-earning ratio, industry benchmark comparisons, and various others.

Many economic experts and corporate leaders have recognized the need for some evolution. Lowell L. Bryan, Harvard MBA and Director of McKinsey and Company in New York, explains it well. After criticizing the industrial-age methods used in measuring financial performance, he points out this gap:

> Companies fill their annual reports with information about how they use capital but fail to reflect sufficiently on their use of the "thinking-intensive" people who increasingly drive wealth creation in today's digital economy. . . . [I]t's time to recognize that financial performance increasingly comes from returns on talent, not on capital.[1]

Profit Per Employee

One newer financial metric that continues to gain favor as an improved method for measuring company performance in today's business world is called "Profit per Employee."[2] Rather than focusing on returns on capital, this measure calls attention to returns on talent, which implies that companies should emphasize creation and use of intangibles, which are often the key to growth in our knowledge economy. Bryan suggests that this financial metric is a robust, conservative measure that can easily support benchmarking between corporations:

> Profit per employee therefore focuses companies on intangible-intensive value propositions and, in turn, on talented people— those who, with some investment, can produce valuable intangibles.

In their book, *Mobilizing Minds: Creating Wealth from Talent in the 21st Century*, Bryan and Claudia Joyce report findings based on the "profit-per-employee" metric. Their research involved information from hundreds of top companies (by market value) in many industry categories. While the top 30 companies employed thousands more people on average, they showed a much higher profit per employee ratio than the next 30 companies. Economists would traditionally predict that more employees (meaning more complex internal structure) would result in a lower profit per employee, just as Bryan and Joyce found using 1984 financials. However, the study of more current numbers—especially from more organizations with more workers with jobs requiring subjective thinking and problem solving—suggested something very different for the 21st century.

> Suddenly we could see why some companies could earn higher profits per employee: The value of thinking-intensive workers is derived from the value of their minds—the ideas they develop and the decisions they make—and from the intangible by-products of that work, such as knowledge, reputations, and relationships they create.
>
> This, of course, helped confirm our earlier research, which had indicated that intangibles had become more valuable due to changes in the global economy. The value of such "mind work" is not highly correlated just to the volume of hours worked but also to quality. The economic conditions of the 21st century are enabling some companies to create wealth by employing ever larger numbers of thinking—intensive workers who translate mind work into high-quality, high-return intangibles.[3]

The Profit per Employee metric yields new insight into the continuing financial success of the top companies, and provides a more complete method for measuring performance and understanding the value of intangible assets.

Innovation Metrics

More than ever, companies are creating wealth by transforming intangibles—knowledge, research, new product development, people/relationships, reputation, creativity—into tangible products, brands, software, and patents. Although there is a growing acceptance of intangible capital value and much "lip service" given to innovation, these can be very difficult to account for. There is

growing interest in improved innovation metrics to strengthen decision making, including metrics for innovation. Unfortunately, many
corporations do little to measure innovation.[4]

Robert Tucker, president of The Innovation Resource, offers
this overview[5]:

> The best metrics, I believe, are stunningly simple and carefully
> thought through before implementation. The more complex they
> are the more likely they are to be misused . . . or unused . . .

While the specific metrics useful for each organization may
differ, some guidelines apply to all. Tucker offers recommendations
for measuring the innovation process:[6]

- Look at innovation as an end-to-end discipline, a holistic
  process . . . innovation needs to be managed as a discipline. . . .
- Create metrics to measure your progress, but use them for
  comparison purposes, not as a stick to "motivate" compliance.
- Measure your yearly revenue from new products, your success
  rate, your pipeline and your times-to-market. . . .
- Find out what metrics Innovation Vanguard firms are using
  and then choose from that menu the metrics that have the
  most buy-in in your organization.

To that list, we would add a few specific suggestions. Innovation
metrics should really be a "family" of different measurements.
Understand your objectives, and clearly define your innovation
goals. Consider specifics such as:

- Royalty and licensing income from patents
- Percentage of capital invested in innovation
- Percentage of executive time spent on innovation
- Percentage of employees or managers who have received
  training, tools, and methodologies for innovation
- Percentage of product/service or strategic innovation pro-
  jects which have assigned executive sponsors
- Percentage of the R&D community actively participating in
  Community of Practice meetings related to innovation
- Percentage of revenue from products launched in the past
  three years

- The number of new products/services/businesses launched in new markets during the past year
- Existence of formal processes to support innovation
- Number of ideas moving from one stage to another.
- Cycle time for innovations
- Percentage of "outside" vs. "inside" inputs.

Corporate financial performance in relation to the value of intangible assets is still widely under-measured. However, the interest and need is growing stronger. With the continuing efforts to develop purposeful, maintainable, understandable metrics, innovation's value as an engine for creating wealth will be more clearly recognized and encouraged.

How Financials May Hinder Innovation

Tough Times Make Slashing R&D Budgets More Tempting

The most obvious threat to the corporate innovation process comes from a less-than-stellar financial statement. As in times of economic downturn, most companies tend to become more conservative. Executives naturally focus on cost cutting, and innovation teams become threatened. Even in companies committed to innovation, new product development will be scrutinized. Symptoms of innovation fatigue may become apparent. Indeed, as this book goes to press in 2009, we seem many large companies giving in to the easy temptation to slash innovation efforts, while those with more vision recognize this as the time to ramp up innovation for prolonged future success, in spite of the present pain.

The reality is that, without innovation, the status quo may decline rapidly. As we discussed under Fatigue Factor #6, the real return from innovation should not be viewed relative to the status quo, but relative to the decreased revenues that are likely to be faced if innovation is not delivered. The wrong financial metrics often make innovation seem far less essential or attractive than it actually is and exacerbate fatigue for the employees within a corporation.

Even when financial reports are stellar, they can motivate leaders to focus on immediate financial growth rather than development of the long-term capabilities needed for the future.[7] Financial success can sometimes disguise the weakness in innovation facing a company and motivate leaders to focus on core competencies rather than needed new competencies.

Focus on Innovation Can be Lost During Reorganizations or Mergers

The basic ways to create growth are to improve products/services or to expand market share. These are most often achieved through internal organization improvements or through mergers and acquisitions. The challenge of combining different corporate cultures can distract attention from innovation efforts. Further, in many cases, prospective innovators from at least one of the two companies in a merger find the changes to be discouraging, sometimes giving them less voice and influence than they once had in driving innovation.

In one case we know of, the R&D community of a large company was excited with the technological potential brought by a newly acquired company and couldn't wait to begin interacting with the scientists and product developers in the newly acquired company. Scientists in the acquiring company made requests to get involved but the intellectual assets of the newly acquired company were largely sealed off except for one team within the large company due to some obscure internal politics. The synergies in innovation capabilities between the two companies were largely unexplored and much of the talent of the acquired company eventually felt unappreciated and many left. A terrible waste.

The innovation community of the acquiring company should be involved in plans for best realizing synergies with the company being acquired. As with open innovation, acquired capabilities will not realize their potential unless value is added with the help of creative minds within the corporation.

Special attention to innovation is demanded after a merger or acquisition. It requires deliberate efforts and discipline, for the easy default path is to focus on the urgent while even more important but less urgent areas such as innovation are neglected.

How Financials Can Help Drive Innovation

Unlike the executives we discussed earlier who reflect the most common reaction to tough financial feedback ("We have to tighten our belts—Let's cut R&D!"), there is another group who express a more enlightened, positive attitude ("Times are tough—It's more important than ever that we innovate!"). While examining the top 25 organizations in the third annual *BusinessWeek*-Boston Consulting Group ranking of the World's Most Innovative Companies, Jean McGregor observed that the most innovative companies recognized the need to keep innovating and building for the future even during economic downturns.[8] We think Jeff Bezos, CEO of Amazon .com (No.11 on the top 25 list), sums it up well: "Constraints drive innovation."

Good company leaders enjoying positive financials know better than to rest on their laurels. Smart decision-makers facing negative performance results know they simply can't afford to. Strong companies understand that they must value and nurture their creative people even when times are bad, and that tough economic times are times to become well-positioned for future growth. "During a recession, [strong companies] invest," according to Eric Schmidt, chairman and CEO of Google, a leader in innovation.[9] As one example, 3M, with one of the world's most successful cultures of innovation, has kept R&D spending to over 6 percent of sales, even in tough economic times. This has been part of a disciplined plan to achieve goals of 12 to 14 percent earnings per share and double-digit sales growth.[10]

As this book goes to press, we are entering a severe economic crisis. Some companies are on the brink of collapse, but fortunes will be made by some who boldly innovate. During the recession of 1975, a small startup named Microsoft was launched. During the Great Depression, Hewlett-Packard was formed. General Electric was founded during the turbulent panic of 1873. This is not the time to abandon innovation, but to accelerate it while remaining cost effective (this includes use of low-cost IA tools, as discussed in Chapter 18).

While conventional thinking might lead competitors to cut back on innovation when times are rough, the winners of the future will make the short-term sacrifices necessary to ramp up innovation. At a minimum, more good talent will be available to enrich your innovation community. This is precisely the wrong time to shut down internal innovation, as your competitors are likely to do.

Possibilities for Positive Organizational Change

There are a variety of ways positive organizational change can be pursued to create business strategies in which attention to financials can enhance rather than hinder innovation. The Balanced Scorecard approach, for example, is described by Robert S. Kaplan and David P. Norton described in *The Strategy-Focused Organization: How Balanced Scorecard Companies Thrive in the New Environment.* Recognizing the danger that a focus on financial performance metrics can lead managers to make decisions that looked good in the short-term at the expense of achieving long-term goals, Kaplan and Norton propose that companies establish specific financial and strategic objectives, then measure company performance based on tracking the results of both.

Another recent approach with the potential for dramatic change is "Value-Based Management" (VBM) which seeks to overcome the weaknesses of traditional financial metrics. Rather than focusing on improving cost and gross margin, VBM uses "value trees" to identify opportunities for improvement and to create clear benchmarks. Well-implemented VBM projects have often delivered 5 to 15 percent gains in bottom-line results.[11]

Another non-traditional approach is Discovery Driven Planning, based on the work of Rita Gunther McGrath and Ian MacMillan[12], in which the focus is not easy-to-tweak financial projections but the assumptions behind the projections. With the spotlight on the critical assumptions and key uncertainties, management can apply their analytical and decision making skills more effectively. This approach can help ensure that the most important questions are asked and the most critical assumptions are tested. There is still a need to consider costs and returns, but such approaches can at least give more of a fighting chance to significant, game-changing innovation, rather than giving unfair weighting to safe, incremental innovation.

Of course, any program needs to tailored to specific business and innovation systems.

Enhancing Corporate Culture

Corporate culture is an expression of a company's internal climate and outward personality, reflecting its history, values, and traditions. It influences every choice, every business transaction, and every interaction with others. If you aren't sure what your corporate culture is, you need to carefully analyze your environment and define it. Whatever you discover, it's safe to say there will be room for improvement.

In terms of innovation and growth, what do you see when you really take a close and honest look at your organization's corporate culture? Is there an unhealthy political or competitive atmosphere? Is there a "not-invented-here" mindset? Do creative employees feel betrayed? Is the tenuous thread of "the will to share" frayed or broken? Do you sense a tired, "can't-wait-to-get-out-of-here" attitude? Who would want to spend eight to ten hours a day in that kind of setting? On the other hand, do you find a corporate culture that's motivational, encouraging, enjoyable, ethical, or even fun?

Google, for example, describes their corporate culture as being intensely innovative with "a small company feel" in which employees mingle and interact in many ways, where there is little corporate hierarchy and many opportunities to be involved in diverse projects and exciting activities.[13] Is that just corporate hype? We don't think so. Many sources confirm that part of their innovation power comes from the unique culture of innovation they have created. Their approach may not be appropriate for some companies, but many companies have yet to make serious efforts toward improving their cultures to enhance innovation. Too often we hear messages such as, "We don't need incentives for innovation or creation of intellectual assets—it's part of the expectations for our employees." Expecting innovation in an innovation-hostile climate is like expecting rich bounties from a garden you never visit except at harvest time. Even if you sprinkled a few seeds at the beginning of the year, your expectations may not be rooted in reality.

Notes

1. Lowell L. Bryan, "The New Metrics of Corporate Performance: Profit per Employee," *McKinsey Quarterly*, 2007, no. 1, pp. 58–59, www.interknowledgetech.com/profit%20per%20employee.pdf (or http://tinyurl.com/boyxsz) (accessed Oct. 22, 2008).
2. Ibid., pp. 59–61.
3. Lowell L. Bryan and Claudia I. Joyce, *Mobilizing Minds: Creating Wealth from Talent in the 21st Century* (New York: McGraw Hill, 2007).
4. Jessie Scanlon and Reena Jana, "The State of Innovation," *BusinessWeek*, Dec. 19, 2007, www.businessweek.com/innovate/content/dec2007/id20071219_302022.htm (or http://tinyurl.com/d4oa9m) (accessed July 21, 2008).
5. Robert Tucker, *Driving Growth Through Innovation: How Firms are Transforming Their Futures* (New York: Berrett-Koehler Publishers, 2008).

6. Joyce Wycoff, "Innovation Metrics: Embedding Innovation in an Organization's Systems—An interview with Robert Tucker," *Innovation Network Newsletter*, www.triz-journal.com/archives/2003/03/d/04.pdf (accessed Nov. 3, 2008).
7. L. Gary Boomer, "Development or Growth? The Challenge for Firms is the Same As It Is in Public Companies: How Do You Balance Short-Term and Long-Term Goals?", *Accounting Today*, June, 4, 2007.
8. Jena McGregor, "The 25 Most Innovative Companies: Smart Ideas for Tough Times," *BusinessWeek*, April 28, 2008.
9. Ibid.
10. "3M—Where Innovation Rules," *R&D Magazine*, April 2003, http://tinyurl.com/3mgrowth (accessed Oct. 28, 2008).
11. Richard Benson-Armer, Richard Dobbs, and Paul Todd, "Putting Value Back in Value-Based Management," *McKinsey on Finance*, Number 11, Spring, 2004.
12. Rita Gunther McGrath and Ian C. MacMillan, "Discovery-Driven Planning," *Harvard Business Review*, July–Aug. 1995, http://harvardbusinessonline.hbsp.harvard.edu/flatmm/files/95406_b2b.pdf (accessed July 5, 2008).
13. Google, "The Google Culture," www.google.com/intl/en/corporate/culture.html (accessed Nov. 3, 2008).

CHAPTER

23

Guidance to Government and Policy Influencers

External fatigue factors can be the most difficult to change, but to those who can drive change, we offer a few further suggestions.

Listen to the Voice of the Innovator

We have seen how the unexpected consequences of well-intended actions can cause innovators to give up, entrepreneurs to abandon their nation, and corporations to decelerate. Many times, the actions of government have not properly considered the impact on innovation. When government leaders and policy influencers such as NGOs seek guidance on policies and their impact, there is a tendency to turn to the elite and well-connected for guidance. Unfortunately, the fatigue experienced by the real engines of innovation in companies may be unknown to or neglected by those at the top. We feel there must be a concerted effort for government to listen to what we call "the Voice of the Innovator." This is the polyphony of voices we have considered here: the lone inventor; corporate employees tasked with innovation, researchers in the educational community, the entrepreneur seeking to bring a new product or service to the market, and others, including some in senior management with a passion for innovation. Panels and commissions of this kind should be tasked with reporting on the impact of existing legislation and regulation, and should also be queried regarding proposed legislation and regulation. With their perspectives and connections, a broader understanding of unintended consequences may be available. Governing bodies and regulating agencies may make wiser, more informed decisions, and may even have the direction needed to repair harm from previous actions.

Many nations are now experimenting with government positions such as "Minister of Innovation" to help government more actively understand and promote innovation. Such an office could sponsor "voice of the innovator" panels or sessions, and could provide data and reports on innovation at the personal level, not just from the eyes of CEOs and politicians. "Voice of the Innovator" commissions could also provide data collection channels to allow innovators at many levels to share feedback, and lead national discussions on the vitality of innovation.

Existing Framework

Several helpful initiatives already exist in the U.S. that could provide the right kind of forums to initiate reforms and strengthen awareness in government of the burdens that innovators face. The National Science Foundation, for example, is funding research into innovation and technology transfer though a program called Science of Science and Innovation Policy (SciSIP). Founded in 2006, SciSIP supports fundamental research to create tools and models describing the processes through which investments in science and engineering affect society and the economy. While several aspects seem highly academic, their planned activities include developing a community of experts across academic institutions focused on program objectives, including the development of "fruitful policies."[1] Perhaps this could be one route for progress in addressing innovation fatigue. NSF also supports university-industry collaboration through national R&D centers (e.g., Science and Technology Centers) and other programs.

We are also encouraged by initiatives under the U.S. National Academies of Science. For example, the NAS's Board on Science, Technology, and Economic Policy (STEP) is a standing committee serving as a forum for dialogue among economists, technologists, and industrial managers seeking to integrate understanding of scientific, technological, and economic elements in the formulation of national policies affecting the economy. The program centers on macroeconomic and microeconomic variables, and their impact on industry, including manufacturing and service sectors and on scientific and technological advancement. Policy areas considered include trade, human resources, fiscal, research and development, and intellectual property. We believe STEP could work with other agencies or groups to provide added forums for considering the voice of the innovator and addressing the various unintended consequences of various policies that engender fatigue, while seeking to promote encouragement of innovation at all levels.

An organization already actively pursuing the issue of industry-university relationships is the University-Industry Demonstration Partnership (UIDP) which seeks to nourish and expand collaborative partnerships between university and industry in the United States. The UIDP is crafting collaborative experiments on new approaches to sponsored research, licensing arrangements, and the broader strategic elements of a healthy, long-term university-industry relationship. Their work will be increasingly important for industry-university collaboration to be more efficient and profitable. Similar partnerships may be of value in the European Union and for other regions of the world.

Diversity: The Need to Value and Encourage Innovation from Many Sources

Individual creativity and the diversity of human thought is ultimately behind innovation. The inventions and new businesses that shape the future often come from surprising sources, not from the big companies with the most money or from the most famous professors in big-name schools. A farm boy plowing a field in Idaho unlocked the wonder of electronic television; a penniless Serbian immigrant brought the mystery of efficient electric power to the shores of America. In the United States, for example, immigrants are among the most important sources of innovation and entrepreneurism, providing a disproportionately large number of start-ups. About 25 percent of all start-ups are formed by foreign born innovators—35 percent for the semiconductor industry, according to Vivek Wadhwa in a Kauffman Foundation study on U.S. engineering and technology firms started from 1995 to 2005.[2] That study also found that in Silicon Valley, over 50 percent of all start-ups have foreign-born CEOs or chief technology officers. Many of the future innovators of any nation may currently be in other nations, waiting for a chance to share their skills and vision. However, for the United States, Wadhwa warns that immigration policy may be an intractable barrier. He found that many companies have increasing numbers of foreign applicants on their patent applications, often highly skilled workers waiting for visas. Unfortunately, there are far more skilled professionals seeking entry than there available visas under current US law. Only 7 percent of the available visas can go to any one nation under U.S. law.

> So immigrants from countries with large populations like India and China have the same number of visas available (8,400) as those from Iceland and Mongolia. We estimate that more than one-third of the million workers in line for permanent resident visas are from India. This means that immigrants from the most populous countries who file for permanent resident visas today could be waiting indefinitely. In the meantime, they can't start companies or lay deep roots in American society.[3]

Wadhwa points to the threat of a reverse brain drain in which prospective innovators who are trained in the United States grow frustrated with delays in visas and return home. The United States then loses the investment in their education, and faces competition from the nations that receive the benefit of their talent. In this case, immigration policy itself can be an external fatigue factor that drives prospective innovators away from a nation's shores. The recent economic crisis in the US may also work to drive highly educated immigrant innovators away.[4]

In addition to encouraging both native and foreign-born innovators, innovation policies should recognize the diversity of social classes and economic levels contributing to innovation. An example of broad-spectrum efforts to promote innovation comes from India. While the Ministry of Science & Technology is working to strengthen innovation related to universities and educated professionals, there are rich bounties of innovation being harvested at the grassroots level. Dr. Anil K. Gupta, recognizing the extent of innovation across India by farmers, housewives, craftsmen, and others, has launched an internationally acclaimed effort to mine and foster innovation at the grassroots level. Dr. Gupta, often called the "Gandhi of Innovation," organizes volunteers who join him twice a year in walking barefoot through rural sectors of India to identify innovations that can be protected and marketed, to the benefit of inventors who may not have recognized they were inventing.[5] Clever tools for processing garlic or climbing poles have been uncovered; new medicinal uses for plants have been identified; and green technologies for converting biomass to energy have been found. His "Honeybee Network" of interested and supportive parties assists in finding the potential of the innovations they spot (see Sristi.org).

Effective efforts to promote innovation must recognize the importance of diversity and the many classes of individuals who may be next in line to transform our world. Focusing efforts exclusively on any one category may only increase the barriers for some innovators.

Ultimately, efforts to encourage diversity should implicitly advance the important but easily overlooked goal of diversity of thought. A wealth of backgrounds and mindsets can increase the creative potential of a group and expand the network of innovation resources.

Support Innovation with a Global Vision of Success

While multinational corporations have been drawn to emerging economies for low labor costs and manufacturing capacity, the intellectual prowess of these nations is increasingly contributing to innovation—but still less than might be expected, largely due to external fatigue factors such as political complexities, inadequate infrastructure, poorly developed logistics, and inadequate protection for intellectual property.

Today labor costs are rising in these nations. Salaries of programmers in Bangalore, India, a global center for programming outsourcing, are rapidly approaching equality with salaries in the US, leaving India with less of a competitive advantage based on labor alone. The future of emerging economies is not prosperity through low labor costs, but prosperity through innovation, driven by lone inventors and small startups, larger corporate efforts, and collaborative efforts between entrepreneurs, inventors, knowledge workers, universities, and others. Look for increasing numbers of new pharmaceuticals, agricultural advances, and clever consumer products to have origins in China and India. Look for Ph.D.s trained at the finest universities, including China's leading universities or schools like the Indian Institutes of Technology (IITS) as well as prominent schools in the West, to increasingly flock to Asian R&D centers. Look for small smart-ups in nations like Brazil and Russia to find partners with capital who can drive rapid growth. Innovation will increasingly be the lifeblood of many nations. Their success, however, will depend upon government officials and occasionally international agencies who recognize the value of innovation and encourage it.

There is much room for acceleration. For example, China and India rank 49th and 50th in terms of productivity growth, hampered by inadequate infrastructure, and challenging regulatory environments.[6] We expect China and India to both accelerate their rise in innovation and productivity, and if external fatigue factors can be minimized with wise government policies and strengthened IP enforcement, there is no limit to what can be achieved with the resources, intellect, and creativity available. The same applies to many other nations. Mexico, for example, has rapidly growing and sophisticated universities capable of sustaining advanced technological innovation in collaboration with industry, and we have had exciting interactions with business leaders in Mexico who "get it" when it comes to the need for innovation, including open innovation. The opportunities there and in many other nations are great, especially when an innovation-friendly environment can be maintained to give encouragement to local talent and talent that will emigrate to new lands of opportunity.

Sometimes the first steps needed are very simple. In much of Africa, as we saw at the beginning of this book (Chapter 1), a need exists for improved lighting to permit children to become better educated. Charitable innovation such as Empower Playgrounds' electricity-generating playground equipment may trigger the rise of future innovators in these nations. We hope policy makers, development agencies, and charities worldwide will remember that laying the foundation for innovation is vital for the future of every people. Innovation is a delicate creature, though, and needs much to prosper: a culture of innovation, incentives such as enforceable property rights, reduction of burdens from political uncertainty and corruption, and policies that encourage commercial activity. These are seeds worth planting and nurturing for many years.

Thoughts on Removing External Fatigue Factors

Regulators, politicians, and others with influence need to remember that vital innovation can be opposed by a host of factors.

Unwieldy regulatory and taxation burdens, policies that weaken intellectual property rights, bureaucratic and slow patent systems, and anything arbitrary in the protection of rights can discourage innovators and entrepreneurs. The result can be a weakened economy, lost employment, and many other lost opportunities.

We urge politicians to carefully consider the impact of reforms that they may be tempted to make. Bayh-Dole, for example, provided valuable stimulus to university pursuit of IP, but in the long run may discourage private research in the United States relative to foreign universities. Susan Butts provides a variety of suggestions for modifying the Bayh-Dole Act to enhance innovation. Regarding the problem of university insistence on owning IP from collaborative research, she says:

> This problem could be mitigated by the addition of language which further clarifies the intent of Congress relative to university research supported with private, rather than government, funding. In particular, clarification of circumstances under which private and federal funding of related research can exist simultaneously without Bayh-Dole rights and obligations being triggered would be very helpful.[7]

Further, tax rules in the United States and elsewhere should be examined for their impact on innovation (listening to the voice of the innovator at many levels) and revisions made when appropriate. In addition to removing legislative roadblocks that might hinder open innovation, improving the operations and policies of patent systems could do much to promote innovation. Innovative approaches such as the Peer-to-Patent pilot program hold promise for reducing delays while also strengthening patent quality.

Keep It Simple

Sometimes even when government agencies strive to promote innovation, they create unintended barriers through bureaucracy and competing or overlapping programs that can confuse and bewilder. In Britain, there are over 3,000 business support initiatives, but the Business Support Simplification Programme (BSSP) is working to reduce these to 100 by 2010 with all services channeled through a single Business Link office. Innovation support programs are in need of similar simplification, according to a recent report from

Britain's Centre for Cities.[8] The fragmentation of innovation support services and the complexity of these programs has been cited as a major barrier to innovation in the UK, though they are intended to help.[9] Insights from the voice of UK innovators are helping to spur changes that should lead to reduced barriers. The need to simplify support efforts probably applies to many nations around the globe. In the United States, plans to bring innovation into the Cabinet at the executive level of government under President Obama could also provide an opportunity to strengthen and simplify innovation initiatives, as well as provide new opportunities to listen and respond to the voice of the innovator.

Notes

1. National Science Foundation, "Program Solicitation: Science of Science and Innovation Policy (SciSIP)," 2007, www.nsf.gov/pubs/2007/nsf07547/nsf07547.htm (accessed Oct. 25, 2008).
2. Vivek Wadhwa, "Foreign-Born Entrepreneurs: An Underestimated American Resource," Kauffman Foundation, 2008, www.kauffman.org/uploadedFiles/WadhwaTBook09.pdf (see also www.kauffman.org/entrepreneurship/foreign-born-entrepreneurs.aspx) (accessed Nov. 22, 2008).
3. Ibid.
4. Kauffman Foundation, "Kauffman Foundation Study Presents Insights into Why U.S. is Losing Growing Number of Immigrants Who Spur Innovation and Economic Growth," March 2, 2009, http://www.kauffman.org/newsroom/united-states-losing-immigrants-who-spur-innovation-and-economic-growth.aspx (or http://is.gd/n4tU) (accessed March 12, 2009).
5. Correspondence of Anil K. Gupta with Jeff Lindsay, Nov. 2008. See also Sristi org.
6. Nandan M. Nilekani, "Obstacles To Innovation In China And India," *BusinessWeek*, Sept. 25, 2006, www.businessweek.com/magazine/content/06_39/b4002421.htm (or http://tinyurl.com/capv8s) (accessed Sept. 16, 2008).
7. Susan Butts, "Testimony Before the Subcommittee on Technology and Innovation, Committee on Science and Technology, U.S. House of Representatives: Bayh-Dole—The Next 25 Years," July 17, 2007, Washington, DC, http://democrats.science.house.gov/Media/File/Commdocs/hearings/2007/tech/17jul/butts_testimony.pdf (or http://tinyurl.com/bgxw7g) (accessed March 7, 2009).
8. Chris Webber, "Innovation, Science and the City," Center for Cities, Oct. 2008, www.centreforcities.org/assets/files/Innovation%20science%20and%20the%20city.pdf (or http://tinyurl.com/cwebber) (accessed Nov. 14, 2008).
9. B. Perry, T. May and A. Monoghan, *The Ideas Business: the Real Innovation Nation* (London: British Chambers of Commerce 2008), as cited by Webber, "Innovation, Science and the City."

Summary

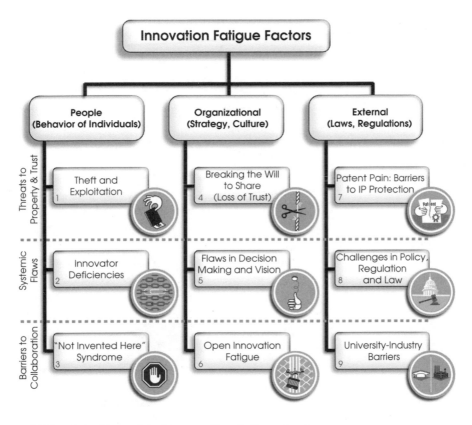

Exhibit 24.1   The grid of innovation fatigue factors

The journey of the innovator and entrepreneur has always been challenging. For many, success comes when others recognize the potential of the person or the technology and take steps to provide, in the word of Thomas Jefferson, "a liberal encouragement." Peers, partners, employers, and regulators can all play a role in providing such encouragement, or can help create fatigue factors that discourage innovation.

We have sought out the voice of the innovator in understanding fatigue factors and ways to overcome them. The successes of some, like Neal Verfuerth at Orion Energy or Paul Rasband and his team at MeadWestvaco that created Vue Technology, provide numerous insights into innovation success. The bittersweet stories of others, like Philo Farnsworth or numerous contemporary inventors and entrepreneurs who remain anonymous in this book, show us the pathos that can befall bright inventors and entrepreneurs when they remain immigrants and second-class citizens in the world of business. Many of them could have had much more success, and done much more for the rest of us, if they had had the right guidance and assistance.

The metaphor of the innovator as an immigrant in a strange land asks us to consider whether we wish to encourage these immigrants to succeed and become an integral part of our economy, or whether we can accept a subservient role for them. We hope that the wall of fatigue factors can be torn down at least enough to allow ingenuity to flourish. Likewise, the metaphor of the "Horn of Innovation™" (Chapter 2) reminds us of the need to keep innovators in the loop, allowing them to hear and sense feedback from the market and to have a hand in what is finally delivered. Thus, their vision and artistry can guide the execution, as sound innovation systems help transform their "buzz" into orchestrated marvels that avoid wasting nearly all of their breath in punishing funnels. Their voice can be heard and transformed into productive innovations that enrich us all.

We have explored a variety of solutions and workarounds for overcoming fatigue factors, and have provided more general energizing factors. We offer these final "Top 5" lists for those who are would-be innovators, organization leaders, and policy makers and influencers in government.

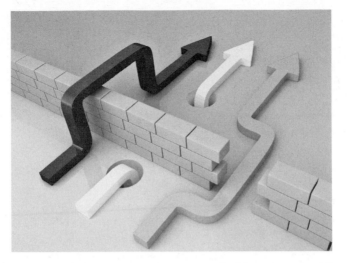

Exhibit 24.2 Diverse approaches are needed to overcome the barriers to innovation success

Top 5 Energizing Factors for Individual Innovators

1. Develop the right skills and fill in gaps with expert help. Continually build multidisciplinary skills and expanded networks that can support innovation at many levels and help you complete the Circuit of Innovation™.

2. Develop a holistic intellectual asset portfolio (360 IA™) that can protect your business, lay a foundation for future growth, be a basis for licensing, and confound the competition. Be sure to include low-cost intellectual assets such as defensive publications that add value to the rest of your estate.

3. Have realistic expectations but dogged determination when the potential is there.

4. Learn to understand the lens of risk that others use when viewing and marketing your innovations.

5. When faced with painful fatigue factors, especially external ones, overcome them with further innovation. Consider ways to position your innovation disruptively. Explore new markets and partners that could bring life to your innovation. Pursue innovation in the business model.

Top 5 Energizing Factors for Corporations

1. Listen to the "voice of the innovator" in the organization. Consider the impact of policies on innovation, and maintain close communication with those in the innovation community. Ensure that your prospective innovators do not feel like immigrants excluded from mainstream society. Keep them in the loop, following applicable principles from the Horn of Innovation™ model.
2. Earn the trust and loyalty of your innovation community, then carefully nourish it. The "will to share" must be kept intact.
3. Pursue added-value open innovation with universities, companies, and individuals, relying on internal expertise to add value to external opportunities. Include and rely on multidisciplinary innovation leaders, following the "Da Vinci in the Board Room" concept.
4. Develop and apply the right metrics, including metrics to track innovation systems and innovation performance. Use improved financial metrics in making decisions, especially those that impact innovation and business growth. Follow up on red flags such as symptoms of innovation fatigue.
5. Recognize the limited value of input from stockholders in guiding the long-term future of your company, and learn to listen to the right voices, including the "voice of the innovators" in your ecosystem.

Top 5 Recommendations for Policy Makers

1. Implement steps to regularly consider the "voice of the innovator" to understand the impact of current or proposed policies and regulations on innovation. Be aware of the risk of unintended consequences for all actions and seek to promote a climate where innovators and entrepreneurs can flourish.
2. Keep intellectual property systems strong and efficient, recognizing that rapid but proper prosecution of high quality patents and the attendant reduction of questionable patents can be a boon to the economy. Systems like the U.S. Peer to Patent program may hold promise for improving quality and speed.

3. In standards for financial reporting, seek improved ways to value intangible assets and encourage meaningful valuation of R&D.
4. Be wary of policies that may reduce protection and respect for intellectual property rights. Provide balanced policies and enforcement systems that reduce the theft of intellectual property.
5. Consider alliance-encouraging revisions to laws and tax codes that affect university-industry partnerships.

The journey of the innovator is one filled with perils and discouragements, much like the journey of many immigrants to strange foreign lands. However, when ingenuity is encouraged rather than worn down with numerous fatigue factors, the innovators in our midst can help transform the world for good. There are many who focus on current crises and shortages, viewing the future as a place of increasing scarcity and gloom. Such pessimism misses the power of creativity and the riches that can flow from the diversity of human thought. Like those who build precious fiber optic cables from abundant sand, like those who turn wind, sun, and the waves of the sea into electricity, and like those who tap the endless realms of the Internet to enrich the lives of millions with information, services, and ties to others, the innovators in our midst can add untold value and even beauty to the world around us, especially if given a little help in conquering innovation fatigue.

Index

1434:The Year a Magnificent Chinese Fleet Sailed to Italy and Ignited the Renaissance (Menzies), 246–247
360° IA (intellectual assets), xvi, 208–210, 271

academia, 30, 55, 74, 181–187, 193, 197–200, 262. *See also* universities
accounting rules, 97–100, 250–252
Adams, Scott, 59–60
Allee, Verna, 240
Amazon, 256
American Forest and Paper Association (AF&PA), 200–201
Apple, Inc., 93–95, 212
apple harvesting analogy, 96, 100
Appleton (Appleton Papers), 195
Appleton, Wisconsin, 69, 191–192, 198
Arab nations, 77, 246–247
Armada Effect, 91–93
Arner, Erika, 138
Asia, 143, 192, 199, 265. *See also specific countries*
assets
    intangible, 98–100, 232, 273 (*see also* intellectual assets)
    intellectual (*see* intellectual assets)
    tangible, 98, 232, 252 (*see also* intellectual property; financial reporting)
Atkinson, Timothy, 181
attorneys. *See* lawyers
Auto ID Center, 119–120
automotive industry, 39–40, 164–165

Bachstrom, John, 109
barriers, 160
    to disruptive innovation, 224–228
    to drug approvals, 160–162
    to external innovation, 103–110
    to intellectual property protection, 7, 129–144
    to open innovation, 7, 103–110
    organizational, 67–84, 108 (*see also* fatigue factors, organizational level)
    See also fatigue factors; innovation fatigue
Bauer, Don, 121
Bayh–Dole Act, 182–184
Bear Stearns, 166
Beijing, China, 142
Bemis Manufacturing, 169
Best Buy, 115, 121
Bezos, Jeff, 256
biofuels, 186, 194, 196, 200, 203, 265
bioproducts, 192–194, 196–197

biotech, 162, 182, 238. *See also* pharmaceutical industry
Blane, Sir Gilbert, 109
Bogle, John C., 159–160
Boise, Idaho, 85–87
bonds, tax-free, 184–185
Boston Consulting Group, 5, 256
Brassica Protection Products LLC, 150, 152, 154–155
brainstorming, 45, 81, 86–88, 225
Brigham Young University, 10, 33, 117
Brigham Young University-Idaho, 10
Britain, 54, 108–110, 164, 267–268
broccoli and broccoli sprouts, 148–150, 157
Bryan, Lowell L., 251
bureaucracy, 61, 108, 164, 232, 267
Burnside, Beth, 186
business method patents, 136–140, 209, 225–227
business models, 10, 95, 116, 170–177, 219, 221–225
BusinessWeek, 5, 256
Butts, Susan, 183, 185, 267
Byrne, Patrick, 166

Calavo Growers, 163
Campero, Rich, 121, 124
Cantu, Homaro, 196
Capstone Turbine, 172
Carnegie Institute of Washington, 181
case studies
    Apple, Inc. (iPod®), 93–95 (*see also* iPod®)
    British Navy and scurvy, 108–110
    Corning, 74–75
    Da Vinci as open innovator, 245–248
    discovery of penicillin, 77–78
    Empower Playgrounds, 9–11
    Farnsworth, Philo, 29–36
    Hampel, A.J. and the Invention Horn, 21–23
    Hewlett–Packard, 85–90
    Kimberly–Clark Corp., 220–221, 226–228
    Kraft Foods, 105, 215
    MeadWestvaco, 113–125
    Orion Energy Systems, 169–178
    paper industry, 191–204
    Procter and Gamble, 107–8, 195
    recording of the human voice, 41–42
    Semmelweis, Ignaz, 215–217
    Sunrise Farms, 147–157
    Tesla, Nikolai, 11–13
    Tucker, Preston, 164–165
    Schwarz Pharma, 238–239
    Vanguard Mutual Funds, 159–160
    Vue Technology, 113–125

champions of defeat, 59.
Checkpoint Systems, Inc., 116.
Chesbrough, Henry, 15, 103
Chester, Jonathan, 220
Chevron, 203, 234–237
China, 129, 142–143, 188, 201, 235, 246–248,
    264–266
Christensen, Clayton, 24, 93, 97, 203, 221–224,
    226–228
Chrysler, 39
Circuit of Innovation™, xvi, xvii, 170, 208–210, 271
Cisco, 99, 107
closed innovation, dangers of, 109–110, 239–240
CoDev, 105, 237
collaboration, 7–8, 11, 22, 31, 43, 46, 73, 82,
    121–123, 203, 235–240
    barriers to, 7–8, 184–185
    with universities, 182–185, 188, 199–200,
        262–267
Collins, Jim, 83
communication, 23, 90, 110, 202, 216, 233–234
community, 139, 203
    innovation, 7, 20, 74, 82, 84, 90, 92, 100,
        193–195, 241, 255, 272
    of practice, 241, 253
    R&D or technical, 72, 80–82, 197, 203, 240, 253,
        255
Compaq Computer Corp., 88–89. *See also*
    Hewlett–Packard
Conant, James Bryant, 181
Congress. *See* United States, Congress
connections, 22, 34, 36, 55, 62–63, 66, 113,
    121–125, 240, 273
consultants, 74, 232
consumer(s), 5, 20, 35, 42, 64, 149,162, 211,
    220–223, 226, 265
consumer product companies, 5, 58, 80, 105–108,
    220–221
contamination from external innovation, 103–106
Coppola, Francis Ford, 165
Cornell University, 115
Corning and the Craft of Innovation (Graham and
    Shuldiner), 75
corporations
    culture, 6, 60, 121–122, 224, 233–234
    dangers of cost cutting on innovation, 95,
        99–100
    facing innovation fatigue, 5, 76, 91–92, 103–110
    inventors in, 207–217
    performance management systems, 81–83
    policies that discourage innovation, 85, 160–163
    risks faced with external innovation, 63–65
    strengths, as potential weakness, 75–77, 232
    unintended consequences of actions, 70, 79
    and the will of employees to share ideas, 70
    See also specific corporations
cost cutting, 95, 99–100, 192, 197, 199, 234, 254
counterfeiting, 132–133, 162
Court of Appeals for the Federal Circuit (CAFC),
    133, 135–136, 154
court decisions
    In re Bilski, 136, 138
    KSR v. Teleflex, 133–134
    *State Street Bank & Trust Co. v. Signature Financial
        Group*, 136–137

creativity, 6, 75, 113, 172, 224, 273
Crikelair, Frank, 148–157
culture, 6, 9, 60, 77, 80–81, 125, 231–234, 257–258
The Culture Code (Rapaille), 80

Da Vinci, Leonardo, 178, 212–214, 225, 245–248
dairy industry and dairy science, 150, 177
The David Sarnoff Library Blog, 34–36
de Soto, Hernando, 136
decision making, 7–9, 59–61, 91–101, 254–256
defensive publications, 85–86, 157, 209–210, 217,
    225–226, 271
Despres, Waynne, 201–202
devaluation of innovators or inventors, 6, 13,
    73–74, 76, 80–81, 109–110, 240
development of new products, 54, 64, 113, 124–125
di Giorgio, Francesco, Martini, 246
Diedrich, Linda, 170
Dilbert and the Way of the Weasel (Adams), 59–60
disruptive intellectual assets, xvii, 219, 224–228
disruptive innovation, 24, 77, 93–94, 219–228, 234
Distant Vision (Farnsworth), 33
diversity, 78–80, 84, 263–265
Dow Chemical, 183
Driving Growth Through Innovation (Tucker), 253
Drucker, Peter, 54
Dugal, Doug, 203
Duchesne, Ernest, 77–78

East of Eden (Steinbeck), 135
EastIP, 142
economic downturn, innovation in, 177, 254–256
The Economist, 136
ecosystem, 84–86, 99–100, 213,231, 240, 245, 272
Edison, Thomas, 11–12, 35, 41–42, 213
education, 9–11, 30, 35, 51, 80, 212–214, 235
electricity, 9, 11, 30, 35, 169–170, 273
Empower Playgrounds, 9–11, 266
encouraging innovation, 3, 73, 77–78, 84–85, 107,
    117–119, 164, 188, 202, 217, 233, 248, 258,
    263–273
endurance, 23, 29–36, 215–216. *See also* persistence
energizing factors to overcome fatigue, 9, 24, 90,
    219–228, 271–273
    applying disruptive innovation theory and
        obtaining disruptive IA, 219–228
    applying sound innovation metrics and finan-
        cials, 252–254
    business model innovation, 95, 116, 136–140,
        170–175
    completing the Circuit of Innovation™, 170,
        208–210, 271
    creating a culture of innovation, 231–234, 241
        (*see also* culture)
    developing multidisciplinary skills, 213–214, 217
    listen to the voice of the innovator, 23, 25,
        83–84, 90, 100, 202, 261–263, 268
    pursuing Added–Value OI and open innovation
        generally, 237–239, 246–247
    valuing innovators and their input, 13, 70–73,
        77–80, 82, 86, 89, 198, 232, 234
energy
    exploration for, 234–237, 241–242
    of innovation, 21, 208–210, 238
engineering, 9, 76, 80, 117, 125, 235, 262

engineers, 35, 76, 86, 233–237, 262. *See also* scientists; inventor(s); innovator(s)
Enron, 163
entrepreneurs, 4–7, 17, 35–36, 46, 54, 148, 177, 188, 210, 213–214, 261, 265
  challenges faced, 124, 132, 166, 267, 270 (*see also* barriers; fatigue factors)
  in down markets, 177, 254–256
  encouragement for, 247–248, 270, 272
  need for broad skills, 124, 213–214
  See also inventor(s); innovator(s); voice of the innovator
Environmental Markets Association, 173
Ericsson, 117
Europe, 22, 78, 137, 161, 181, 201, 246, 263. *See also specific countries*
European Patent Convention/Office, 137, 143
Ewing Marion Kauffman Foundation, 185, 242, 263
exploitation, 7, 39–49
exploration
  early stage, 15, 20, 116, 124, 225
  oil and gas, 234–237, 241–242
external fatigue factors, 6, 7, 129–144, 159–167, 181–189
  from patent pain, intellectual property challenges, 129–144
  from regulatory and tax burdens, 159–167, 174–175
  from university–industry barriers, 181–189
external innovation(s), 6, 58–59, 62–65, 103–110, 202, 237–239, 241. *See also* open innovation
ExxonMobil, 9

The Farnsworth Invention (Sorkin), 33–35
Farnsworth, Philo T., 29–36, 78, 214, 270
fatigue factors, xvii, 4–8
  Armada Effect, 91–92
  chart of, 8, 27, 67, 127, 269
  from deficiencies in innovators, 7, 51–55
  from errant metrics, 95–100, 254–256
  external level, xvii, 6, 129–144, 159–167, 181–188 (*see also* regulation and regulatory issues)
  from government policy, 127–143, 159–167, 174–175, 181–188
  individual level, xvii, 5, 27–65
  from intellectual property barriers, 129–144, 147–157
  from listening to the wrong voices, 93–95
  lost relationships of trust, 69–84, 91–93
  from NIH ("not invented here") syndrome, 57–66
  organizational level, xvii, 6–8, 67–84, 103–110
  from open innovation barriers, 103–110
  people fatigue, 5–6, 8, 27–65
  process-related, 6, 91–93, 231–232
  from questionable patents, 147–157
  from theft and exploitation, 7–8, 39–49
  from university-industry barriers, 181–187
FDA. *See* United States, Food and Drug Administration (FDA)
Federal Circuit Court. *See* Court of Appeals for the Federal Circuit
feedback loop, 18, 19, 24–25, 90, 210–211
Ferrazzi, Keith, 241
fiber optic cables, 273

Financial Accounting Standards Board (FASB), 98, 250
financial reporting, 97–99, 249–258, 273
financial returns, 9, 97, 254–257
Finn Power robotic machining, 172
Fiorina, Carly, 87–89
Fischer, Bobby, 76
Flambeau River Biorefinery, 196–197
Flash of Genius, 39
Fleming, Alexander, 77–78
Florida Power and Light, 174
Florence, Italy, 135
food innovation, hindered by regulation, 162–163
Ford Motor Company, 39–40
Forest Products Laboratory, 194
forests and forest bioproducts, 192–196, 201.
  See also paper industry
Fortune 100 or 500, 43, 79, 104, 240
Foster, James, 160
Fox Cities, Wisconsin, 69
France, 77–78, 188
free markets, 60–62
French horn, 16–17
funnel model for innovation, 15–16, 24
fusion, nuclear, 29, 33, 35

Galvus®, 161
Gao, Lulin, 142
Garnier, Jean-Pierre, 5, 214, 233
Gatorade® Syndrome, 52, 181
Genentech, 182
General Electric, 81, 256
General Motors, 100
Generally Accepted Accounting Principles (GAAP), 99, 250
Georgia Tech, 192, 200
germ theory, 215
Germany, 22, 211
Ghana, 9, 10
Gillette, 116
Gladwell, Malcolm, 248
GlaxoSmithKline, 5, 214, 233
Gleick, James, 137
Glomb, John, 116
Goers, Steve, 105
Good to Great, 83
Google, 182, 256
government 6–8, 33, 167, 181–189, 261–268
  and intellectual property rights, 129–144, 166
  regulation, 150, 165, 174–175
  See also regulation and regulatory issues; fatigue factors, external level
Government Accounting Standards Board, 250
Graham, Margaret, 75
Great Depression, 256
greed, 5, 34, 63
Greece, 23, 78
green energy, 169–178, 194, 196, 203, 265
Greenspan, Alan, 57
Gupta, Anil K., 264–265
Gustafson, Helen, 220

Haber, Carl, 41
Hampel, A.J., 22
hand, unseen (economic theory), 60–62

hand stopping (horn technique), 17–19, 22, 24
hand washing practices, 215–217
*Hanky Panky: An Intimate History of the
    Handkerchief*, 220
Harvard, 181, 221, 251
Harvard Business Review, 96–97
Hassan, Fred, 161
healthcare, 54, 77–78, 162, 165, 215–217
Heins, Steve, 170, 173, 176
Hewlett-Packard (HP), 85–90. 256
Hise, Ronnie, 118
Hilden, Mikael, 160
Holland, 109
Hon Hai Precision Industry Co., 143
Honeybee Network, 265
Hong Fu Jin Precision Industry Co. Ltd., 143
Horiuchi, Vince, 31
Horn of Innovation™, 15–25, 42, 61, 74, 210, 215,
    233, 242, 270
Hot Property (Choate), 132
Huawei Corp., 143
Hungary, 215–217
Hutchinson, Kay Bailey, 164

IA. *See* intellectual assets
IBM, 54, 73, 88, 98–99
Idaho, 10, 30, 32, 85–90, 263
immigrants, 11–13, 31, 34, 77–78, 215–217,
    263, 265
    important source of innovation and entrepre-
        neurism in U.S., 263–264
    inventors and innovators as, xviii, 3–4, 11–13,
        30–31, 78–82, 89, 207–208, 214–216
In re Bilski, 136, 138
incentives,
    altruistic, 8–13
    financial, for innovation, 12, 13, 45, 71, 99, 224
    to innovate through respect for IP rights, 141,
        143
    intrinsic, 8–9, 11–13, 71, 240
    in universities, 185–187, 242
incumbents, 94–95, 97, 222
Inficomm, 236–237
India, 78, 131, 143, 188, 235, 264–266
industries
    agriculture, 147–157
    apparel and textiles, 105–6, 132, 220
    automotive, 39–40, 164–165
    computers, 93–95
    consumer products, 80, 105, 220–221
    electronics, 34, 93–95, 113–125
    energy, 234–237, 241
    financial services, 159–160
    food, 105, 148, 150, 163
    glass, 74–75
    healthcare, 54
    information technology (IT), 188
    lighting, 35, 165, 169–178
    mature, 204
    music, 93–95
    oil and gas (*see* industries, energy)
    pulp and paper, 113–115, 160, 191–204
    pharmaceutical, 5, 15, 160–163, 182, 233,
        238–239
    television, 34

industry, collaboration with universities, 6–8, 10,
    181–189, 262–267
ingenuity, 8, 73
innovation
    in business models, 10, 95, 103, 116
    closed, 109–10
    definition of, 4
    discouraging, xvii, 5, 42, 163 (*see also* fatigue
        factors)
    disruptive (*see* disruptive innovation)
    encouragement for, 3, 186, 247–248, 258,
        270–273 (*see also* energizing factors)
    external, 63 (*see also* open innovation)
    fatigue factors (*see* fatigue factors; innovation
        fatigue)
    funnel, xvi, xvii, 15
    game-changing, 78, 94, 220, 257
    incremental, 71, 94, 98, 194, 257
    metrics for evaluation of, 95–100, 252–254
    networks, 49, 240, 252–254 (*see* networks and
        networking)
    open (*see* open innovation)
    radical, 77, 94, 115–116
    social aspect of, 4, 13, 23, 42, 79, 172, 215–216
    sustaining, 222–224
    systems, 18, 25
    targeted, 19–21, 170, 225
innovation fatigue, xvii, 4–8
    from barriers to university-industry
        collaboration, 182–187
    categories of, 5
    in corporations, 5, 43–45, 95–100, 249–258
        from flaws in decision making and vision,
            95–100
        from improper metrics and financial tools,
            95–100, 249–258
        from lost trust among employees (*see* will to
            share)
        from NIH ("not invented here") syndrome,
            57–65, 257
        from open innovation barriers, 103–110
        from poor performance management, 81–82
    factors, 5–8 (*see* fatigue factors)
    from counterfeiting and pirating, 132–133
    among innovators and inventors
        from devaluation by others, 73–74, 80–82
        from exploitation, 39–48
        from NIH ("not invented here") syndrome,
            57–65
        from opposition and skepticism, 11, 31–33,
            92–94, 117–121, 171–173
        from personal deficiencies, 51–55
    from regulatory burdens, 159–167
    symptoms of, 60, 88–89, 91, 254, 272
    unintended, 12, 70, 79, 82, 85–90, 130, 160,
        162–164, 177, 182–184, 261
    from weak intellectual property rights,
        140–142
    See also fatigue factors
Innovation Resource, 253
Innovation Spectrum™, 231–232
Innovationedge, 46, 208–211
InnovationEdge.com, 210
InnovationFatigue.com, blog, xviii, 134, 210
innovator(s)

as immigrants, 3–4, 11–13, 31, 79–82, 89, 207–208, 214–216
deficiencies to avoid, 6–8, 35–36, 42, 51–57, 79, 207, 216–217
devaluation of, 6, 13, 73–74, 76, 80–81
employees, 6, 18, 63, 70–74, 207–217, 232
journey of, 3–4, 30, 217, 270, 273
multidisciplinary, xvii, 213–214, 225, 234–237, 245–248
training of, 21, 45, 55, 86
university, 242 (*see also* universities; academia)
visionary, 29–36, 41–42, 150, 170–171, 178, 214, 238, 245
The Innovator's Dilemma (Christensen), 221
The Innovator's Solution (Christensen and Raynor), 24, 221
innovestment, 191, 196
Institut Pasteur, 78
Institute for Information Law and Policy, 139
Institute of Paper Chemistry. *See* Institute of Paper Science and Technology
Institute of Paper Science and Technology (IPST), 192, 197–200, 204
intangibles, 98–100, 198, 232, 239–240, 249–251, 273. *See also* assets, intangible
Intangibles: Management, Measurement, and Reporting (Lev), 98–99
Intel, 83, 212
intellectual assets (IA), xviii, 6, 63, 208–211
    at Check Point, 116
    to create an IA story, 209
    defensive publications, 85–86, 157, 209–210, 217, 225–226, 271
    disruptive, 219, 224–228
    domain names, 209
    holistic, xvi, 34, 209–210, 271
    low-cost, vxi, xvii, 209, 211, 225–228 (*see also* defensive publications)
    protecting, 46, 49, 132–133
    review boards for, 234
    and strategy, 33–34, 53, 248
    See also intellectual property; trademarks; publications; patents
intellectual property
    in China, 142–143
    and copyrights, 211
    in developing nations, 140–143
    and enforcement fatigue, 132–133
    issues in university-industry relationships, 182–187
    ownership of, 182–184, 188, 209, 212
    patent barriers, 6–8, 129–143, 147 (*see also* patents)
    and property rights, 132–136, 140–141
    trade secrets, 53, 85–86, 134–135, 221
    trademarks, 46–47, 53, 99, 211–212, 217, 221
    See also intellectual assets; patents
Intellectual Ventures, 214, 248
International Accounting Standards Board (IASB), 250
International Paper, 119
International Sprout Growers Association, 149
invention(s)
    of agricultural equipment, 246–248
    of air traffic control systems, 29

of alternating current motors, 11–13
of the alternating windshield wiper, 39–40
of antibiotics, 77–78
inflated value of, 42, 52, 186 (*see also* Gatorade® syndrome)
of the iPod®, 94–95
of movable type, 246
of numerous Renaissance devices, 246–247
patentability of, 133–135
of the phonograph, 41–42
skills and resources required to bring to market, 35, 113, 124–125
of the television, 27–36
theft of, 7, 39–49
of voice recording, 41–42
inventor(s)
    corporate, 20, 207–217 (*see also* innovator(s), corporate)
    deficiencies, 7, 51–55, 216–217
    devaluation of, 6, 73–74, 76
    exploitation of, 7, 39–49
    fear of theft, 40
    inclusion of, 86, 234
    lone, 3, 17, 34, 207–217, 261
inventorship, 22, 40–45, 187
investment, 5, 52, 55, 82, 91–92, 192, 196–196, 200–204, 262
investors, 93–95, 99, 166
IP. *See* intellectual property
IP.com, 157, 210
iPod®, 42, 93–95, 212
Ireland, 188
irrational acts, 57
IRS. *See* United States, Internal Revenue Service (IRS); taxation
Italy, 135, 246
iTunes®, 93–95

Japan, 79, 137, 143
Jefferson, Thomas, 3, 270
Johns Hopkins University, 150–153
Johnson, Avery, 161
Johnson, Lyndon B., 36
journey of the inventor or innovator, 3–4, 30, 217, 270, 273
Journal of Product Innovation Management, 219
Joyce, Bryan and Claudia, 251–252

Kaplan, Robert S., 257
Kauffman Foundation, 185, 242, 263
Kearns, Robert W., 39–40
Kettering, Charles F., 51
Kimberly-Clark Corp., xix, 24, 83, 192, 199–200, 220–221, 226–228, 234, 241, 253
Kleenex® facial tissue, 24, 220–221
Kodak, 147
Kraft, Norman, 215
Kraft Foods, xvi, 105, 215
kraft pulping, 194
Kromholz, Joe, 148
KSR v. Teleflex, 133–134

law
    fatigue factors related to, 6–8, 163–164, 166, 182–184

law *(continued)*
    unintended fatigue factors from, 160, 163–164,
        182–184, 261
    See also legislation; patents
Lawrence Berkeley National Laboratory, 41
lawsuits, 32, 39–40, 150–157
lawyers, 32, 44, 46, 129, 135, 139, 148, 152–153,
        186, 227. *See also* patent(s), agents and
        attorneys
layoffs, 88, 147, 163, 235, 239
leaders and leadership
    blocking flow of information, 62
    CEO views on innovation, 73–74
    corporate, 12, 62, 73, 231–242
    flaws in judgment and vision, 7–8, 70–77, 81–83,
        91–100
    government, 164, 166, 261–268
    university, 185
    visionary, 35–36, 83, 94, 113–114, 150, 170–171,
        178, 214, 224, 233, 238
Leavitt, Ted, 224
legislation, 6, 8, 160, 163–164, 176, 182–184, 194,
        262, 267
legislators, 130, 162, 184, 194. *See also* United
        States, Congress
Lehman, Bruce, 141
lens of risk, 63–66, 104–5, 187, 207, 271
Leonard-Barton, Dorothy, 76
Lev, Baruch, 98–99, 240
liberty, personal, 61
licensing innovation or patents, 52–54, 152,
        183, 253
    compulsory in some nations, 131, 162
    risks faced, 63–65
    television patent, 31, 33
    from universities, 182–187
lights and lighting, 10–11, 35, 165, 169–178
Lincoln, Abraham, 130
Lind, James, 109
The Lion King, 69–70
Litan, Robert, 242
litigation, patent, 32, 39–40, 133–134, 143,
        148–157
Lock, Robert, 124
Los Alamos National Laboratory (LANL), 234–237
Los Angeles Times, 138
Lott, Frank, 69
Lotus Development Corp., 98
A Love Affair with Electrons, 33
Lucent Technologies, 116
Ludwig, Steven, 129
Luke, John, 118
Luke, Maryland, 115
Lyon, France, 77

MacGyver, 178
MacMillan, Ian, 257
MacRumors.com, 94–95
Made in Japan (Morita), 79
Madison, Wisconsin, 194
Magellan, 246
Magoun, Alexander B., 34–36
management, 24, 75, 83, 231–242. *See also* leaders
        and leadership
Manitowoc, Wisconsin, 170
market(s), 21, 25, 60–62, 64, 177, 220, 253–256

marketers and marketing, 35, 54–55, 76, 122, 199,
        202, 209, 220
marketplace, 17–18, 24, 64–65, 208, 220,
        223–225, 238
Markham, Ben, 9–11
Maryland, 115, 152–153
Massachusetts, 116–117
Mayo, Merrilea, 185–186
mavericks, requirements for success, 79
McGrath, Rita Gunther, 257
McKinsey and Company, 251
Mead Corporation. *See* MeadWestvaco
MeadWestvaco, 113–125, 270
Medicis and funding for innovation in the
        Renaissance, 247
memorandum of understanding, 46
mental illness, corporate, 62
mentoring of innovators and inventors, 30, 35, 63
Menzies, Gavin, 246
mergers and acquisitions, 197–200, 235, 255–256
merry-go-rounds, 10–11
Messing, Ralph, 75
metrics for innovation, 95–100, 240, 242, 252–255.
        See also financial reporting
Metso Paper, 202
Mexico, 266
Middle Ages, 135
Minalogic, 188
Minnesota, 115
microencapsulation, 194–195
Microsoft, 117
Milwaukee, Wisconsin, 148
Minister of Innovation position, 262
mission, religious, 9
MIT, 115, 117, 119–120, 186
Mitchell, Lesa, 242
Mobilizing Minds (Joyce and Joyce), 251–252
Morita, Akio, 79
Mormon, 31
Moto Restaurant, 196
Motorola, 117, 119, 223
MP3 players, 42, 93–95, 212
multidisciplinary talent, xvii, 213–214, 234–237,
        245–248
mutual funds, 106, 159–160
Myhrvold, Nathan, 214

Nagshead, South Carolina, 91
naked short selling, 166
Nanofilm, 237
nanotechnology, 188, 194–195, 213, 237–238
National Academies. *See* United States, National
        Academies
National Institutes of Health. *See* United States,
        National Institutes of Health
National Science Foundation. *See* United States,
        National Science Foundation (NSF)
Neenah, Wisconsin, 148
net present value (NPV), 97
networks and networking, 49, 55, 62, 66, 90, 167,
        186, 213, 240, 252–255, 265. *See also* ecosys-
        tem; community
Never Eat Alone (Ferrazzi), 241
New Jersey, 34
New York, 115, 139–140, 251
New York Law School, 139

New York Stock Exchange, 115, 163–164
New York Times Magazine, 137
Nickerson, William M., 154
NIH (Not Invented Here) syndrome, 7–8, 57–66, 103, 257
Nintendo, 172, 223
Nobel Prize, 77
Nokia, 117
non-disclosure agreements (NDAs), 46
Nong Shu (Wang), 246–247
Northwestern University, 211
Norton, David P., 257
Novartis, 161
Noveck, Beth, 139, 140
nuclear power, carbon credits from, 174–176

Obama, Barack, 268
obviousness (patent law), 133–134, 210, 227
Ocean Tomo, 52
Office of the Alien Property Custodian, 11
Office Depot, 121
Ohio, 237
oil and gas exploration, 234–237
open innovation (OI), 6, 15, 103–110, 236–238, 246–247
    Added Value OI (AVOI), 246–247
    dealing with contamination risks, 107
    as an energizing factor, 237–239
    fatigue, 6–8, 103–110, 239–241
    for mature industries, 204
Open Innovation (Chesbrough), 15, 103
Open Business Models: How to Thrive in the New Innovation Landscape (Chesbrough), 103
Orion Energy Systems, 169–178
organizational fatigue, 7–8, 67–110
Orozco, David, 211
Overstock.com, 166

packaging, 116, 211
pain, 254
    from disruptive innovation, 222 (*see also* disruptive innovation)
    patent, 7, 130–143
    regulatory, 7, 159–167
paper, 116, 194–196
paper industry, 160, 191–204
    biofuels from, 194, 196–197
    cost cutting in, 192, 197
    decline of, in U.S., 192, 196–197, 200
    energy recovery in, 194
    engineering and science in, 195
    external fatigue factors in, 200–202
    financial metrics, short-term, 197
    history of innovation in, 192–195
    hope for, 182
    leadership needs, 202–204
    open innovation needs, 202–203
    products, 116, 194–196, 220–221
    spin-off of a high-tech company from, 113–125
Paper Industry International Hall of Fame, 191
Paprican, 202
parachute, 246
Parks, Chris, 117
partner(s), 23, 34, 46, 49, 65, 238
patent law
    changes in, 129

as social compact, 130, 135, 140–141
Patent and Trademark Law Amendments Act. *See* Bayh-Dole Act
patent(s)
    gents and attorneys, xix, 44–45, 129, 135, 139, 142, 148, 227 (*see also* lawyers)
    allowance rates (USPTO), 131
    auctions, 52–53
    barriers to, 7, 129–134
    benefits to society, 130, 135, 140–141, 183
    business method, 136–140, 226 (*see also* business method patents)
    delays in obtaining (latency), 130–131, 139
    in developing nations, 141–143
    difficulty in obtaining, 129–130
    drafting, 48, 52, 134, 141, 211, 227
    duty of candor, 140
    facilitators or coordinators, 86
    history of, 134–135
    hostility toward, 139, 141–142
    law, 129–143, 166
    obviousness challenges, 133–134, 227
    peer review pilot (*see* Peer to Patent)
    and property rights, 134–136, 140–142
    prior art, 139, 152–153, 210
    provisional, 47–48, 107
    questionable, 147–157
    reform, 130
    software, 136–140, 226 (*see also* business method patents)
    USPTO challenges, 130–132
    story telling in, 134
    strength of, 52, 141–142
    for the television, 30, 32–33
    validity of, 33, 44–45, 133–134, 139–140, 147, 152–157
    See intellectual property; intellectual assets
atience, 54, 63, 65, 216–217. *See also* persistence
Payless Shoes, 211
Peer to Patent, 139–140, 272
PeerToPatent.org, 139
penicillin, 77–78
performance management, 6, 71, 79, 81–83
people fatigue, 5, 7
personal factors in innovation, 5, 7, 234
persistence, 62–63, 113, 119–120, 156, 170, 172, 174–175, 207, 217, 271
PG.com, 108
pharmaceutical industry, 5, 15, 160–163, 182, 233
    compulsory licenses for medicines, 131, 162
    delays in drug approvals, 161–162
    fatigue from regulatory burdens, 15, 163
    regulatory burden, impact on drug development, 160–163
Pingle, Laura, 116, 118
playgrounds, 9–11
Polaroid, 147
policy
    challenges in, 7–8, 159–167
    impact of unexpected changes in, 159
    innovation fatigue arising from, 7, 8
    influencers, xviii, 261–267, 270
    makers, xviii, 166
    tax, 6, 184–185, 273
The Post-Crescent, 198
poverty and link to property rights, 136

price, mechanism of, 61–62
pride, 6–7, 34, 57, 59
Pride Rock, 69–70, 73
Pringles® potato chips, 196
printable electronics, 115–116
Procter and Gamble, 107–8, 195–196
product(s)
    development of, 15, 20, 21, 54
    new, 9, 10, 93–95
    reaching non–users, 93–94, 221–224, 227
    release to market, 20
    skills and resources to bring to market, 35, 113,
        124–125, 208
professors, 10, 17, 55, 182, 185–188, 193, 215, 221,
    242, 263
profit
    disdain of, 11
    motive, 9
    not always an incentive for innovation, 8–13
    per employee, 251–252
property rights, 134–136, 140–142. See also intel-
    lectual property
prototypes, 30, 44, 64, 121–123
provisional patent application. See patent(s),
    provisional
Provo, Utah, 10, 31
PTO. See United States, Patent and Trademark
    Office.
publications, defensive, xviii, 85, 157, 209–210,
    217, 225–226, 271
Punto, Giovanni, 22
Pygmalion Effect, 76

Rao, A.S., 188
radio, 11, 31, 214, 223
radio–frequency identification (RFID), 114–125,
    226
Ramada Inns, 92
Rapaille, Clotaire, 80–81
Rasband, Paul, 115–125, 270
RCA, 31–33
reason to believe, 104, 171, 209
recognition for invention(s) or innovation(s), 22,
    29, 33, 40–45, 60
recording of the human voice, 41–42
recycling, 95, 172, 191, 194
Reedy, E.J., 242
regulation and regulatory issues, 6–8, 47, 159–167,
    232, 266
    business threatened by unexpected change in,
        159–160
    cost–benefit analysis often lacking, 160–163
    enforcement, 166–167
    need to anticipate, 150
    unintended consequences of, 160
relationships
    with the business ecosystem, 99–100, 240
    with customers, 178
    between employees and management, 69–84,
        92, 198, 240
    with external innovators, 107–8, 237, 240
    between government and universities, 181
    between inventors and influencers, 217
    between innovators and management,
        69–84, 92

needed for innovation success, 35, 90 (see also
    connections)
    with suppliers or vendors, 177
    between universities and industry, 181–189,
        240–241
Renaissance, 246–247
reorganization, 91–93
research and development (R&D), 73–74
    budget cuts, 254–255
    community, 80
    impact of financial report rules, 98–100, 250–252
    need to invest in, for survival, 192
    outsourcing of, 240
    productivity of, 5, 70–73, 160–161, 163
    reorganizing of, 91–93 (see also Armada Effect)
    at universities, 183, 185, 267
researchers, 153, 155, 187–188, 233, 241. See also
    scientists; inventor(s); engineers
returns, likely to decline without investment in
    innovation, 97–100, 192, 197, 200, 204, 254
RFID. See radio frequency identification (RFID)
Rice, Woody, 199
Rickert, Scott, 237–238
risk(s), 16, 42–43, 225
    avoiding, 59–61, 77, 225
    of contamination from outside concepts, 103–106,
        110
    danger of excessive aversion, 160–163
    for inventors, innovators, entrepreneurs, 4
    of competitive disruptive innovation, 93 (see
        disruptive innovation)
    in patent litigation, 134
    and value, related, 52
    See also lens of risk
Robins, Kaplan, Miller and Ciresi, 134
Rodney, Lord Admiral George Brydges, 109
Rogers, Everett M., 13
Rosenthal Effect, 76
Royal Dutch Shell, 241–242
royalties, 41, 152, 182, 187, 253
Russia, 31, 34, 78, 266. See also Soviet Union, 234
Rust, Robert, 153, 155

safety standards, 149–150, 160–163
Sanofi–Aventis, 161
Sappi, 192
Sarbanes–Oxley Act, 163–164, 250
Sarnoff, David, 31–36
Scott, Edouard-Leon, 41–42
schools, 9–11
Schering-Plough, 161
Schmidt, Eric, 256
Schumpeter, Joseph, 8, 54
Schwarz Pharma, 238–239
scientists, 71, 92, 123, 153, 163, 177, 184, 191, 233,
    262
    at Corning, 74–75
    devaluation by management, 92–93
    external recognition important for, 233
    at LANL, 236
    multidisciplinary, 213–214, 233, 245–248
    product finders, 233
    See also engineers; inventor(s); innovator(s);
        professors
Scott, Robert, 110

scouts, 241
scurvy, 54, 108–110, 162–163
search and development, at Schwarz Pharma, 238
Security Exchange Act, 250
Seeing What's Next (Christensen et al.), 221
self–interest, 57–58, 60–72
semiconductor industry, 263
Semmelweis, Ignaz, 54, 215–217
Sensormatic Electronics Corp., 124
Serbia, 11–13, 78, 263
share, the will to. *See* will to share
shareholders, 5, 93–95, 142, 159, 202, 251, 272
SharpIP.com, 243
Shaw, George Bernard, 76
Sheboygan, Wisconsin, 169
Shell, 241–242
Shuldiner, Alec, 75
Silicon Valley, California, 263
Singapore, 188
smart shelf, 115, 120–121
Smith, Adam, 60–61, 213
social aspect of innovation, 4, 13, 23, 42, 79, 172,
    215–216
social classes, 264
social networks, 186 (*see also* networks and network-
    ing; Value Network Analysis)
software, 136–140, 175
Sony, 79, 223
Sorkin, Aaron, 33, 35
South Africa, 182
Soviet Union, 234. *See also* Russia
Spedden, Rick, 118, 120
Spence, Jean xv–xvi
Spiegelberg, Harry, 192
sprouts, patent dispute over, 148–157
Sputnik, 234
Sristi.org, 265
stage–gate process, 98
start–ups, 17, 46–47, 113–125, 183, 187–188, 238,
    256, 263–265
*State Street Bank & Trust Co. v. Signature Financial
    Group*, 136
Steinbeck, John, 135
Stigler, Stephen, 40
Stigler's Law of Eponymy, 40
stockholders. *See* shareholders.
strategy
    corporate, 57, 91–100, 118, 231–232
    disruptive intellectual asset, 224–228
    flaws in, 7, 8, 231–232
    for innovation, 231–232
    intellectual asset, 33–34, 53, 226–228
    marketing, 53
The Strategy– Focused Organization (Kaplan and
    Norton), 257
strengths, and potential weakness, 75–77, 254
students, 9–11, 17, 22, 76, 80, 187–188, 193,
    197–198, 215, 235, 242
Sunrise Farms, 148–157
supply and demand, 61

Taiwan, 132
tangibles, 232, 252
tax credits, 188
taxation

impact on competitiveness of industry, 200
impact on research funded at universities,
    184–185
on innovation (effectively), 130
policy, 6, 184–185
and tax–free status of public facilities, 185
teacher–expectancy effect, 76
teams, 8, 17, 202, 224–225
technology councils, 49
technology transfer, 49, 55, 182–187, 193, 197,
    242, 262
television, 27–36
Tesla, Nikolai, 4, 11–13, 214
Tesla, Master of Lighting (Uth), 214
Tesco, 121
Television: The Life Story of a Technology (Magoun),
    34
Texas, 89, 164
theft
    and exploitation, 7–8, 36, 39–49
    of inventions, intellectual property 5,7, 32, 36,
        40, 46
Thorp, Ben, 197, 200
Tiffany, 212
Time, 33
Toyota, 100
trade practices, international, 200
trade secrets, 53, 85–86, 134–135, 221
trademarks, 46–47, 53, 99, 211–212, 217, 221
training of innovators, 21, 45, 55, 86
trust, 6, 12, 64–65, 71, 84, 198, 232, 258. *See also*
    will to share
Tucker '48 automobile, 164–165
Tucker: The Man and His Dream, 165
Tucker, Preston, 164–165
Tucker, Robert, 252
Tuscany, 247
Tyco International, 114, 124
typhoid, 78

UCB Group, 239
United States
    Board on Science, Technology, and Economic
        Policy (STEP), 262–262
    Congress, 138, 161, 164
    Constitution, 140
    Court of Appeals for the Federal Circuit
        (CAFC), 133, 135–136
    corporations, ability to partner, 238
    Customs Office, 132
    District Court in Maryland, 153
    Federal Circuit Court, 136
    Food and Drug Administration (FDA), 149–150,
        160–163
    Government Accounting Standards Board
        (GASB), 250
    immigration policy, 264
    Internal Revenue Service (IRS), 184–185
    National Academies, 185, 262
    National Institutes of Health, 184
    National Science Foundation (NSF), 262
    numerous federal agencies tasked with enforc-
        ing IP laws, 132
    Patent and Trademark Office (USPTO), 32,
        130–131, 136–140, 152–153, 156, 210

United States *(continued)*
  patent law, 129–144
  Postal Service, 33
  regulations, 159–167, 250
  Science and Technology Centers, 262
  Science of Science and Innovation Policy
      (SciSIP), 262
  Securities and Exchange Commission (SEC),
      159–160, 165, 166, 250
  Supreme Court, 133, 154
  University–Industry Demonstration Partnership
      (UIDP), 263
universities, 6–8, 49, 55, 262–267
  building and tax policies, 184–185
  collaboration with industry, xvi, 6–8, 10,
      181–189, 262–267
    and Bayh–Dole Act, 182–184
    and tax policies, 273
  fatigue factors within, 187–188
  funding for research at, 185–186
  professors *(see* professors)
  profit-motivated activities, 184
  publication pressures, 187
  and tax-exempt bonds, 185
  technology transfer at, 49, 55, 182–187, 193, 197,
      242, 262
University of Arkansas, 181
University of California–Berkeley, 186
University of California–San Diego, 186
University of Florida, 52
University Industry Demonstration Partnership
      (UIDP), 183
U.S. News & World Report, 33
USPTO. *See* United States, Patent and Trademark
      Office (USPTO)
Utah, 10, 31, 33

Valley View, Ohio, 237
value
  chain, 194, 223 *(see also* Value Network Analysis)
  from intellectual assets, 45
  from inventions, 4–5, 97, 252
  shareholder, 5, 250–251
  trees, 257
Value Network Analysis, 240. *See also* Allee, Verna;
      social networks; intangibles
Van As, Eugene, 192
Vanguard Mutual Funds, 159–160
Veitinger, Klaus, 238–239
Venice, Italy, 135
Verfuerth, Neal, 169–178, 270
Vioxx®, 160–161
Virtual Power Plant, 173, 176–177
vision, 7, 11, 18, 20, 35–36, 41–42, 53, 91, 113, 156,
      159–160, 232

Vitruvian Man, 245
voice of the innovator, xv, xvii–xviii, 23, 25, 83–84,
      90, 100, 202, 261–263, 268, 270
  harms when not listened to, 130
  input on regulation, 272
  input on tax policies, 267
  need for government to consider, 261–262
  need for leaders to listen to, 73, 202
  need for officials to listen to, 160, 261–262
  panels for providing policy input,
      261–262, 268
  and the will to share, 73
Vue Technology, 113–125, 270. *See also*
      MeadWestvaco; Rasband, Paul

Wadhwa, Vivek, 263–264
Wang, Zhen, 246
Washburn, Jennifer, 184
Watson, Thomas, 54
Wausau Paper Company, 196
WE Energy, 174
weakness, 254
  converting into strengths, 122
  from corporate strengths, 75–77
The Wealth of Nations, 61
Werner, Johann, 22
West Virginia Paper Company, 115
Westinghouse, George, 12
Westvaco. *See* MeadWestvaco
Weyerhaeuser, 203
WHBD Associates, 201
Wii®, 223–224
will to share, 6, 43, 69–84, 92, 198,
      232–234, 258
  and the Armada Effect, 92–93
  and impact on productivity, 72, 258
  and incentives, 71
  and sense of inclusion, 71, 234
  and trust, 71, 73
  and performance reviews, 71, 79, 81–83
windshield wiper, 39, 165
Winslow, Ron, 161
Wired Magazine, 30
Wisconsin, 69, 148, 169–170, 174, 191–192, 194,
      197–197
World Intellectual Property Organization, 142
World Trade Organization (WTO), 131

Yamaha, 212
Yoches, Robert, 138

Zhen. *See* Wang, Zhen
Zhezhiang University, 143
ZTE Corp., 143
Zworykin, Vladimir, 31–35